GENDER AND CHOICE IN EDUCATION
AND OCCUPATION

Despite many years of ostensible equality between the sexes in educational provision and occupational opportunity, sex segregation persists in both educational subject choice and in occupations: for example, around 90 per cent of nurses are female, and 90 per cent of engineers are male.

Gender and Choice in Education and Occupation presents cutting-edge research on 'brainsex' and its effects on personality, education and choice. It targets concepts such as job attributes, work flexibility, long-term life planning, home–work conflict, prestige versus occupational interest, and intrinsic motivational mechanisms to explain the relative failure of intervention policies to date despite many attempts at national levels to reduce sex segregation in both Western Europe and the United States.

John Radford and eminent contributors, all with a wide range of academic and professional experience, challenge the myth of androgynous work, examine intra-sex differences as well as male–female differences and similarities, and offer practical ways of improving fairness in selection processes.

Gender and Choice in Education and Occupation will be of interest to students and practitioners in education, management, psychology, the social sciences and social services, and to all those interested in social equality.

John Radford is Emeritus Professor of Psychology at the University of East London. He received the Award for Distinguished Contributions to the Teaching of Psychology from the British Psychological Society in 1996. Widely published, his books include *A Textbook of Psychology*, second edition (ed. with Ernest Govier, 1991) and *Quantity and Quality in Higher Education* (with Kjell Raaheim, 1997).

GENDER AND CHOICE IN EDUCATION AND OCCUPATION

Edited by John Radford

London and New York

First published 1998
by Routledge
11 New Fetter Lane, London EC4P 4EE

Simultaneously published in the USA and Canada
by Routledge
29 West 35th Street, New York, NY 10001

Typeset in Galliard by RefineCatch Limited, Bungay, Suffolk
Printed and bound in Great Britain by Clays Ltd, St Ives PLC

British Library Cataloguing in Publication Data
A catalogue record for this book is available from the British Library

Library of Congress Cataloguing in Publication Data
Gender and choice in education and occupation / edited by
John Radford.
Includes bibliographical references and index.
1. Sex role. 2. Sex differences (Psychology) 3. Sex differences
in education. 4. Sexual division of labour. 5. Sex discrimination
in employment. 6. Choice (Psychology) – Sex differences.
I. Radford, John.
HQ1075,G4575   1998
306.3'615 – dc21   97–37180

ISBN 0–415–15394–8 (hbk)
ISBN 0–415–15395–6 (pbk)

CONTENTS

CONTENTS

FIGURES

TABLES

CONTRIBUTORS

Pauline Anderson is a Chartered Occupational Psychologist and a Partner with consultants Anderson Lewis Associates. She has extensive experience in the areas of career development and psychometric research. She works internationally and has jointly led the parallel development of a personality measure in eight European countries. Her specialism is gender, ethnic and cultural issues.

Ann Colley is Professor of Psychology and Head of the Department of Psychology at the University of Leicester. Her research interests are in the areas of social cognitive explanations of gender stereotyping effects, and gender differences in educational settings. Her research publications cover gender differences in academic subject choice, adolescent sport participation, educational computer use and the use of technology in music.

Paul Creighton, Recruitment and Assessment Services Ltd (now working with Pearn Kandola Occupational Psychologists, Oxford), is a Chartered Occupational Psychologist and has work and research interests in assessment and development in occupational settings, in equal opportunities and management of diversity issues and in graduate recruitment. He has lectured in Psychology at the University of Jos in Nigeria and has developed graduate recruitment systems for both the British and Bangladesh Civil Services and for multinational companies.

Alan Durndell is a Senior Lecturer in the Department of Psychology, Glasgow Caledonian University. He has been working for more than a decade in the general area of gender and technology. Much of his work has had an emphasis on computing. He also has an interest in the developments in Central and Eastern Europe, where before the collapse of Communism there were many female technologists.

Ernest Govier is currently Deputy Head of the Department of Psychology at the University of East London. His research interests focus on the nature and origins of psychological sex diferences. He is co-editor with Professor John Radford of *A Textbook of Psychology* (1991) (second edition) published by Routledge.

Leonard Holdstock has tried a variety of occupations, all involving playing around with numbers. After making no progress in the penultimate of these (what is now called 'Artificial Intelligence'), he discovered Birkbeck College and Psychology. Later, at the invitation of John Radford, he found a lecturing home for twenty years in an institution which has gone under more than one name and is now known as the University of East London. Retirement has permitted a continued association with UEL and the active pursuit of research interests, especially in the subject matter of the present book.

Viki Holton is a Senior Researcher with Ashridge Management Research Group and Director of the Action Learning for Women Directors programme. Her interest areas include surveying current trends in management and management development, trends and best practice in career development, flexible working, equal opportunities and the development of women managers. She was involved with the research that launched the Opportunity 2000 Campaign, a national business-led initiative to create change for working women.

Estelle King is a lecturer in psychology at Brunel University and has conducted a longitudinal study into older students' interaction with higher education, which has formed the basis of her doctorate submission. As a feminist, her other interests include reflexively exploring power dimensions of the researcher and the researched, resulting in 'The Use of the Self in Qualitative Research', in J.T.E. Richardson (ed.) (1996), *The Handbook of Qualitative Research Methods for Psychologists and Social Scientists*, published by BPS Books. She is currently conducting a comparative study of constructions of the interview as a research tool.

Pauline Lightbody is a Research Fellow in the Centre of Gerontology and Health Studies, University of Paisley. Research interests include gender and career choice, and ageing and health.

John Radford is Emeritus Professor of Psychology at the University of East London, where he was formerly Head of the Department of Psychology and then Dean of the Faculty of Science. His current research interests are high ability, gender differences, and Higher Education. He has published numerous papers and a dozen books including *Child Prodigies and Exceptional Achievers* (Harvester Wheatsheaf, 1990), *A Textbook of Psychology* (with Ernest Govier, Routledge, second edition 1991), and *Quantity and Quality in Higher Education* (with K. Raaheim, P. DeVries and R. Williams, Jessica Kingsley, 1997).

Neil Scott, Recruitment and Assessment Services Ltd (now working with Psychometric Services Ltd), is a Chartered Occupational Psychologist and has worked extensively in the areas of assessment and the development of psychometric tools including tests, personality questionnaires and biodata. His particular research interests are equal opportunities and assessment.

INTRODUCTION

John Radford

We have it on no less authority than that of Counsellor Deanna Troi of the Starship Enterprise (*Next Generation* version) that 'despite centuries of evolution, some behaviour is still gender-linked'. It is perhaps not so surprising that she and Beverley Crusher, the ship's doctor, are the only female bridge officers on board – at least for most of the voyages. To begin with, the security officer also was a woman, Tasha Yar, but she served for less than a year (star time) before perishing in the line of duty, to be replaced by the ultra-macho Klingon, Worf. This is the second version of the Enterprise; in the first, under Captain Kirk, the only woman on the bridge is Lt. Uhura, the communications officer (superior female verbal ability?). In a further spin-off, (*Voyager*), the captain is a woman. So we go on.

Like much science fiction, *Star Trek*, which is reputed to be broadcast somewhere in the world every moment of every day, continuously year on year, in many ways reflects our own cultural assumptions rather than imaginary ones. Troi is a qualified psychologist, although the psychology taught at Betazed University where she graduated about 2357 seems to be some way behind our own, emphasising mainly the need to express one's emotions. Twentieth-century research suggests that gender differences in behaviour might actually be the result of evolution, at least partially. On the other hand, there are certainly widely held views that would include the notion of counselling and medicine as being much more 'suitable' jobs for women than security officer (though Crusher and Troi are mighty handy with their phasers on occasion).

In all human societies that we know of, men and women have generally been brought up and educated differently, and have tended to follow different occupations. The rigidity of the distinction has varied greatly, as has the degree of overlap. Without much doubt, on the whole the range of opportunity available to women has been less than that for men, although it has not always been the case that women have necessarily been disadvantaged. Our own society has really quite recently come to see dissimilar treatment as wrong, and much effort has gone into changing it. Yet marked differences still persist. A large literature has appeared, some of it attempting to elucidate the reasons behind these patterns, but perhaps even more devoted mainly to decrying them. This book is intended to be a contribution to the first type. All the authors have been researching in the area for a considerable time, and their contributions generally are intended to be by way of 'position statements' based on their experience and reflection and their own studies. Naturally their positions are not the same, and there is no attempt to present a unified view to which all subscribe. Nevertheless, perhaps a rather clearer picture is beginning to emerge. It becomes apparent, as is usual with human behaviour, that there is not one simple or even overriding explanation. It is not, certainly, just a matter of the wrongly supposed incapacity of women, or the unjustified dominance of men, although these do come into it. Rather, we have to think of a multiplicity of elements, from genetic variance through physical and mental development to social, religious, economic and other wider cultural factors. And we have to reconcile the fact that human attributes nearly always form continuous dimensions, on which each individual finds a place, with the tendency that societies have to put these individuals in separate boxes, such as black and white, Protestant and Roman Catholic, or men and women, with all sorts of consequences. Not all of these issues are dealt with here in detail, but perhaps a general pattern of how they may fit together is discernible, as is suggested in the final chapter.

One of Dr Johnson's more famous remarks was 'no man but a blockhead ever wrote except for money'. More recently the notion has become familiar that if you pay peanuts you get monkeys. Where this leaves academics is uncertain. Their direct financial rewards for writing are almost invisible if not non-existent. They may legitimately hope to raise the reputation of their institution or themselves, however, it is widely acknowledged that in the assessment of research excellence, 'books don't count'.

There remains the disinterested wish to make ideas and research more widely available, in the persistent belief that the attempt at objective enquiry is a better way than prejudice, hearsay or mere inertia. The present authors hope that this collection will be of interest to those concerned with issues of gender and choice in education and occupation, whether from a research or a practical point of view. As Editor, I am grateful to them for finding time amid the welter of (often entirely non-academic) pressures to make their contributions.

John Radford
London, June 1997

1

BRAINSEX AND OCCUPATION[1]

Ernest Govier

To begin at the beginning, along with both Dylan Thomas
and the King of Hearts, our gender and our choices both
take their origins in hereditary endowment, that which is
constituted at the moment of conception. From that point
on, environment comes into play. The first environment is of
course the foetus, that is to say, the mother's body of which
it is part. After birth, physiological factors, particularly the
hormone system, continue to contribute to the shaping of
the individual. Ernest Govier discusses some of the relationships between these factors and later choice of occupation.

Sex roles: socially learned or biologically determined?

It is, of course, a truism that males and females typically have different roles in
life. It has often been argued in the psychological and sociological literature that
these roles stem from social processes which operate during the development of
children to mould them into behaving in ways that are sex-appropriate (Bandura
1977). This process, in turn, leads people into occupations which are seen as
appropriate for their sex. This view has held sway since about the mid-1960s but
recently it has been argued that, at least in part, sex-role differences, of which
occupational choice is an important component, are the result of differences in
brain structure and organisation. The argument runs as follows: sex-typed brains
which differ in organisation and function will result in sex differences in abilities,
interests, levels of aggression, motives, emotional characteristics, and so on.
These differences will, in turn, influence the social roles, including the occupational role, that the sexes will feel most comfortable in filling (Berenbaum
1978; Harshman *et al.* 1983; Kimura 1992).

This chapter will review the evidence that there are sex differences both in the
function and structure of the human brain and will go on to describe experiments
in cognitive psychology involving procedures called, 'dichotic listening tests'
which have yielded evidence that our brain organisation plays a major role in our
choice of occupation. It follows from this that our 'brainsex' influences our job
choice but, as we shall see, it does not follow that all males will want to follow the

1

same set of occupations and females another set. In fact, there is growing evidence that there is not one single type of brain that all men share and another that all women share. The evidence is rather that the brains of males and females range from those which are very typical for their sex in functional organisation to those which are more typical of the 'opposite' sex. Actually, an analogous state of affairs can be seen in the range of physiques. The body types of males, range from, for example, that of a body-builder which, in terms of muscular development, is at the extreme 'masculine' end of the dimension, to the other more 'feminine' end, at which a male would be slender, with much less muscle development, narrower shoulders and proportionately wider hips. Similarly, the body types of females range from the more 'masculine' bodies of say, female body-builders (masculine in terms of their muscle development) to the very feminine bodies of Hollywood film starlets. These body types indicate the range in muscular development in what might be regarded as the normal population with many men and women overlapping in the development of their musculature. And so it is with brainsex. The dichotic listening data, which will be described later in this chapter, indicate that some males have brains which appear to be organised, at least in some respects, in an apparently female fashion. Similarly, some female brains appear to be more functionally male-differentiated. Thus, 'brainsex' may be a matter of degree, and the simple categories, female and male, when applied to brains, may be an intellectual convenience rather than an accurate reflection of brain organisation. Before developing this point further the experimental research on psychological sex differences will be reviewed.

The experimental evidence

Over the last twenty years, several lines of psychological research have converged on the notion that there are sex differences in the way in which the brain is organised. The research fields which have led to this conclusion include experimental cognitive psychology, neurophysiological and neuroanatomical research, and studies using modern brain-imaging techniques. Hitherto, most of the studies have concentrated on the task of searching for differences between males and females, either in their performance of a wide range of tasks or in the structure and function of their brains. This strategy is an understandable and obvious first step in trying to tease out the complexities of group and individual variations in brain organisation, although it does have the disadvantage of leading to, initially at least, an emphasis on, 'the two sexes'.

Evidence from experimental cognitive psychology

One line of research, which has recently been summarised by Halpern (1992), has focused on cognitive differences between men and women. There is now some measure of agreement that there are several cognitive areas in which the sexes perform differently. For example, female performance in many tests of verbal skill has been shown to be superior to that of males. Females perform better than males in tests of speech fluency, anagram solution and general tests of verbal ability. Indeed, two verbal tasks, those of synonym generation (Hines 1990) and consonant-word matching, (Block *et al.* 1989) have shown such enormous female advantages that tests to determine whether they were statistically significant were unnecessary. That is to say, there was only a modest overlap between the scores of the females and those of the males. The exception to this general pattern was the male advantage in the use of analogies.

There is also a female advantage in arithmetic but a male advantage in geometry and mathematical problem-solving. These mathematical differences are small for the general population but dramatic at the highest levels of ability (the top 6 per cent) where, in mathematical problem-solving, males are thirteen times more likely to be represented than females. This finding has proved to be remarkably robust over a fifteen-year period of careful research (Benbow 1988). Among the spatial skills there is a mixed picture, mainly because researchers in this area are still trying to identify the different types of abilities involved in solving the sorts of problems posed by tests of, 'spatial skill'. A preliminary attempt to analyse the factors involved in tests of visual-spatial ability (Linn and Petersen 1986) has indicated that they seem to be composed of three processes.

First, *spatial perception*: the ability to locate the vertical and horizontal while ignoring distracting context. Examples of tasks which could be said to test this are the 'rod and frame test' and the 'water level test'. In the former, the subject sits strapped in a chair in a darkened experimental cubicle, with a large, illuminated rectangular frame in front of him or her. Inside the frame is an illuminated rod and these are the only things visible to the subject. The chair in which the subject sits can be tilted by the experimenter (who operates from outside the experimental cubicle), a procedure which is somewhat disorienting. The subject can, by moving a control knob, turn the illuminated rod through 360 degrees. The experimental procedure is as follows; the experimenter tilts the chair and sets the frame at an angle to the vertical whereupon the subject is required to adjust the rod to the true vertical. Of course, this requires the subject to make the judgement while compensating for the distracting information from his or her eyes and sense of balance. The error, as measured in degrees of angular deviation of the rod from the true vertical, is noted by the experimenter and the procedure is repeated for a number of trials. In general, the average error for females is greater than the average error for males. In the water level test the subject is shown diagrams of jugs or tumblers depicted as having been tilted from the vertical to varying degrees and his or her task is to draw the water level on the diagram. Again, the error can be measured, and again, the average male error is lower (Thomas *et al.* 1973; Kalichman 1989).

Second, *mental rotation*: the ability to imagine the appearance of rotated objects or how shapes would look when folded or unfolded. Typically, the subject doing a mental rotation test would be presented with a drawn target shape and would be required to choose from among several items the one which represented the target shape in a different orientation, either rotated left/right, or forward/backward, but sometimes both. Or the subject may be presented with pairs of figures and he or she is asked to decide whether the members of each pair are versions of the same figure in different orientations or mirror images (Shepard and Metzler 1971). In these tasks, response time and number correct may be noted. On average, males respond faster and more accurately, to the extent that this sort of test produces arguably the largest male advantage of all the tests of spatial ability and the size of the male advantage is similar to the magnitude of the female advantage on synonym generation tests.

Third, *spatial visualisation*: the ability to see simple shapes within complex patterns. This is tested using 'embedded figures tests'. In these tests the subject is presented with a simple target shape next to a complex line-drawing which 'contains' the target shape and the task is to find the target in the complex drawing. The response time is noted. Again, there tends to be a male advantage in these tests (Hyde *et al.* 1975).

Even in what we might think of as intermediate-level skills there are sex differences. Garai and Scheinfeld (1968) have shown that females' hearing is more acute than males' and about six times as many females as males can sing in tune. McGuiness (1976) has shown that females see better in the dark and are more sensitive to the red end of the spectrum, while males see better in very bright light than females. Males have a narrower visual field but have a better sense of depth. Hutt (1972) and Reinisch *et al.* (1987) have shown that females react faster and more acutely to pain but their ability to withstand chronic discomfort is greater than that of males. McGuiness (1976) has shown that females have a tactile superiority as measured by the ability to detect pressure on the skin, such that the least sensitive female is more sensitive than the most sensitive male. Garai and Scheinfeld (1968) also found that females were more sensitive than males to bitter flavours like quinine and preferred sweeter tastes than males. Reinisch *et al.* (1987) point out that the female sense of smell is superior, a largely ignored field of study but one which underlies extraordinary sex differences in perfume buying behaviour, and possibly in strategies for mate selection. Finally, males are better at simple, manual tracking tasks in which, for example, the subject is required to watch a dot move across a television screen and press a button as it coincides with a line on the screen (Smith and McPhee 1987; Schiff and Oldak 1990). This skill, together with their much higher levels of aggression, may, in part, account for the young male's delight in computer games and the general male obsession with competitive ball games!

It will be apparent from this brief review of the experimental cognitive sex-difference literature that researchers have assumed homogeneity within the categories, 'male' and 'female'. Typically, samples of females and males are recruited, often from among student populations, a test of some skill or ability is administered and the results analysed for between-sex differences. In fact, there is always a range of scores among the males which overlaps with the female range and, depending on the shape of the distributions and the number of subjects used, the statistical analysis will indicate a between-group difference even when there is substantial overlap. This overlap has largely been ignored but represents a large number of people whose brain organisation ought to provide useful insights into the factors which influence men and women to behave in gender-atypical ways. As we shall see later, these people have provided extremely useful insights into the relationship between cognitive organisation and life-choices.

Evidence from neuroscience

Researchers at Yale University have recently used a technique which allowed them to produce pictures of living, active brains showing the areas of greatest activity. The technology which has made this possible is very new and extremely expensive. It is called Functional Magnetic Resonance Imaging (FMRI) and early in 1995 the team at Yale reported what many researchers in the field of sex-difference research see as a landmark study. Sally and Bennett Shaywitz and their colleagues studied nineteen males and nineteen females, each of whom was tested in an FMRI machine. The subjects lay inside the four-foot long tube which, with its accompanying computers, was able to accurately map the activity in the subject's brain while he or she decided whether pairs of nonsense words presented visually on a screen, rhymed. The subjects did not have to say the words out loud, they just had to think about how they would sound. An example of a nonsense word pair was loke and jote. The results were startling; in each of the nineteen male subjects a region in the left inferior frontal gyrus became very active while the subjects were working on the task but in the female subjects not only did that area's activity increase but the equivalent area in the right hemisphere also became more active. This demonstration of bilateral brain involvement in a verbal task in females but not in males is congruent with the female verbal advantage described earlier in this chapter as well as findings from the dichotic listening studies described later. Moreover, although all of the males' brains behaved similarly, only eleven of the nineteen females showed the clear bilateral pattern, eight of the female subjects produced brain activity which was similar to the male pattern; a finding which supports the view that our 'brainsex' is not a simple categorical attribute but rather may better be conceptualised in dimensional terms. Clearly, in this study eight of the females had brains which were, in this respect, more male-like. Again, this finding has important implications for the interpretation of the data from the dichotic experiments described later in the chapter.

Sex differences in the functional activity of the brain have also been found in subjects solving mathematical problems. Positron Emission Tomography (PET) is another form of brain-imaging technique which can discriminate areas of intense brain activity from areas which are less active. A study of twenty-two male and twenty-two female students revealed an intriguing pattern of results. Eleven males and eleven females were chosen because they had scored over 700 on a standard maths test while the other half of each subject sample scored around 540. While they were solving maths problems the high-scoring males showed markedly increased brain activity in the temporal lobes compared to the lower-scoring males but no differences in brain activity were observed between high- and low-scoring females (Haier and Benbow 1995). The mathematically-able females did not seem to be using any more 'neural effort' than the females with average ability while the able males seemed to be using much more than the less-able males. Although it is difficult to interpret these patterns of activity they do indicate functional differences in the way the male and female brains in this sample operated on these particular maths problems.

But, modern brain-imaging techniques have not just been used to investigate the biological correlates of cognitive sex differences. Perhaps the most marked sex differences are in interests, motivation and emotions. Raquel Gur and Ruben Gur have used PET scans to measure brain activity in males and females while they were looking at male and female faces. The subject's task was to judge whether the faces were showing happiness or sadness. Both males and females were equally good at picking out happiness and recognising sadness on male faces but the females were over 30 per cent better than males at recognising sadness on female faces. The PET scans showed that the limbic system in the female brains was less active while they were making these judgments than the limbic system of the male brains (Gur *et al.* 1995).

Mark George and his colleagues PET-scanned the brains of ten males and ten females while they were imagining sad events such as funerals or divorces. The limbic systems of both the male and female subjects increased their activity while engaged on these tasks but the area of increased activity was eight times bigger in the female brains than the male brains (George *et al.* 1996).

Interpretation of the results of these studies is difficult. But, clearly, the answer lies in the tasks in which the subjects were required to engage; the recognition of emotion on the faces of others is very different to experiencing emotion. Nevertheless, it is clear that there are differences in brain activity which are related to sex. In fact, there has been a recent explosion in research into sex differences in brain activity as researchers have discovered that their results are much easier to interpret when male and female results are analysed separately. In one very recent study in which males and females performed a cognitive task, Mansour *et al.* 1996 found seven brain regions showing sex differences in activity. These studies are in their infancy but as they become ever more sophisticated they will be crucial not just in demonstrating that the brains of men and women function differently but in clarifying the functional differences within each sex.

As well as the very modern and powerful brain-imaging techniques, sex-related structural brain differences have been found using the older neuroanatomical methods. Although many minor differences in structure between male and female brains have been noted since the 1880s, differences are now emerging which seem more fundamental. For example, in 1991 Laura Allen and Roger Gorski studied 146 brains from cadavers and found that the anterior commissure, which is an axonal connection between the left and right halves of the cerebral cortex, is generally larger in women than men. This finding has been interpreted as providing some of the physiological underpinning for the view that the two cerebral hemispheres of female brains are capable of more efficient co-operation on some tasks than are the two hemispheres of male brains. This, of course, fits well with the finding of Shaywitz *et al.* (1995) and the dichotic listening experiment described next.

Dichotic studies and occupation

It has been argued (Berenbaum 1978 and Harshman *et al.* 1983) that the sex differences in brain organisation and function described above result in differences in patterns of skills, abilities, interests and motives. These, in turn, ought to be associated with sex-related differences in life-choices, such as occupation. The dichotic listening test has been shown to be an accurate non-invasive predictor of brain organisation (Kimura 1967) and was thus an obvious choice to test for an association between brain organisation and occupation. In the version of the dichotic test described below, the subject was seated wearing a pair of stereophonic headphones. Pairs of nonsense syllables were presented via the headphones, one nonsense syllable to the left ear and a different one to the right. The subjects simply had to listen to each simultaneously presented pair of syllables (an example might be gak and dak) and say what they heard. It was made clear to them that they had to recall what they heard in both ears if they could, but, failing that, they were required to report what they heard in either ear. The experimenter recorded their responses. Doreen Kimura was the first researcher to note that, with repeated presentation of verbal stimuli in such a task, most subjects produced more correct responses from their right ear than their left. This right ear advantage (REA) has been replicated many times and is among the most robust phenomena in the cognitive experimental literature. Kimura also showed that the REA is produced because the right ear is most efficiently connected to the left cerebral hemisphere in which most verbal processing takes place. The left ear, however, is directly connected with the right hemisphere and in Kimura's model of brain organisation verbal stimuli presented to the left ear go first to the right hemisphere and then across the bridge called the corpus callosum between the two hemispheres to the left hemisphere where they are processed. This roundabout route results in errors. Thus, an REA is produced. It is now known that this model does not hold for a significant number of left-handed people, for whom the organisation is reversed, nor for females for whom the REA is much reduced because, as has been confirmed by Shaywitz *et al.* 1995, some verbal processing takes place in the right hemisphere as well as the left. It is this last feature of subjects' performance which has proved to be so useful when looking at sex differences and occupational choice.

Pauline Bobby and the present author decided to test the notion that brain organisation influences occupational choice by comparing dichotic performance in four groups of subjects: males in sex-typical occupations (occupations which are typically carried out by far more men than women); males in sex-atypical occupations; females in sex-typical occupations; and females in sex-atypical occupations. Allocation to occupational group was determined by reference to the 1988 and 1989 Labour Force Survey (1991) published by The Office of Population Census and Surveys. These four groups of subjects were tested using the dichotic technique described above. The results showed that both males and females in male-typical occupations produced similar patterns of dichotic performance which arguably reflect similar underlying brain organisation. These two groups produced larger REAs than males and females in female-typical occupations, indicating the more masculine nature of the organisation of their brain functions, at least of those involved in the dichotic task.

This demonstration of intra- as well as inter-sex differences implies a dimensional interpretation of sex-related brain organisation with extreme 'maleness' and 'femaleness' occupying the ends of the dimension with many men and women occupying the middle ground. Other researchers have also divided males and females into sub groups, for example, in 1983 Valerie Shute *et al.* divided a sample of male students into **high** and **low** androgen groups on the basis of their blood levels of androgens. They found that the **low** androgen group performed better on spatial tests. A group of female students was similarly split into **high** and **low** androgen individuals, (androgens are present in females but at much lower levels than are found in males), and in females it was the **high** group who performed better on the spatial tasks. It would seem reasonable to infer from this that spatial ability develops best in a hormonal environment with an optimal level of androgens which is somewhere around the concentration found in the **low** male sample. Doreen Kimura and Catherine Gouchie have also reported studies based on saliva testosterone levels which demonstrated patterns in sub groups of males and females. They confirmed Shute's findings for testosterone and spatial ability and found that for tests of mathematical reasoning **low** males outperformed high males, with no pattern in the female groups.

This concept is in line with work using other cognitive tasks and measures of sexuality (Weekes *et al.* 1995; Gruzelier 1994; Kimura 1992) which show relationships between hormonal profiles and scores on cognitive tasks. These researchers have identified male-like females and female-like males in the normal population.

Govier and Bobby had used subjects performing a variety of *professional* jobs, e.g. teachers, nurses, accountants, tax inspectors, secretaries, managers, etc. In order to test for education and/or social-class effects, Govier and Attewell (1994) partially repeated the experiment using males who were carpenters, asphalters, bricklayers and lorry drivers, and females who were aerobics instructors, supermarket shelf-stackers, seamstresses and barmaids. The pattern of results was very similar to the pattern found in the 'extreme' professional groups with the males producing much more marked REAs than the females. This study supports the view that the association that Govier and Bobby found between job choice and dichotic performance does not seem to be related to educational experience or social class. In the light of this evidence it is now very difficult to see how experiential factors could be responsible for the occupation/dichotic performance relationship, and it therefore looks more certain that it is indeed founded on the brainsex/occupation relationship and that brainsex itself derives from genetic and biological factors.

With the development of more accurately produced dichotic tapes it has become possible to use dichotic tasks to look for lateralisation effects in groups that would be expected to occupy similar but not identical points on the sexuality dimension. The jobs of hospital doctors and nurses have many similarities; they both involve caring for others who are often distressed, they operate in the same intellectual environment, they work in the same physical environment. However, they differ in the levels of training required, the levels of responsibility they carry and in their positions in the power hierarchy of the medical profession. It could be argued then, that the profession of 'doctor' while being carried out by more men than women (although the gender imbalance is not as sharp as it was twenty years ago) also requires a mixture of typically male and female traits while the profession of 'nurse' is not only carried out overwhelmingly by women but that, apart from a few managerial positions, it requires typically female traits. Thus it follows that male and female doctors should have more male differentiated brains than male and female nurses. This notion was tested by Govier and Boden (1997) who tested twenty-four male and female doctors and twenty-four male and female nurses on a dichotic listening task and found that occupation was related to dichotic listening performance but biological sex was not. Both male and female doctors produced the typical-male large REA while male and female nurses produced a typical-female pattern of dichotic performance. The clear implication from these results is that male and female doctors have brains which are more similar (at least in the distribution of their verbal processing functions) than either male doctors compared to male nurses or female doctors compared to female nurses. The same holds true for male and female nurses.

This view has been supported by a study which found a relationship between scores on the Bem Sex Role Inventory (BSRI) and a dichotic listening task (Weekes *et al.* 1995). In this study, subjects completed the BSRI which is a questionnaire designed to measure how masculine or feminine subjects are regardless of their biological sex. The questions focus on the subjects' interests and lifestyle to produce a 'masculinity' score and a 'femininity' score. In the male subjects the researchers found a significant negative relationship between the left ear scores on the dichotic task and 'masculinity' as measured by the BSRI. This finding is in line with the Govier and Bobby data in which males in male-typical occupations (who are therefore more 'masculine'), produced lower left ear dichotic scores than males engaged in female-typical occupations (who are therefore less 'masculine'). Govier and Bobby also found a similar, although less marked, pattern among their female subjects with increased masculinity, as indicated by occupation, being associated with lower left ear scores.

These results now begin to point to the important implication that our 'brainsex' or cephalosex is an important factor in our psychological lives. In fact, the relationship between gender (which is arguably heavily influenced by cephalosex) and occupation has been confirmed by several studies using Personal Attribute Questionnaires (PAQs) as measures of masculinity and femininity. As long ago as 1978, Wertheim, Widom and Wortzel found that people of both sexes who are drawn to female-dominated professions such as primary education and social work score higher on the PAQ F (expressive or feminine) scale than do their same-sex peers entering male-dominated professions. The latter individuals score higher on the PAQ M (instrumental or masculine) scale.

Genes, hormones and brainsex

As we have seen, our somasex (the sex of our bodies) is very often a good indicator of our brainsex, but it is only that, an indicator. If this is the case, it raises the question of the nature of the mechanism which is responsible for controlling the development of brainsex. In fact, the mechanisms underlying normal sexual development are now quite well understood. Normal male development begins when an X-chromosome-carrying egg is fertilised by a Y-chromosome-carrying spermatozoon (sperm). The resulting zygote, or fertilised egg, then develops more or less bisexually until about the sixth week of foetal life, when a gene on the Y-chromosome triggers the development of testes. The complete differentiation of the testes involves genes on several other chromosomes but the process is started by the gene on the Y-chromosome. Once the testes have formed they produce two hormones, testosterone which causes the primitive internal male plumbing to develop into the male internal sexual apparatus and Mullerian Inhibiting Factor (MIF) which causes the primitive female internal plumbing to disappear. The testes continue to produce testosterone and other androgens which, as we have seen, progressively masculinise both the body and the brain. In female development, which begins with the fertilisation of an X-carrying egg by an X-carrying sperm, the primitive male internal apparatus begins to disappear at about the twelfth week of foetal life because there is no testosterone to preserve it and encourage its development. The primitive female internal apparatus develops and, by about the sixteenth week, both it and the external genitalia develop into the typical female form. Thus the hormonal environment within which male and female embryos develop is very different, with the effects of testosterone producing differences in the brains of the sexes, some of which have been described in this chapter. Thus, we now have a strong candidate for the mechanism which might underlie individual differences in degree of masculinisation of brain organisation. Variations in levels of sex hormones during foetal development are clearly implicated in this process and it is possible to see how such variations could interact with the social environment to bring about the gender range seen in the normal population.

One source of insight into this process has been provided by studies of females who, because of a genetic accident, are exposed to abnormally high levels of male hormone while they are foetuses. The condition that these females have is called, Congenital Adrenal Hypoplasia (CAH) and it has provided researchers with the opportunity to study the psychological development of females whose brains have been 'masculinised'. The way in which this condition arises is, in essence, quite simple. These females lack a particular gene which is responsible for producing an enzyme called 21 hydroxylase (actually, eight different enzymes have been implicated but 21 hydroxylase deficiency is the most common cause). Because this enzyme is missing, abnormally large amounts of the male hormone testosterone are produced from a very early point in foetal development. Thus, the developing brains of affected girls are exposed to abnormally high levels of male hormone until the condition is discovered, which nowadays is usually at birth, when appropriate treatment is given. This involves administering cortisol to prevent the continued over-production of testosterone and surgery to correct genital abnormalities. The first researchers to study the psychological development of these girls were John Money and Anke Ehrhardt who published their findings in 1972 in a book entitled Man and Woman: Boy and Girl. They studied fifteen girls aged between 4 and 15 years. A match (for age, IQ, socioeconomic background and race) was found for each girl and all of the girls were tested with a standard schedule of sex-role preference procedures. Compared to the control group, the CAH girls were more often tomboyish and for much longer periods of their lives. The CAH girls were also more energetic in their play and more often played with boys, joining in team ball games like football and baseball, while the control girls preferred playing with girls. Interestingly, although the CAH girls liked to play the rather rough-and-tumble team games with boys they did not strive to be dominant in the company of boys, possibly because they were wary of rejection, as 'really being girls'. The CAH girls also rejected feminine-style clothes and favoured utilitarian garments. One of the most marked differences was in the attitude of the CAH girls to babies and mothering role-play. The younger ones were indifferent to dolls or openly neglectful of them, preferring to play with cars, trucks and guns. None of them were babysitters whereas all of the older control girls earned money from this. Moreover, the CAH girls were uneasy with babies unlike the control girls who took every opportunity for contact with young babies. The CAH girls expected to have careers which would be the focus of their lives whereas the control girls were looking forward to marriage and children as the focus of their lives. This last finding was especially intriguing in view of the fact that the control girls had been matched for IQ with the CAH girls. Money and Ehrhardt's general conclusions were that the masculinisation of the foetal brain develops brain pathways involved in exploration and territoriality and it inhibits the development of brain structures involved in caretaking behaviour. These findings were confirmed in later studies and the findings were extended by research which looked at the children of women who, for a variety of reasons, had been given female hormones during pregnancy. These studies showed that the male children of these women were less assertive and less athletically able than matched comparison boys (Yalom *et al.* 1973; Reinisch 1977).

So far the discussion has focused on females and has emphasised the importance of the foetal hormonal environment for the development of brainsex-type
and later occupational choice, but there is also evidence that the hormonal profiles of female adults in the normal population are related to the kinds of occupations they choose. In 1979 Purifoy and Koopmans reported that, in their sample
of 20- to 34-year-old women, the professional, technical and managerial group
and the group of students had higher levels of testosterone, free testosterone
(testosterone not rendered inactive by Sex Hormone Binding Globulin) and
another androgen called androstenedione, than homemakers and women in service occupations. Married women graduates have also been found to have higher
testosterone levels than married non-graduate women (Morris *et al.* 1987), and
Schindler (1979) found that higher concentrations of testosterone in a group of
working women were positively correlated with need for achievement and
autonomy. Parallel research with males has shown that men who attain a more
dominant or eminent status within an occupational hierarchy have elevated testosterone levels (Christiansen and Knussman 1987; Udry and Talbert 1988).
Indeed, as might be expected, many aspects of the lives of males have been shown
to be correlated with their testosterone levels, from winning and losing at games
(Booth *et al.* 1989) and engaging in dangerous activities (Ellertsen *et al.* 1978)
to whether they work as church ministers or football players (Dabbs *et al.* 1990).

Finally, Udry *et al.* (1995) have shown that more masculine behaviour in adult
females is influenced by androgen exposure in the second trimester of their foetal
life interacting with their adult androgen levels. The researchers report that these
hormonal effects account for a significant proportion of the intra-sex variance
seen in the gender-typed behaviour of women.

All of the evidence presented above, outlining the genetic and hormonal influences on the development of brainsex and related behaviours has, at its heart, the
implication that one of the most important organising factors in our interaction
with the world is our sense of gender. But what is the evidence that gender has
this intense phenomenological importance which makes men and women feel
themselves to be different in some fundamental sense? And, furthermore, is there
any persuasive evidence that these feelings have their roots in our biology? The
evidence comes from studies of individuals who are *gender dysphoric,* or *trans-
sexual.* That is to say, they feel that they have been born into the wrong body so
that the sex they feel themselves to be does not match the sex of their bodies (Le
Vay 1993). This can happen either way round, so that a biological male may feel
that, really, he is female and a biological female may feel that she really should
have a male body. These feelings of being trapped in the 'wrong' body may be
intense, indeed they may be so intense that the individual may seek gender
reassignment surgery in order to be rid of what they regard as unsightly and
distressing body parts. Such surgery, with its attendant risks, pain and discomfort
is, of course, not undertaken lightly but, nevertheless, affected individuals will
overcome many obstacles so that they can eventually 'qualify' for surgery. Case
studies of gender dysphorics do not usually provide any evidence that there has

been anything in their upbringing which could explain their remarkable psychological state. In fact, they often describe their early home life as ordinary with the only oddness being their private, growing realisation that they had been born into the wrong body. It does not require too much imagination to understand how distressing this feeling must be and affected individuals often describe how they tried to deny their own feelings from early in their lives until they became overwhelmed by them, at which point, if they have sufficient psychological resources, they accept themselves and begin to live in their 'true' sex roles. Sadly, the experience often proves too demanding and the suicide rate among transsexuals is high, a fact which, in itself, indicates the fundamental importance to us of our sense of gender. It is also the case that gender dysphoric people will, if they are able to overcome the social pressure they feel to conform to their biological sex, express their identification with their 'real' sex in every facet of their lives; that is to say, through their mannerisms and body language, their dress, their interests and their occupations. All of this would suggest that our gender is not simply the product of appropriate childrearing practices but rather it is firmly based in our biology. Perhaps it should be noted at this point that a distinction has been drawn between *gender identity* – the sex, male or female that we feel ourselves to be and *gender role* – the sex-typical way in which we behave (Diamond 1977). Clearly, there is such a distinction because, as we have seen, social pressure usually forces transsexuals to dress and behave in the way which is conventionally appropriate for their biological sex, at least for the early part of their lives. Some never step outside that role.

Some thoughts on ethics

It is incumbent on researchers, just as it is on everyone, to consider the consequences of their work. The area of sex differences is, perhaps, an especially sensitive area provoking, as it often does, very strong emotionally charged controversy. The controversy usually becomes polarised between those who believe that it is wrong to investigate differences between the sexes because the results may confirm negative stereotypes of women and those who believe that ignorance can never be preferable to the truth. Halpern (1992) has rehearsed many of the arguments both for and against each of these positions and has concluded that the latter view is likely to lead to the best outcome. Indeed, it is very difficult to see how mutual respect between men and women can be enhanced by ignorance of each other's experiences. Bigotry has always flourished on half-truths and ignorance. The discovery of fundamental psychological differences between the sexes does not imply that one sex should seek to subjugate the other. Rather, it could lead to greater tolerance for, and even delight in, our differences.

Conclusion

The evidence from studies of transsexuals and CAH girls, modern brain-scanning experiments, dichotic listening tasks and a range of cognitive tests, points to the conclusion that humans are not just male and female but that we all find our-selves somewhere along the dimension which is characterised by extreme femi-ninity at one pole and extreme masculinity at the other. We arrive at this point, which may not be completely fixed for the whole of our lifespan, by the complex interplay of genetic, biochemical, anatomical and social factors. There is also growing evidence that the point at which individuals find themselves on the brainsex dimension constitutes the most important facet of their personalities and that it heavily influences their lifestyles and life-choices (see also Holdstock, this volume). All of the research referred to in this chapter has demonstrated a rela-tionship between brainsex, gender and occupation. Each line of research has independently confirmed the separate steps in the chain of logic which runs from brain organisation to life-choices and lifestyle, with occupation as the focus. Although the biologically based cognitive influences on occupational choice have been emphasised, there are many social factors which may be involved in the choice of occupation. People may feel pressure to take a job which is stereotypic-ally appropriate for their sex or they may feel pressure to join a family business or to take a better-paid job. It may be that alternatives are unavailable. But, in spite of these and other social factors, there is abundant evidence that when people are able to choose their type of occupation their brainsex has an important influence on that choice. The particular emphasis of this chapter should not be seen as a denial of the importance of social factors in occupational choice, rather it repre-sents an attempt to add an important ingredient to the complex soup of factors governing the process.

Note

1 The term, 'brainsex' was, as far as the author is aware, first used in this context by Anne Moir and David Jessell as the title of their book on sex differences.

References

Allen, L.S. and Gorski, R.A. (1991) 'Sexual dimorphism of the anterior commissure and massa intermedia of the human brain' *Journal of Comparative Neurology*, 312: 97–104.

Bandura, A. (1977) *Social Learning Theory*, Englewood Cliffs, N.J.: Prentice Hall.

Benbow, C.P. (1988) 'Sex differences in mathematical reasoning ability in intel-lectually talented preadolescents: their nature, effects and possible causes', *Behavioural and Brain Sciences* 11: 169–232.

Berenbaum, S.A. (1978) 'Effects of sample characteristics on group differences in brain lateralization and cognition', Paper presented at the 8th Annual Meeting of the Behavior Genetics Association, Davis, C.A.

Block, R.A., Arnott, D.P., Quigley, B. and Lynch, W.C. (1989) 'Unilateral nostril breathing influences lateralized cognitive performance', *Brain and Cognition* 9: 181–90.

Booth, A., Shelley, G. Mazur, A., Tharp, G. and Kittock, R. (1989) 'Testosterone and winning and losing in human competition', *Hormones and Behavior* 23: 556–71.

Christiansen, K. and Knussman, R. (1987) 'Androgen levels and components of aggressive behavior in men', *Hormones and Behavior* 21: 170–80.

Dabbs, J.M., De La Rue, D. and Williams, P.M. (1990) 'Testosterone and occupational choice: actors, ministers, and other men', *Journal of Personality and Social Psychology* 59, (6): 1261–5.

Diamond, M. (1977) 'Human sexual development: biological foundations for social development' in F.A. Beach (ed.) *Human Sexuality In Four Perspectives*, Baltimore: Johns Hopkins University Press.

Ellertsen, B., Johnsen, T.B. and Ursin, H. (1978) 'Relationship between the hormonal responses to activation and coping' in H. Ursin, E. Baade, and S. Levine (eds) *Psychobiology Of Stress: A Study Of Coping Men*, New York: Academic Press.

Garai, J.E. and Scheinfeld, A. (1968) 'Sex differences in mental and behavioural traits', *Genetic Psychology Monographs* 77: 169–299.

George, M., Ketter, T.A., Parekh, P.I., Herscovitch, P. and Post, R.M. (1996) 'Gender differences in regional cerebral blood flow during transient self-induced sadness or happiness', *Biological Psychiatry* 40, (9): 859–71.

Govier, E. and Attewell, L. (1994) 'Sex, occupation and dichotic listening performance'. Paper presented to the British Psychological Society London Conference.

Govier, E. and Bobby, P. (1994) 'Sex and occupation as markers for task performance in a dichotic measure of brain asymmetry', *International Journal of Psychophysiology* 18: 179–86.

Govier, E. and Boden, M. (1997) 'Occupation and dichotic listening performance', *Laterality* 2, (1): 27–32.

Gruzelier, J.H. (1994) 'Developmental psychopathology: brain asymmetry, gender and maturation', *International Journal of Psychophysiology* 18, (3): 167–78.

Gur, R.C., Mozley, L.H., Mozley, P.D., Resnick, S.M., Karp, J.S., Alavi, A., Arnold, S.E. and Gur, R.E. (1995) 'Sex-differences in regional glucose-metabolism during a resting state', *Science* 267, (5197): 528–31.

Haier, R.J. and Benbow, C.P. (1995) 'Sex differences and lateralization in temporal lobe glucose metabolism during mathematical reasoning', *Developmental Neuropsychology* 11, (4): 405.

Halpern, D.F. (1992) *Sex Differences in Cognitive Abilities* (2nd edition), Hove and London: Lawrence Erlbaum Assoc.

Harshman, R.A., Remington, R. and Krashen, S.D. (1983) 'Sex, language and the brain. Evidence from dichotic listening for adult sex differences in verbal lateralization'. Department of Psychology Research Bulletin No. 588, University of Western Ontario, London, Canada.

Hines, M. (1990) 'Gonadal hormones and human cognitive development' in J. Balthazart (ed.) *Hormones, brain and behaviour in vertebrates. 1. Sexual differentiation, neuroanatomical aspects, neurotransmitters and neuropeptides*, Basel: Karger.

Hutt, C. (1972) *Males and Females*, London: Penguin.

Hyde, J.S., Geiringer, E.R. and Yen, W.M. (1975) 'On the empirical relation between spatial ability and sex differences in other aspects of cognitive performance', *Multivariate Behavioral Research* 10: 289–309.

Kalichman, S.C. (1989) 'The effects of stimulus context on paper-and-pencil spatial task performance', *Journal of General Psychology* 116: 133–9.

Kimura, D. (1967) 'Functional asymmetry of the brain in dichotic listening', *Cortex* 3: 163–8.

—— (1992) 'Sex differences in the brain', *Scientific American* 267: 80–7.

Le Vay, S. (1993) *The Sexual Brain*, Cambridge, MA: MIT Press.

Linn, M.C. and Petersen, A.C. (1986) 'A meta-analysis of gender differences in spatial ability: implications for mathematics and science achievement' in J.S. Hyde and M.C. Linn (eds) *The Psychology of Gender: Advances through Meta-analysis*, Baltimore: Johns Hopkins University Press.

McGuiness, D. (1976) 'Sex differences in organization, perception and cognition' in B. Lloyd and J. Archer (eds) *Exploring Sex Differences*, London: Academic Press.

Mansour, C.S., Haier, R.J. and Buchsbaum, M.S. (1996) 'Gender comparisons of cerebral glucose metabolic rate in healthy adults during a cognitive task', *Personality and Individual Differences* 20 (2): 183–91.

Moir, A. and Jessel, D. (1989) *Brainsex*, London: Mandarin.

Money, J. and Ehrhardt, A.A. (1972) *Man and Woman: Boy and Girl*, Baltimore: Johns Hopkins University Press.

Morris, N.M., Udry, J.R., Khan-Dawood, F. and Dawood, M.Y. (1987) 'Marital sex frequency and midcycle female testosterone', *Archives of Sexual Behaviour* 16: 27–37.

Purifoy, F.E. and Koopmans, L.H. (1979) 'Androstenedione, testosterone and free testosterone concentrations in women of various occupations', *Social Biology* 26: 179–88.

Reinisch, J.M. (1977) 'Prenatal exposure of human foetuses to synthetic progestin and oestrogen affects personality', *Nature* 266: 561–2.

Reinisch, J.M., Rosenblum, L.A. and Sanders, S.A. (eds) (1987) *Masculinity and Femininity*, New York: Oxford University Press.

Schiff, W. and Oldack, R. (1990) 'Accuracy of judging time to arrival: effects of modality, trajectory, and gender', *Journal of Experimental Psychology, Human Perception and Performance* 16: 303–16.

Schindler, G.L. (1979) 'Testosterone concentrations, personality patterns and occupational choice in women'. Ph.D. dissertation, Department of Psychology, University of Houston.

Shaywitz, B.A., Shaywitz, S.E., Pugh, K.R., Constable, R.T., Skudlarski, P., Fulbright, R.K., Bronen, R.A., Fletcher, J.M., Shankweiler, D.P., Katz, L. and Gore, J.C. (1995) 'Sex differences in the functional organization of the brain for language', *Nature* 373: 607–9.

Shepard, R.N. and Metzler, J. (1971) 'Mental rotation of three dimensional objects', *Science* 171: 701–3.

Shute, V.J., Pellegrino, J.W., Hubert, L. and Reynolds, R.W. (1983) 'The relationship between androgen levels and human spatial ability', *Bulletin of the Psychonomic Society* 21, (6): 465–8.

Smith, G.A. and McPhee, K.A. (1987) 'Performance in a coincidence timing task correlates with intelligence', *Intelligence* 11: 161–7.

Thomas, H., Jamison, W. and Hummel, D.D. (1973) 'Observation is insufficient for discovering that the surface of still water is invariantly horizontal', *Science* 181: 173–4.

Udry, J.R. and Talbert, L.M. (1988) 'Sex hormone effects on personality at puberty', *Journal of Personality and Social Psychology* 54: 291–5.

Udry, J.R., Morris, N.M. and Kovenock, J. (1995) 'Androgen effects on women's gendered behaviour', *Journal of Biosocial Science* 27: 359–68.

Weekes, N.Y., Zaidel, D.W. and Zaidel, E. (1995) 'Effects of sex and sex role attributions on the ear advantage in dichotic listening', *Neuropsychology* 9, (1): 62–7.

Wertheim, E.G., Widom, C. S. and Wortzel, L.H. (1978) 'Multivariate analysis of professional career choice', *Journal of Applied Psychology* 63: 234–42.

Yalom, I.D., Green, R. and Fisk, N. (1973) 'Prenatal exposure to female hormones', *Archives of General Psychiatry* 28: 554–61.

2

GENDER AND SUBJECT CHOICE IN SECONDARY EDUCATION

Ann Colley

Over a period of some decades, at least, girls and boys have continued to make differential choices of subjects to study, even when they are ostensibly equally free to choose any of those on offer. This clearly has direct consequences for Higher Education and for occupational opportunities. The introduction of a National Curriculum in the UK after 1988 has meant that up to the age of 16 all students take the same subjects. But immediately after that they become free to choose, and preferences immediately become apparent. Ann Colley explores some of the possible reasons for this, paying particular attention to the adult social roles of men and women, the abilities that are considered typical of these roles, and the consequent gender-related stereotypes of academic subjects, according to which some subjects are more appropriate for males and some for females.

The issue of the influence of gender upon subject choice in education has remained high on the research agenda for many years, partly because marked differences in what girls and boys choose to do persist, despite the introduction of a core of compulsory subjects in the UK National Curriculum in 1988. The subject areas which show the most marked differences in male and female enrolment are the physical sciences in which boys dominate, and English, art and modern languages, in which girls dominate. The problem is illustrated in Table 2.1 which shows enrolments for Advanced level examinations (normally taken at 17–18 years) in 1995. The influence of the National Curriculum with its core compulsory areas conceals such effects earlier in the school career, although patterns of preferences presenting a similar picture have been reported by researchers.

The choice of educational routes and achievement in different subject areas by males and females is influenced by a number of factors: perceptions of what males and females are good at, which are influenced by stereotypes of male and female abilities and roles, educational factors, including school environment, teacher

Table 2.1: Enrolments for A level entry
1995

	% *male*	% *female*
Physics	78.2	21.8
Mathematics	64.9	35.1
Chemistry	56.2	43.8
Art	39.0	61.0
German	31.8	68.2
English literature	30.7	69.3
French	29.6	70.4

Source: From Elwood and Comber (1996)

beliefs and behaviour, styles of course delivery, syllabus, content, assessment procedures, and individual differences such as patterns of achievement, gender stereotyping, educational experiences and family background. The most fundamental of these are perceptions of male and female attributes and roles, which have an influence both within and across groups in the form of attitudes and beliefs about what males and females are good at, and at the level of the individual and his or her identification with stereotypical beliefs. However, contextual factors, and in particular the educational environment, can moderate these effects.

In order to understand how gender influences the choices made in education, it is necessary first to examine the content of stereotypes of male and female attributes and behaviour, and how these are internalised. The discussion will then examine the gender stereotyping of different school subjects before reviewing moderating influences from the educational environment. The conclusion will be informed by the results of studies of strategies designed to moderate the effects of gender stereotyping on choice and attainment.

Perceptions of gender roles

A large literature which commenced in the early 1970s has explored our stereotypes of males and females by identifying attributes which are perceived to be characteristic of each sex (e.g. Bem 1974, 1981; Spence and Helmreich 1978). Two major dimensions reflecting respectively the positive attributes of masculinity and femininity have emerged. Masculinity encompasses attributes such as self-reliance, individualism, ambition, dominance, the ability to lead, which have been summarised as instrumental (Bem 1981; Spence and Helmreich 1978) or agentic (Bakan 1966; Eagly 1987). Femininity encompasses kindness, being affectionate, being eager to soothe hurt feelings, reflecting a dimension of expressiveness (Bem 1981; Spence and Helmreich 1978) or communality (Bakan 1966; Eagly 1987). These dimensions are central to our perceptions of gender-role appropriate behaviour, but where do they come from? They are certainly more complex and culturally based than simple biological sex differences. One explanation lies in the interaction between biological predispositions and cultural pressures: biological differences between the sexes predispose them to different roles, which have then been reinforced by the needs of society and embodied in family, economic and political systems. It has been argued that differences in the reproductive roles of males and females have emphasised involvement in key societal roles by the former who take the responsibility for providing resources, and involvement in childcare and the family by the latter. Within the roles they occupy, independence and aggressiveness are attributes necessary for males, while nurturance is necessary for females.

Eagly (1987) has developed this view and proposed that perceptions of normative male and female characteristics and adult sex differences can be explained in terms of social roles, which are themselves influenced by biological predispositions and socialisation by parents and peers. Social roles have a proximal effect upon our perceptions of gender roles, while biology and socialisation have a more indirect distal effect. Males tend to occupy roles which are controlling within our society and economy, which have agentic attributes at their core, while females predominate in caring, nurturant roles, which have communality at their core. The importance of the traditional division of labour for our perceptions of gender-related behaviour was demonstrated by Eagly and Steffen (1984) in a study of judgements of the attributes of males and females occupying roles as full-time employees or homemakers or having no occupation specified. The occupational role was a strong determinant of the degree to which agentic or communal attributes were assigned, with the non-specified individuals being perceived stereotypically. Further support comes from cross-cultural and anthropological evidence, which, according to Singleton (1986) can only support a conclusion that gender-role socialisation in any society can be predicted from the work requirements for each gender. These social roles and the attributes attached to them provide stereotypes of normative male and female behaviour. Importantly, they also provide different opportunities for learning skills associated with fulfilment of role demands, encouraging the divergence of gender-role stereotypes.

Our understanding of how gender roles and their stereotypes are learned and internalised focuses upon the socialisation process which prepares children for future adult roles by encouraging appropriate behaviour and interests. Two similar but different theoretical approaches to understanding gender-role socialisation, Social Learning Theory (Mischel 1966, 1970; Bandura 1977), and Cognitive Developmental Theory (Kohlberg 1966), have respectively focused upon modelling and reinforcement – a primarily passive process, and the active acquisition of cognitive structures to make sense of the world. In the former, the child's attitudes and behaviour are moulded by the environment: parents and significant others provide models for observation, positively reinforce appropriate behaviours and negatively reinforce inappropriate behaviours. In the latter, the child, as an actor within a social environment, assimilates and internalises information which is crucial to understand and act within that environment. In both, albeit with different emphases, childrearing practices provide an important context for presenting the information to be internalised and the role of parents is, therefore, central. A considerable number of empirical studies have examined whether parents treat their male and female offspring differently (e.g. Fagot 1978; Langlois and Downs 1980). A recent meta-analysis of studies of the differential socialisation of boys and girls by parents (Lytton and Romney 1991) has shown that the active involvement by parents is confined to differential encouragement in areas of play and household chores, which are probably the most significant for developing perceptions of gender roles. It is tempting to regard such findings as indicative of an explanation of later role differentiation in terms of learning and cultural pressures. However, as Lytton and Romney point out, the interpretation of differential parental behaviour is not straightforward. It may arise from parents' own internal models of masculine and feminine behaviour, reinforcement of biologically based preferences and behaviours in their children, or reinforcement of preferences arising from internal models of gender appropriate behaviour already acquired by their children.

In both the social learning and cognitive developmental approaches variations in socialisation, and in particular in the degree to which gender distinctions are prominent, could result in individual differences in adherence to gender-stereotyped behaviour. This notion is also inherent in Bem's (1981) Gender Schema Theory, in which it is proposed that the degree of gender stereotyping acquired during socialisation determines the extent to which gender is used as a construct to differentiate behaviours in others and as a basis for classifying one's own attributes. Of relevance to educational choice is the possibility following on from this, that the gender-stereotyping of subject areas is more of an attraction/deterrent to some pupils than others.

Measures of gender-role identity reflect the degree to which individuals describe themselves in gender-stereotyped terms. Measurement normally is undertaken using a self-description inventory such as that of Bem (1974) in which an individual provides self ratings of the typicality of a list of behavioural characteristics which have been found to be stereotyped as masculine or feminine. Total scores for both masculinity and femininity can then be derived providing a measure of psychological sex-typing. Associations have been found between masculinity and femininity scores and preferences for particular subject areas. A particularly robust association has been found between higher masculinity scores and sport participation at all levels, including recreational sport, among secondary school pupils (e.g. Gregson and Colley 1986). Colley *et al.* (1994a) in their study of the ranking of school subjects in middle school found a positive association between femininity and the ranking of humanities and music, and a negative association with rankings of PE. Masculinity was negatively associated with rankings for English. Such associations may be indicative of subtle effects of socialisation contributing to individual differences in preferences.

The issue of possible biological substrates for differential behaviours and, indeed, for differential abilities and preferences for different subject areas in the educational system is important but will not be the focus of the present discussion, because, following Eagly's argument (Eagly 1987), biological influences must be regarded as distal rather than proximal factors with respect to their influence upon choices in education. There is an argument that gender differences in cognitive abilities, in particular better verbal abilities in girls and better mathematical abilities in boys, may contribute to subject preferences, although the magnitude of these has been shown by recent meta-analyses to be less than previously thought (Feingold 1988; Hyde and Linn 1988). It is also the case that the link between sub-test scores from psychometric tests of verbal and mathematical abilities and attainment in the educational system is not a straightforward one. Attainment in English national examinations shows only a partial link with gender preferences. In GCSE examinations at 16, girls have gained a higher proportion of top grades (A*–C) than boys (Elwood and Comber 1996). Only in biology are boys markedly ahead of girls. In English, French and technology, girls are ahead of boys, with maths, physics and chemistry showing negligible differences. At Advanced (A) level at 18, boys are outperforming girls in general, although in some subjects the gap is very small. In English, boys have an advantage, while in maths and physics the gap is negligible and in favour of girls. The statistical information from GCSE and A levels indicate that ability *per se* does not underlie gender differences in enrolment (for a fuller discussion of gender differences in cognitive abilities the reader is referred to the chapters by Govier and by Holdstock in this volume), although gender stereotypes of abilities are undoubtedly relevant. The crossover in the performance of boys and girls at the two levels has been attributed to a number of specific educational factors, including syllabus content and assessment schemes (Elwood and Comber 1996), emphasising the influence of such factors upon gender differences found in the educational system.

Subject preferences and choice

Studies of pupils' perceptions of school subjects in British schools have either used rating scales or lists ranked in preference (Archer and Macrae 1991; Colley *et al.* 1994a, 1994b; Weinreich-Haste 1979, 1981). There is considerable consistency in the gender differences that have been found which mirror the enrolment data presented earlier. The physical sciences, male-stereotyped crafts, and mathematics are regarded as the most masculine subjects and tend to be preferred more by boys, while English, French and RE are regarded as the most feminine subjects and are preferred more by girls.

There is some slight evidence that gender differences in preference have diminished in the last decade. Archer and MacDonald (1991) reported the results of interviews with 10–15-year-old girls about their own school subject likes and dislikes and those of other girls. Their own likes and dislikes were both split fairly evenly between stereotypically masculine and stereotypically feminine subjects, providing little evidence of the traditional gender split, and their views of the likes and dislikes of other girls were only slightly more stereotyped. Although this study does apparently provide evidence of a reduction in stereotyping among girls, it was based upon a small sample and large age range. Recently, Colley *et al.* (1994a) examined the rankings of nine curriculum subjects from 11–13-year-old pupils in a comprehensive middle school. English received the highest average rank for girls followed by humanities. For boys, PE received the highest average rank followed by science. For all four of these subjects a statistically significant gender difference was found in the rankings of boys and girls indicating that some subjects remain 'gendered'.

Course enrolments and subject preferences of male and female students follow the stereotypes of academic disciplines. Some areas have consistently been stereotyped as masculine while others have been stereotyped as feminine. Weinreich-Haste (1979, 1981) asked 13–14-year-old secondary school pupils to rate subjects on several scales: masculine–feminine, difficult–easy, interesting–boring, useful–useless, complicated–simple, about people–about things, involves feeling–involves thought. She found that of the academic subjects rated, physical sciences and maths were perceived as the most masculine and French and English as the most feminine subjects. However, the most strongly stereotyped subjects were vocationally related: cookery and typing were feminine, woodwork and metalwork were masculine. Inevitably, occupational stereotypes have a powerful effect upon perceptions of related areas in education, and the recent increase in provision for vocational training through the GNVQ system warrants careful scrutiny in this context. Weinreich-Haste's findings were followed up in 1991 by Archer and Macrae using 11–12-year-olds. Their findings were similar: craft design and technology, IT and physics were rated as significantly masculine while personal and social education, RE, typing and home economics were rated as significantly feminine. The intercorrelations between the scales found in both studies throw some light on the perceptions of gender-stereotyped subjects of male and female pupils. For girls, masculine–feminine correlated with difficult–easy and complicated–simple, so masculine subjects were seen as difficult and complicated while feminine ones were seen as easy and simple. For boys, masculine–feminine was correlated with interesting–boring and about things–about people, so masculine subjects were seen as interesting and about things, while feminine subjects were seen as boring and about people. Archer and Macrae suggest that the pattern of correlations also indicates that masculine subjects may be seen as of higher status than feminine ones.

Preference for and choice of subjects in the educational system influence and are influenced by desired career path. A clear gender gap in the career aspirations of 14-year-olds was recorded by Kelly (1989), demonstrating a distinction between occupations which are associated with machines or technology among boys and for people-oriented occupations for girls. Among the top ten ideal jobs for boys were engineer, pilot and computers, and for girls, nurse, teacher and hairdresser. There is a clear association here and in the perceptions of masculine and feminine school subjects with the traditional division of labour between males and females, and their occupational and familial roles. The association of feminine subjects with 'about people' and masculine subjects with 'about things' is linked to both female participation in occupations which require extensive contact with others and to their preferences for subject areas which concern or are about people rather than those which deal with inanimate entities or systems.

Some subject areas with a particularly masculine image have been more intensively studied from the point of view of liking and participation by boys and girls, and the findings from these studies have identified factors which may underlie different patterns of subject choice between males and females more generally. One area which is of particular interest in this context is computing in which interaction occurs with a machine rather than another human. The computer can be perceived as a machine or a tool, or animistically, reflecting a relationship between the machine and its user. Nelson *et al.* (1991) investigated differences in relational style when interacting with computers and found that females who thought of computers as machines rather than as animate (with connotations of being friendly and interactive) were more likely to drop out at the start of an introductory computing course. The reverse was true of males. Computer studies is one of the most gendered curriculum subjects in terms of voluntary course enrolments, and one in which the recent situation appears to be worsening rather than improving (only 14 per cent of entrants to university computing courses in 1992 were female [UCCA, 1992]). The major problem for girls appears to be a lack of confidence and increased anxiety in using computers. This is reduced with experience (Chen 1986) but presents a significant barrier to the use of computers in a variety of settings. There is an abundance of literature examining factors which contribute to the gender gap in computing and its masculine image (e.g. Campbell 1988; Ware and Stuck 1985). There is no indication that girls and women who use computers are any less competent than their male counterparts, but the manner in which formal introduction occurs and the types of task for which computers are used appear to be very important in encouraging their use. It also seems that the presence of boys in the learning environment, with their greater experience and confidence discourages girls, and disadvantages them in the competition for resources (Comber *et al.* 1997). A similar observation to that often made in the science classroom has been made with respect to computers: 'There's two computers and the boys always use them, the girls never use them. I did it once and that was OK, but I never got the chance to do it again because the boys were always on it' (quote from a 12-year-old girl, Colley *et al.* 1997: 7).

Female participation in science and mathematics has also attracted a substantial amount of attention. Mathematics has traditionally been preferred by boys (Fennema 1980); indeed, girls are more likely than boys to perceive it as irrelevant to their interests and not useful for their future lives or careers. There is a large international literature investigating strategies for overcoming females' mathematics anxiety (e.g. Marr and Helme 1987). Similarly, physical science which is perceived as complex and abstract shows a marked gender gap, although biology attracts slightly more girls than boys and has not been stereotyped as masculine in the empirical studies of preferences. The focus of school biology upon living organisms rather than upon abstract laws and formulae removes the association with masculinity. The importance of relevant syllabus content to male and female concerns is illustrated in a study by Sjoberg (1988), who found that boys performed better than girls in physics and chemistry, but that biology showed little difference between the sexes. More detailed investigation of performance in the different areas revealed that girls scored higher on questions about human reproduction, the effects of hormones and heredity, while boys scored higher on questions on such topics as electricity, mechanics, sound and light. The growing abstractness and complexity of science through school results in an increase in negative attitudes for both sexes, but particularly for girls (Doherty and Dawe 1988). Weinreich-Haste (1979) published a review entitled 'What sex is science?'. The answer apparently depends critically on the content and focus of the syllabus: it is not science that is masculine but the study of abstract, complex, inanimate processes and objects.

Unlike physics, computing and mathematics, physical education is not complex and abstract but nevertheless is strongly stereotyped for males in preference studies. The explanation given has focused upon its close association with male gender-role socialisation which emphasises the psychological attributes such as competitiveness and independence, and the physical competencies acquired through boys' play which is more group-based and less constrained to the home (e.g. Birrell 1983). Physical education has come under scrutiny as part of a more general interest in differences in male and female sport participation over the lifespan, and in particular in the reduction in female participation which occurs at adolescence. The reduction in sporting interest for girls which occurs at the age of 14 was recorded by Van Wersch et al. (1992). Their study indicated that the lower status of physical education as a school subject may have contributed to the reduction in interest because at that stage in school studies start to focus upon public examinations. The lesser effect of this consideration upon boys probably reflects the fact that physical education is more significant in the male role, starting in childhood: as Archer's (1984) analysis of developmental pathways suggests, one of the inconsistencies in the male role description arises from the concentration on physical toughness and prowess during childhood which is modified to focus upon occupational success later. Another factor contributing to the differential perceptions of physical education by males and females arises from their motivational patterns with respect to sport and exercise; females value the social contact which accompanies some sport participation more highly than males, reflecting their orientation towards people rather than the more abstract rewards of competition which are more highly valued by males (e.g. Tappe et al. 1990).

There is evidence that participation in activities stereotyped for the opposite sex may induce role conflict. Such incompatibility of the female role with male-stereotyped activities has been recorded for girls who participate in sport (see Birrell 1983). The perceived negative concomitants of participation or achievement in traditionally masculine areas have also been emphasised by Horner (1974) in her discussions of 'fear of success' among females. These consist of problems in fulfilling traditional role expectations and in social interactions. Similarly, Lage (1991) found that 14–15-year-olds saw girls' involvement with computers as indicative of a lack of femininity and loneliness. Other investigators have suggested that strategies are adopted to reduce the apparent conflict: for example, Measor (1984) reported that girls in science classes feign clumsiness in order to protect their feminine image.

The about things–about people dimension which has been found to differentiate between academic subjects appears to be fundamental to their gender stereotyping and the degree to which they attract participants of each sex. However, recent changes in the way in which some subjects are taught indicate that subject enrolments are sensitive not only to the overall image of a discipline but also to modifications of that image through changes in the curriculum and methods of delivery. Of particular interest is the change which has occurred in the uptake of music GCSE (optional at 16) by boys as a result of a shift of emphasis from traditional instrumental musical skills to greater participation through the use of computers and electronic musical instruments. These have allowed pupils to compensate for a lack of traditional musical training which attracts more girls (DES 1991) and have resulted in a gradual closing of the gender gap in GCSE enrolments. The shift to a greater use of male-stereotyped technological skills has not been enthusiastically received by girls, many of whom still prefer the use of traditional instruments (Comber *et al.* 1993; Colley *et al.* 1997).

Skill areas associated with the opposite sex inevitably reduce self-efficacy beliefs which play a major role in motivation (Bandura 1982). Gender differences in self-efficacy beliefs have been found in male-stereotyped areas such as mathematics (Pajares and Miller 1994) and computing (Miura 1987). The increasing use of technology in female-dominated areas such as music, while encouraging the participation of boys, may result in the gradual exclusion of girls from part of the syllabus, and this has been raised as an area of concern. It seems that choice can be affected by the perceived skill requirements of a particular subject, and this conclusion opens up the possibility that teaching methods and syllabus content can play a significant role in modifying existing patterns of choice.

The learning environment

One important source of variation in the extent to which stereotyping takes place lies in the context in which behaviour is enacted. Deaux and Major (1987) drew attention to the role of context in shaping gender-linked behaviour which results from an individual's expectancies and self-identity: gender-related behaviour may be salient or irrelevant in a given situation. While gender stereotypes of some subject areas emerge consistently, it is also evident that their effects can be moderated by the learning environment. One of the major issues to emerge from changes in the structures of schools over the past few decades arises from the debate over the relative advantages and disadvantages of single-sex vs. mixed teaching for both sexes, first at the level of overall academic achievement and social development, and second, at the level of choice and enjoyment of specific subject areas.

Single sex vs. co-educational schools

In the 1960s and 1970s in both Britain (except Northern Ireland) and the US trends in education led to a marked reduction in the number of single-sex state-funded secondary schools. As a consequence, single-sex schools are now a small minority in the state sector although they have remained popular in the private sector. The whole issue of the advantages and disadvantages of single-sex vs. mixed secondary education has recently come to prominence in the UK due to the publication of examination result league tables which have shown that single-sex schools, particularly girls' schools, are over-represented at the top of the leagues for both the GCSE results of 16-year-olds and for the A level results of 18-year-olds. One issue which has been resurrected as a result of these data is that of the potential benefits of single-sex education for girls in particular.

The demise of the single-sex school in the state sector was largely due to social pressures to encourage cross-sex contact and socialisation in a more 'natural' environment. In terms of educational reform, there was also a strong impetus to make schools enjoyable and the traditional concentration on order and discipline was regarded as oppressive and potentially stifling for the development of many children. Selectivity was also gradually abandoned in favour of mixed-ability comprehensive education. Ironically the pendulum has now swung back and many parents are now buying an education for their children which is modelled upon the post-war single-sex grammar schools. Of particular relevance to this chapter are the advantages and disadvantages, both academic and for social development, of the two kinds of education for boys and girls. Research in the 1970s, particularly that of Dale (1969, 1971, 1974) tended to emphasise the social benefits of co-education, and the possible disadvantage of lower achievement in girls was not given much emphasis. Even the notion that there are social benefits has been challenged with respect to girls (Mahony 1985). A debate has since ensued in which a clear picture of potential disadvantages, both academic and social, of co-education for girls has emerged, although methodological points have been hotly contested.

Dale's research, which was undertaken in schools in England and Wales, appeared to find that students from co-educational schools were less anxious than their peers in single-sex schools, that boys had lower neuroticism scores and higher levels of academic achievement, particularly in mathematics. He concluded that co-education was beneficial for boys and probably had little effect on girls. More recently single-sex schools have been found to foster higher academic achievement (Finn 1980; Willis and Kenway 1986) but when differences in intake have been allowed for this difference largely disappears (Steedman 1984).

27

Studies in the 1970s and 1980s examining possible social advantages of co-education (e.g. Feather 1974; Schneider and Coutts 1982) also acknowledged their failure to control pre-existing differences which may have accounted for any school-type differences found.

Marsh *et al.* (1989) undertook a five-year longitudinal study of the merger of a girls' and boys' school into two co-educational schools. They found some benefit of the change for the self-concept of both sexes and no evidence of any effect on academic achievement. This study, because it is longitudinal and examines the same participants in both kinds of school setting, does not have the problem of non-equivalent groups which proved so problematic in previous studies. The authors acknowledge the limitation of basing conclusions upon only two schools. However, they interpret their findings as being supportive of Dale's conclusions and of extending the generality of his findings to an Australian setting. While examining a transition from one system to another may be informative, there are inevitable problems in interpreting the data. The transition will inevitably be seen as a positive one, and the teachers involved clearly saw it as such. Expectations engendered in the pupils will presumably have been very positive and it is not surprising therefore that the effect on self-concept was positive. The special circumstances will also have encouraged teachers to manage the transition carefully with respect to the academic needs of the pupils so the circumstances are unlikely to truly reflect life in the two school systems.

One methodological issue in particular which has caused problems in the interpretation of data from studies which use a single-sex vs. co-educational school comparison, concerns the scarcity of single-sex schools within the state system in the main English-speaking countries in which such studies have taken place: the USA, Australia and England. As a result, some prominent studies (e.g. Lee and Bryk 1986) have used schools which have some form of selection, by the school, the parents or both, which are fee-paying, which are Catholic schools with a particularly traditional approach to education, or which have some combination of these three characteristics. The applicability of the results to the state-funded sector and the possibility of some school-related factor other than sex of intake being responsible for statistically significant findings have both been raised as potential problems.

Lee and Bryk (1986) examined academic achievements and attitudes among pupils enrolled in co-educational and single-sex Catholic private high schools using data from a national survey. The choice of schools was determined by pragmatic factors. Single-sex secondary education is rare in the US public system and the non-Catholic private schools sampled in the survey were too different to each other for data to be pooled and too few in number to provide a meaningful comparison. In a series of regression analyses in which statistical adjustments were made for socioeconomic and ethnic variations between pupils and between schools, results were obtained which provided evidence of benefits of single-sex schools for girls in particular. Girls in single-sex schools were more likely to associate with academically oriented peers, and have an interest in both mathematics and English. A similar but non-significant trend was found for boys. Pupils in boys' schools were more likely to have more positive attitudes to socially active peers and student athletes. A more 'academic' ethos seemed to prevail in the single-sex schools in which pupils, especially girls, did more homework. Boys in boys' schools took more mathematics and science courses and fewer vocational courses than their peers in co-educational schools. Measures of academic achievement again showed positive effects for single-sex schools, although the effect diminished from sophomore to senior years for boys and increased for girls. Of particular note were the gains made in girls' schools in reading and science achievement. Measures of self-concept, locus of control and educational aspirations produced significant effects in favour of girls' schools with non-significant effects for boys. Lee and Bryk felt that their statistical adjustment countered many concerns about selection with respect to their sample, and pointed out that in many of the communities sampled there was only one type of Catholic school available, although they conceded that factors other than those they adjusted for may have been present. Their data taken together are indicative of academic and other benefits for girls educated in single-sex secondary schools, but the evidence for boys was much weaker. The freedom from social pressures arising from the presence of the opposite sex was offered as one possible explanation of the benefits for girls, with other possible factors being the similarity in the gender composition of the staff and student bodies and the more academic nature of courses in single-sex schools.

However, these findings were rapidly challenged. Marsh (1989b) criticised Lee and Bryk for a number of methodological inadequacies, including their use of one-tailed significance tests, failure to control for pre-existing differences, and failure to test for sex differences in outcome variables rather than relying on inspection of the data from boys and girls respectively. Marsh conducted analyses of data from the same database which attempted to control for background variable and found little evidence of school-type effects. A debate then took place in the literature (Lee and Bryk 1989; Marsh 1989b) with each set of authors taking different methodological stances and drawing different conclusions from the data. In stressing the advantages of co-educational schools, Marsh also reiterated the findings of other investigators (Feather 1974; Schneider and Coutts 1982) that students prefer co-education which, he concludes, is a 'compelling advantage' in their favour. It is possible only to draw tentative conclusions from this recent debate because methodological issues, particularly those of sampling, remain problematic. The most recent evidence of an academic advantage for single-sex education, and especially for girls, comes from data in the public domain – the annual school league tables of public examination results published in the press. These, however, suffer from similar problems of sampling to studies in the educational literature: there is no account taken of catchment area, selection policies or of the degree to which such schools are chosen by ambitious middle-class parents.

In addition to possible effects upon social development and achievement, there is evidence of an effect of school type upon subject preferences and choice. The findings in this area support the view that greater gender polarisation occurs in co-educational than in single-sex schools. Ormerod (1975) examined the subject choices of a large sample of pupils from single-sex and co-educational grammar and comprehensive schools. The pupils were selected to be similar in terms of expected GCE O level entry. Across the sample as a whole, the usual popularity of mathematics and physical sciences for boys, and English and French for girls emerged, but less polarisation was found among the single-sex pupils. A more recent study by Stables (1990) investigated attitudes to school subjects and, in particular, science subjects, among 13–14-year-olds from mixed and single-sex comprehensive schools. Again evidence of less polarisation among single-sex pupils was found. Physics was preferred by girls in single-sex schools and boys in co-educational schools, while French was preferred by girls in co-educational schools and boys in single-sex schools. Lawrie and Brown (1992) investigated the perceptions of the gender stereotyping of school subjects among 14–15-year-old pupils from single-sex and mixed secondary schools. There were some differences found in the rated enjoyment and difficulty of mathematics according to the sex of the pupils and the school type. Girls from the mixed school perceived mathematics to be more difficult than their male counterparts. They also enjoyed mathematics less than male pupils from the mixed school and female pupils from the single-sex school. A level enrolments also varied according to school type: the proportion of girls choosing mathematics in the single-sex school was more than twice that of girls in the co-educational school, while enrolment for English was substantially lower in the single-sex school. This tendency for greater gender polarisation in the mixed school was also present for boys, for whom enrolments in modern languages were substantially higher, and for physics substantially lower in the single-sex school. Since Lawrie and Brown sampled from only one school for each type, it is possible that some apparent school-type differences are in whole or in part due to differences specific to individual schools or even to individual subject teachers. However, all three schools had the same catchment area and were selective in intake.

Single-sex teaching within mixed schools has been found to have positive benefits for girls in science and mathematics. For example, Whyte (1986) reported on the teaching of Year 3 science in girls-only classes in one of the participating schools in the Girls into Science and Technology (GIST) initiative. The outcome was a significant increase in the number of girls choosing physics in Year 4 and indications of more positive attitudes to science. The location of the effect – upon pupils, teachers, or both – is not clear. Whyte points to the role of such classes in making teachers aware of girls' potential and also of their different ways of working. A similar conclusion was drawn by Smith (1986) who conducted a longitudinal study of the use of single-sex groups in the teaching of mathematics. Little evidence was found of increased achievement, but once the teachers were made aware that girls need not underachieve, improvements were evident in both single-sex and mixed groups.

Although the picture emerging from the literature on single-sex teaching is somewhat murky in places, a cautious conclusion that less gender polarisation occurs may be drawn. There may also be some advantage in the achievement levels attained, particularly by girls. So what can account for these benefits of single-sex teaching? The most obvious explanation derives from the fact that gender is not a salient part of the teaching and learning environment, and so its influence on the behaviour of both pupils and teachers is reduced. Gender is a powerful influence upon classroom interactions (e.g. Baker 1987; Whyte 1984) and attributions of success and failure (Swim and Sanna 1996), both of which in turn influence choice and achievement.

Addressing the problems: strategies for overcoming gender stereotyping

As has been shown in the discussion so far, a number of factors appear to contribute to or moderate the gender stereotyping of academic subject areas. One of the major goals of any educational system ought to be to try to promote equality of opportunity and choice. On the one hand, the fact that boys and girls tend to take different pathways through the educational system may not be regarded as particularly problematic provided they have access to different specialisms, and that there is evidence that achievement in all areas is possible. However, there is significant concern that science and technology in particular are failing to attract females. The concern has arisen for a number of reasons. There is no doubt that some of the impetus has come from the more general debate about access by women to key occupational areas which carry power and status. The increasing importance and centrality of science and technology in our lives has emphasised the need for wide participation. Ironically, recruitment to some areas of science is poor and particularly poor among females, again raising the lack of take-up of courses as a significant problem. The poor recruitment of males to modern language courses has attracted far less attention, although one might argue that communication across national and language boundaries is essential to our economic well-being. However, lack of linguistic competence can be supported by translations and the possession of language skills provides the basis for delivering a service rather than being an absolute necessity to function effectively in many multilingual environments. Such skills may therefore be regarded as less essential and of lower status than those associated with the main professions and science by many males.

Given the greater significance attached to the lack of females opting for science and technology, some of the educational literature reports the results of strategies designed to increase female participation or counter female underachievement. These vary from interventions within a single classroom to large initiatives such as GIST (Girls into Science and Technology) or WISE (Women into Science and Engineering). GIST was successful in reducing the masculine stereotyping of science among children, although its effect upon choice was more dependent upon local circumstances within a given school (Kelly *et al.* 1987). The most interesting outcomes from the larger initiatives derive from observations or findings from smaller-scale observations or interventions, and coincide with the results of smaller, more piecemeal studies. In general, there is evidence that classroom organisation, the use of familiar material which is felt to be relevant, and structured presentation of material may encourage girls in the learning of scientific or technological material. For example, Fish *et al.* (1986) had some success in using a range of intervention strategies to increase the participation of girls in computing activities. In particular, girls were encouraged by having girls-only computing sessions, having a girls' computer committee and undertaking activities emphasising social contact with other girls. They were discouraged if female friends were absent from the computer room. In other words, their participation was encouraged by undertaking computing activities on their own terms and in a manner which fits with their preferred style of working. It is also interesting to note the preference for engaging with others while working – the antithesis of the solitary 'computer nerd'. A similar finding emphasising the importance of collaborative work emerged from a study of the educational use of science software by Char *et al.* (1983). The liking of girls for the software only equalled that of boys when it was used collaboratively and for activities with some personal relevance.

Familiarity with tasks and materials has been found to increase the performance of girls on science practical tasks. Toh (1993) examined the performance of 13-year-old boys and girls matched for attitude, aptitude and prior knowledge on three problem-solving tasks. Girls outperformed boys when the tasks were familiar as a result of pre-exposure. Structured teaching has also been found to encourage girls, as demonstrated by Arch and Cummins (1989) who compared two forms of introduction to computers: structured training in class vs. unstructured voluntary exposure with assistance available. Females who had received the unstructured introduction perceived themselves as less competent, had more negative attitudes to computers and used computers less than peers who had received the structured introduction or males who had received the unstructured introduction. Science and computing are strongly stereotyped as domains of male competence, and exposure through leisure to relevant skills is far greater than for females. Under such circumstances the importance of structure and familiarity to females in the learning environment is understandable.

Conclusion

Why do the subject preferences and enrolments of males and females in secondary school vary? The theme running through this chapter stresses the reflection of adult male and female social roles and the abilities and attributes assigned to males and females on the basis of these roles in the gender stereotypes of academic subject areas. The information contained in these stereotypes is acquired during socialisation and reinforced by prevailing beliefs, observation of the *status quo*, and educational practices which themselves are influenced by the same stereotypes. Much of the research relevant to the discussion has been driven by the interest in potential female disadvantage, which derives in turn from broader concerns about access to occupations and institutions dominated by males enacting their traditional social roles. There has been little concern expressed about the possible disadvantages for males of the effects of academic gender stereotyping. The most problematic areas for girls are mathematics, physical science and technology, and interventions have been designed to address concerns about their masculine image and perceived remoteness from everyday life. There is evidence from school-based studies and from action research interventions such as GIST that teaching methods and syllabus content are influential, and there is much systematic work to be done at classroom level to continue to discover and disseminate methods that counteract prevailing stereotypes and their inevitable influence upon choice in secondary education.

References

Arch, E.C. and Cummins, D.E. (1989) 'Structured and unstructured exposure to computers: sex differences in attitude and use among college students', *Sex Roles*, 20: 245–54.

Archer, J. (1984) 'Gender roles as developmental pathways', *British Journal of Social Psychology* 23: 245–56.

Archer, J. and McDonald, M. (1991) 'Gender roles and school subjects in adolescent girls', *Educational Research* 33: 55–64.

Archer, J. and Macrae, M. (1991) 'Gender-perceptions of school subjects among 10–11-year-olds', *British Journal of Educational Psychology* 61: 99–103.

Bakan, D. (1966) *The Duality of Human Existence: An Essay on Psychology and Religion*, Chicago: Rand McNally.

Baker, D. (1987) 'Sex differences in classroom interactions in secondary science', *Journal of Classroom Interaction* 22: 6–11.

Bandura, A. (1977) *Social Learning Theory*, New Jersey: Prentice-Hall.

—— (1982) 'Self efficacy beliefs in human agency', *American Psychologist* 37: 122–47.

Bem, S.L. (1974) 'The measurement of psychological androgyny', *Journal of Consulting and Clinical Psychology* 45: 155–62.

—— (1981) 'Gender schema theory: a cognitive account of sex-typing', *Psychological Review* 66: 354–64.

Birrell, S. (1983) 'The psychological dimensions of female athletic participation', in M.A. Boutilier and L. San Giovanni (eds) *The Sporting Woman*, Champaign, Ill.: Human Kinetics Publishers.

Campbell, N.J. (1988) 'Correlates of computer anxiety of adolescent students', *Journal of Adolescent Research* 3: 107–17.

Char, C., Hawkins, J., Wootten, J., Sheingold, K. and Roberts, T. (1983) 'The voyage of the Mimi: classroom case studies of software, video and print materials'. Report to the US Department of Education, Centre for Children and Technology.

Chen, M. (1986) 'Gender and computing: the beneficial effects of experience on attitudes', *Journal of Educational Computing Research* 2: 265–82.

Colley, A., Comber, C. and Hargreaves, D.J. (1994a) 'Gender effects in school subject preferences', *Educational Studies* 20: 13–19.

—— (1994b) 'School subject preferences of pupils in single-sex and co-educational secondary schools', *Educational Studies* 20: 379–85.

—— (1997) 'IT and music education: what happens to boys and girls in co-educational and single-sex schools', *British Journal of Music Education* 14: 1–9.

Comber, C., Hargreaves, D.J. and Colley, A. (1993) 'Girls, boys and technology in music education', *British Journal of Music Education* 10: 123–34.

Comber, C., Colley, A., Hargreaves, D.J. and Dorn, L. (1997) 'The effects of age, gender and computer experience upon computer attitudes', *Educational Research* 39: 1–11.

Dale, R.R. (1969) *Mixed or Single-Sex School? Volume 1: A Research Study about Pupil–Teacher Relationships*, London: Routledge and Kegan Paul.

—— (1971) *Mixed or Single-Sex School? Volume 2: Some Social Aspects*, London: Routledge and Kegan Paul.

—— (1974) *Mixed or Single-Sex School? Volume 3: Attainment, Attitudes and Overview*, London: Routledge and Kegan Paul.

Deaux, K. and Major, B. (1987) 'Putting gender into context: an interactive model of gender-related behavior', *Psychological Review* 94: 369–89.

DES (1991) *Music from 5 to 14: Curriculum Matters 4*, London: HMSO.

Doherty, J. and Dawe, J. (1988) 'The relationship between developmental maturity and attitudes to school science: an exploratory study', *Educational Studies* 11: 93–107.

Eagly, A.H. (1987) *Sex Differences in Social Behavior: A Social Role Interpretation*, Hillsdale, N.J.: Erlbaum.

Eagly, A.H. and Steffen, V. (1984) 'Gender stereotypes stem from the distribution of women and men into social roles', *Journal of Personality and Social Psychology* 46: 735–54.

Elwood, J. and Comber, C. (1996) *Gender Differences in Examinations at 18+*. Final Report to the Nuffield Foundation, London.

Fagot, B.I. (1978) 'The influence of sex of child on parental reactions to toddler children', *Child Development* 49: 459–61.

Feather, N.T. (1974) 'Co-education, values and satisfaction with school', *Journal of Educational Psychology* 66: 9–15.

Feingold, A. (1988) 'Cognitive gender differences are disappearing', *American Psychologist* 43: 95–103.

Fennema, E. (1980) 'Sex-related differences in mathematics achievement: where and why?' in L.H. Fox, L. Brody and D. Tobin (eds) *Women and the Mathematical Mystique*, Baltimore: John Hopkins University Press.

Finn, J.D. (1980) 'Sex differences in educational outcomes: a cross-national study', *Sex Roles* 6: 9–25.

Fish, M.C., Gross, A.L. and Sanders, J.S. (1986) 'The effect of equity strategies on girls' computer usage in school', *Computers in Human Behavior* 2: 127–34.

Gregson, J.F. and Colley, A. (1986) 'Concomitants of sport participation in male and female adolescents', *International Journal of Sport Psychology* 17: 10–22.

Horner, M.S. (1974) 'Performance of women in non competitive and interpersonal competitive achievement-oriented situations' in J.W. Atkinson and J.O. Rayner (eds) *Motivation and Achievement*, New York: Halsted.

Hyde, J.S. and Linn, M.C. (1988) 'A meta-analysis of gender differences in verbal abilities', *Psychological Bulletin* 107: 53–69.

Kelly, A. (1989) '"When I grow up I want to be . . . ": a longitudinal study of the development of career preferences', *British Journal of Guidance and Counselling* 17: 179–200.

Kelly, A., Whyte, J. and Smail, B. (1987) 'Girls into science and technology: final report', in A. Kelly (ed.) *Science for Girls*, Milton Keynes: Open University Press.

Kohlberg, L. (1966) 'A cognitive-developmental analysis of children's sex role concepts and attitudes', in E.E. Maccoby (ed.) *The Development of Sex Differences*, London: Tavistock.

Lage, E. (1991) 'Boys, girls and microcomputers', *European Journal of Psychology of Education* 6: 29–44.

Langlois, J.H. and Downs, A.C. (1980) 'Mothers, fathers, and peers as socialisation agents of sex-typed play behaviors in young children', *Child Development* 51: 1217–47.

Lawrie, L. and Brown, R. (1992) 'Sex stereotypes, school subject preferences and career aspirations as a function of single/mixed sex schooling and presence/absence of an opposite sex sibling', *British Journal of Educational Psychology* 62: 132–8.

Lee, V.E. and Bryk, A.S. (1986) 'Effects of single-sex secondary schools on student achievement and attitudes', *Journal of Educational Psychology* 78: 381–95.

—— (1989) 'Effects of single-sex schools: Response to Marsh', *Journal of Educational Psychology* 81: 647–50.

Lytton, H. and Romney, D.M. (1991) 'Parents' differential socialisation of boys and girls: a meta-analysis', *Psychological Bulletin* 109: 267–96.

Mahony, P. (1985) *Schools for boys? Co-education reassessed*, London: Hutchinson.

Marr, B. and Helme, S. (eds) (1987) *Mathematics: A New Beginning*, Melbourne: State Training Board.

Marsh, H.W. (1989a) 'Effects of attending single-sex and co-educational high schools on achievement, attitudes, behaviors, and sex differences', *Journal of Educational Psychology* 81: 70–85.

Marsh, H.W. (1989b) 'Effects of single-sex and co-educational schools: a response to Lee and Bryk', *Journal of Educational Psychology* 81: 651–3.

Marsh, H.W., Owens, L., Myers, M.R. and Smith, I.D. (1989) 'The transition from single-sex to co-educational high schools: teacher perceptions, academic achievement and self-concept', *British Journal of Educational Psychology* 59: 155–73.

Measor, L. (1984) 'Gender and sciences: pupils' gender-based conceptions of school subjects' in M. Hammersley and P. Woods (eds) *Life in Schools: the Sociology of Pupil Culture*, Milton Keynes: Open University Press.

Mischel, W. (1966) 'A social learning view of sex differences' in E.E. Maccoby (ed.) *The Development of Sex Differences*, London: Tavistock.

—— (1970) 'Sex typing and socialisation' in P.H. Mussen (ed.) *Carmichael's Manual of child psychology. Volume 2*, New York: Wiley.

Miura, I.T. (1987) 'The relationship of computer self-efficacy expectations to computer interest and course enrollment in college', *Sex Roles* 16: 303–11.

Nelson, L.J., Wiese, G.M. and Cooper, J. (1991) 'Getting started with computers:

Experience, anxiety, and relational style', *Computers in Human Behavior* 7: 185–202.

Ormerod, M.B. (1975) 'Subject preference and choice in co-educational and single-sex secondary schools', *British Journal of Educational Psychology* 45: 257–67.

Pajares, F. and Miller, M.D. (1994) 'Role of self-efficacy and self concept beliefs on mathematical problem solving: a path analysis', *Journal of Educational Psychology* 86: 193–203.

Schneider, F.W. and Coutts, L.M. (1982) 'High school environment: A comparison of co-educational and single-sex schools', *Journal of Educational Psychology* 74: 898–906.

Singleton, C.H. (1986) 'Biological and social explanations of sex role stereotyping' in D.J. Hargreaves and A.M. Colley, (eds) *The Psychology of Sex Roles*, London: Harper and Row.

Sjoberg, S. (1988) 'Gender and the image of science', *Scandinavian Journal of Education Research* 32: 49–60.

Smith, S. (1986) *Separate Tables*, London: HMSO.

Spence, J.T. and Helmreich, R.L. (1978) *Masculinity and femininity: Their Psychological Dimensions, Correlates and Antecedents*, Austin: University of Texas Press.

Stables, A. (1990) 'Differences between pupils from mixed and single-sex schools in their enjoyment of school subjects and in their attitudes to science and to school', *Educational Review* 42: 221–30.

Steedman, J.(1984) 'Examination results in mixed and single-sex schools', in D. Reynolds (ed.) *Studying School Effectiveness*, London: Falmer Press.

Swim, J.K. and Sanna, L.J. (1996) 'He's skilled she's lucky. A meta-analysis of observer's attributions for women's and men's successes and failures', *Personality and Social Psychology Bulletin* 22: 507–19.

Tappe, M.K., Duda, J.L. and Menges Ehnwald, P. (1990) 'Personal investment predictors of adolescent motivational orientation towards exercise', *Canadian Journal of Sports Sciences* 15: 185–92.

Toh, K-A. (1993) 'Gender and practical tasks in science', *Educational Research* 35: 255–65.

UCCA (1992) *UCCA Statistical Supplement 1991–2*, Cheltenham: The Universities Central Council on Admissions.

Van Wersch, A., Trew, K. and Turner, I. (1992) 'Post-primary pupils' interest in physical education: age and gender differences', *British Journal of Educational Psychology* 62: 56–72.

Ware, M.C. and Stuck, M.F. (1985) 'Sex-role measures vis-a-vis microcomputer use: A look at the pictures', *Sex Roles* 13: 205–16.

Weinreich-Haste, H. (1979) 'What sex is science?' in O. Hartnett, G. Boden and M. Fuller (eds) *Women: Sex Role Stereotyping*, London: Tavistock.

—— (1981) 'The image of science' in A. Kelly (ed.) *The Missing half: Girls and Science Education*, Manchester: Manchester University Press.

Whyte, J. (1984) 'Observing sex stereotypes and interaction in the school laboratory and workshop', *Educational Review* 36: 75–86.

Whyte, J. (1986) *Girls into Science and Technology: The Story of a Project*, London: Routledge and Kegan Paul.

Willis, S. and Kenway, J. (1986) 'On overcoming sexism in schooling: to marginalise or mainstream', *Australian Journal of Education* 30: 132–49.

3

USING STEREOTYPES TO DISPEL NEGATIVE PERCEPTIONS OF CAREERS IN SCIENCE AND TECHNOLOGY

Pauline Lightbody and Alan Durndell

Men and women are in various degrees behaviourally as well as physically different. In particular, they continue to make differential choices of subjects to study and occupations to enter. Much attention has been paid especially to the low take-up of sciences and technologies (with certain significant exceptions) by women. Pauline Lightbody and Alan Durndell relate this to the career aspirations of school children, which in turn involve their views both of what they are and what they can do, and of the nature of subjects and careers. They suggest ways in which both these aspects might be altered so as to make a wider range of opportunity open to both women and men.

Despite an overall rise in the proportion of undergraduates that are female, courses in the physical sciences and technology have failed to attract female students in large numbers. Three Scottish studies are outlined in this chapter. In the first study the career aspirations of school pupils, aged 16–18, were investigated to identify disparities between pupils' own aspirations and their schematic representations of social and technical roles. The second study, which also involved school pupils, illustrates the disjunction between pupils' personal career aspirations and the 'anyone can do anything' point of view. The third study which focused on women entering the 'professions' found that they were often drawn towards a role which they perceived to be 'socially useful' and involved human contact. Results are linked to the 'we can, but I don't want to' formulation, lenses of gender, and social identity theory. Discussion is then oriented towards intervention policies which would not only identify and target potential 'technical' students but also revise course content in order to increase the attraction of technological courses to students of both genders.

Introduction

The last two decades have seen increasing enrolment in institutions of Higher Education, particularly in the case of females who now account for 48 per cent of all undergraduates compared to only 31 per cent in 1971 (UCCA Statistical Supplement 1971; UCAS Annual Report 1995). Nevertheless, research suggests that occupational trends have remained remarkably stable. Gendered option choice in schools, leading to a traditional pattern of 'gender-appropriate' career paths has been resistant to intervention policies aimed at attracting females to previously male-dominated disciplines. UCAS figures show that in the UK, in 1995, female admissions to engineering, computer studies and the physical sciences were all below 19 per cent of total admissions to each subject; female applications to computer science having fallen from 24 per cent in 1979 to 18 per cent in 1995 (UCCA Statistical Supplement 1979; UCAS Annual Report 1995).

In this chapter we will initially highlight a number of issues which have been attributed to the continuing pattern of gendered subject choice in schools leading to a gendered dichotomy in Further and Higher Education. Following this brief introduction we will focus on a number of recent studies carried out in Scotland, before concluding with some ideas concerning the importance of recognising young people's stereotypical perceptions of different careers in order to attract increasing numbers of applicants to courses with a high technological content

The current position

The persistence of gender-stereotyping within education and thereafter in the labour market has been extensively researched in recent years (e.g. McTeer 1986; Griffin 1985; Kelly 1989; Shemesh 1990; Taber 1992; Colley *et al.* 1994; Lightbody *et al.* 1996a). Many studies have shown that, within school, boys prefer science and technology subjects, while girls tend to prefer language, social studies and humanities (e.g. McTeer 1986; Shemesh 1990). It can be seen from Table 3.1, which shows the percentage of female presentations for the revised Scottish Higher Grade examinations in 1993, that in Scotland females were more highly represented in English, French, modern studies and art. In the sciences, girls tend to opt for biology rather than the physical sciences, which are more popular with male pupils.

Table 3.1: Scottish Higher Grade 1993,
females as a percentage of all presentations

Subject	Female %
French	73
Biology	73
Art and design	61
English	57
Modern studies	60
History	60
Maths	47
Chemistry	46
Physics	30
Computer studies	23

Source: Scottish Examination Board (1993)
Note: Scottish Highers are taken by pupils aged
16–18 years.

A number of explanations have been proposed for this imbalance, including the sex-stereotyping of science and technology (Pratt *et al.* 1984; Cockburn 1985; Whyte 1986; Culley 1988; Gati 1992). It has also been suggested that the 'hidden curriculum' within schools actively reinforces gender stereotypes; that young people have preconceived ideas about careers in science and technology (Fuller 1991); and that the main influence in subject choice comes from peer pressure which may be towards subjects which are perceived to be gender-appropriate (Newton 1986). Research shows that both school pupils and Further/Higher Education students continue to regard some subjects, including engineering, the physical sciences and mathematics, as masculine, and others, including English, French, biology, psychology and sociology, as feminine (Archer and Freedman 1989; Radford and Holdstock 1995). However, it should be noted that other studies have suggested a decline in the gender-stereotyping of school subjects (Archer and MacRae 1991; Archer 1992).

It is not the case that girls are underachieving at school, in fact the success rate of girls in the upper school is greater than that of boys. In Scotland, a higher proportion of girls than boys remain at school beyond the period of compulsory schooling. Of those gaining at least three Higher Grade passes in the same year, 55 per cent were female and 45 per cent male; 53 per cent of those going to college or university were female (School Leavers Destination Report: 1992–93 Cohort 1994). Nevertheless, gender divisions persist in the choice of Higher Education courses in that boys continue to predominate on courses in computing/maths, construction and engineering (School Leavers Destination Report: 1992–93; Cohort 1994).

Technology at home and abroad

The inclusion of computing in the group of subjects where females have not made very much progress indicates that it may be something about dealing with machines and objects rather than science *per se*, as females are attracted into biological sciences in large numbers as shown by their success in entering competitive professions like veterinary science, medicine and physiotherapy. As indicated above, there is little sign of gender neutrality arriving in the area of computing (see Durndell and Lightbody 1993; Durndell and Thomson 1997).

This situation is not universal, however. For example, many of the countries of Central and Eastern Europe that used to be part of the Communist world are of special interest. While they were still Communist, it became apparent that in general their educational systems were producing very large numbers of females who were choosing to study in areas which in Britain and North West Europe featured hardly any females at all at that time, such as engineering. This continued, to a lesser extent, into the world of work. Researchers visiting Russia and Bulgaria found that blankness greeted attempts to engage their hosts in analysis involving gender. There was no issue, the problem had been solved, equality was proclaimed by the state (Walford 1983). In 1987 the educational authorities in Bulgaria were restricting the proportion of engineering students who were women to 50 per cent, a situation inconceivable in Britain (Durndell 1991). There was also concern in Bulgaria over the extent to which girls were outperforming boys in education, referred to as 'the feminisation of the intelligentsia', predating the raising of this issue in Britain.

Why such countries had these experiences is an interesting question. Clearly the answers are complex, but issues such as the status of engineering and the poor quality of technology in these countries have to be relevant, as are the presence of a core curriculum in schools, formal teaching methods and the dominant ideology (see Durndell 1992). Furthermore, this appeared to be achieved without any concessions to altering the nature of engineering to make it more attractive to females, one of the persistent themes of Western debate in this area. Whether the relative gender neutrality of science and technology will survive the collapse of Communism is an interesting and at present unresolved question (Durndell *et al.* 1997).

Interventions

The imbalance between the sexes in the UK has been acknowledged by the government which is committed to promoting growth in science, technology and computer studies in order to tackle a projected skills shortage which is seen as an obstacle to the development of industry and Britain's position in the world economy (White Paper 1993). In order to achieve this aim a number of incentives have been initiated via the education and training system with a view to encouraging both male and female participation in the fields of science and technology:

- Changes to the curriculum which ensure that all pupils, females as well as males, study at least one technical subject up until the age of 16.
- All pupils will receive impartial and accurate careers guidance.
- A new range of vocational qualifications has been introduced which are equivalent to the standard certificates of education, i.e. GCSEs and A levels in England, and Standard Grade and Highers in Scotland.
- College and university funding policies have been modified to provide an incentive to recruit more students to science and engineering courses as opposed to the arts.

(White Paper 1993)

Despite these initiatives many institutions continue to report a shortage of good quality applicants to read for first degrees in science and technology.

What went wrong?

The limited success of intervention policies designed to increase female participation in science and technology suggests that perhaps they have been incorrectly targeted. The tendency to base initiatives exclusively on the Department of Education's perception of 'sex-stereotyping' may result in other possible interpretations being overlooked. Research shows that boys as well as girls hold less positive attitudes towards the physical sciences and technology during their teens than at any other time (Goodwin *et al.* 1981; Whyte 1986; Lightbody 1993), and that any difference between the performance of boys and girls is small in comparison to the variation within each group (Robertson and Stark 1992; Gardner 1974, 1975).

Alternative explanations

Our own research has rejected the vision of young women sitting in the back of science classes unable to participate, or attract the 'stereotypically male' teacher's attention. We believe that such assumptions are unrealistic and outdated. While there may be lingering inhibitions due to the effects of early socialisation and/or discrimination in the labour market, there is ample evidence that women are now ascending the career ladder in areas of their choosing.

It can be seen from Figure 3.1 that while female admissions to engineering courses and the physical sciences rose only marginally between 1979 and 1995, female admissions to veterinary science, medicine, dentistry and law increased to the point where females now outnumber males (UCCA Statistical Supplement 1979; UCAS Annual Report 1995). These disciplines, which were also previously male dominated, have stringent entry requirements, the top three requiring

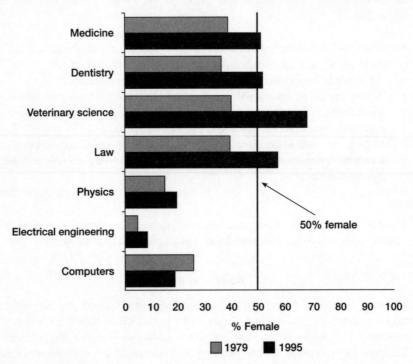

Figure 3.1 Percentage of female applicants accepted by subject in the UK in 1979 and 1995

the 'prestigious' science qualifications which are frequently cited as the reason for lack of female participation in technological careers. Well-qualified female applicants appear to be rejecting courses in the physical sciences and technology on the basis of something other than gendered option choice within schools and/or inadequate qualifications. Thus it is time to seek either an alternative explanation for female avoidance of careers in the fields of science and technology or another means of addressing the disparity.

Recent Scottish research

The following section contains a synopsis of three studies carried out in Scotland within the past four years. Full details can be found in Lightbody and Durndell 1996a, 1996b; Lightbody *et al.* 1995 and Lightbody *et al.* 1996b.

Self-stereotyping and the importance of self-concept

Choosing a suitable career is one of the most far-reaching decisions that a young person will be required to make; however, the decision to follow a particular career is not only based on the expected tasks involved, but also on the inter-action between an individual's social identity and their representation of that profession. The social categories used to group people, and the status or value assigned to these groups, are an important source of identity (Garza and Herringer 1987), and while the importance of self-concept in occupational choice has been recognised for a long time (e.g. Super 1957), it is worth bearing in mind that the more fluid gender roles in the 1990s imply that the self-concept of male and female school-leavers today will be markedly different from those of school-leavers of a decade or more ago.

In order to investigate the role of self-concept in career choice we carried out a study, based on Social Identity Theory (Tajfel 1981), and Self-Categorisation Theory (Turner 1985, 1987), with school pupils aged 16–18 years, attending Scottish secondary schools. Q-methodology provided a framework on which to base an investigation of school pupils' schematic representations of 'technical' and 'socially' oriented career areas. The study also sought to identify any dis-parities between the career aspirations of male and female school pupils, and to compare the pupils' own aspirations with their schematic representations of social and technical roles. (For a full description of this research see Lightbody and Durndell 1996a, 1996b.)

Schematic representations of 'social' and 'technical' roles

The results of our research allowed us to develop a 'picture' of the school pupils' perception of the characteristics associated with 'social' and 'technical' career areas. It was apparent that the majority of school pupils, over 80 per cent, viewed 'technical' workers (labelled *technical stereotype*) as being motivated by financial reward, security and, not surprisingly, an interest in technology. Public contact and social concern were considered to be the least, or most uncharacteristic, attributes for this group. The more 'socially oriented' worker (*social stereotype*) was perceived to be someone who would enjoy working with the public and was concerned about the needs of society in general; they were characterised by a desire to enjoy their course or career. 'Gender' was found to be less salient than other personality characteristics when dealing with a hypothetical situation.

When the pupils' *own* career aspirations were investigated we were able to identify four separate categories, or career 'types', two of which encompassed more males than females and two of which encompassed more females than males. Further investigation of the four career 'types' showed that 22 per cent of the sixth-year pupils, who were currently contemplating their future careers, shared similar attitudes and aspirations to the technical stereotype, particularly in their interest in new technology. Thirty-five percent of pupils shared a similar pattern of attitudes as the social stereotype. It was interesting to note that when we looked at the gender balance of the pupils who fell into these two categories, only 20 per cent of those who shared similar attitudes to the technical stereotype were female, whereas 70 per cent of those who shared similar attitudes to the social stereotype were female. These figures are remarkably similar to the gender dichotomy typically found in course choice within secondary school and Higher education.

Further investigation of the two career 'types' which did not correspond to the technical, or social stereotypes, revealed that one category comprised 24 per cent of pupils who were characterised by a strong desire to make money; they were very instrumental, seeking status and power from their future occupation (we labelled this group *instrumental*). Thirty-five per cent of this group were female. The final category comprised only 8 per cent of the pupils, 75 per cent of whom were female. This group exhibited a rather confused picture, being fairly ambitious but with little direction. They seemed to be practical, looking for some sort of skills training rather than a broad education – perhaps these are the pupils who ultimately opt for a stereotypically suitable career (we subsequently labelled these as *don't knows*).

In many ways the social and technical stereotypes appeared to depict opposite ends of a 'caring'/'material reward' spectrum; however, it would be unwise to focus exclusively on differences at the expense of acknowledging similarities. Shared attitudes and values were identified among pupils in all career 'types' – we will return to this point later.

Choosing subjects at school

Another study carried out in Scottish schools (Lightbody *et al.* 1996b) sought to investigate pupils' experiences when choosing which subjects to study at Standard Grade (age 15), and Higher (age 16–17), and to examine some of the issues which pupils may consider important for their future career. Results indicated that there was little difference between the experiences of males and females when choosing their subjects at school. There was no evidence that girls were being channelled towards sex-stereotyped subjects. In general, pupils agreed that girls were encouraged to break with traditional gender boundaries more often than boys; in fact one pupil claimed that the girls were 'fed up' being told that they should choose more technical subjects.

During group discussions with the school pupils they firmly rejected the notion that some jobs are better suited to males or females; the responses from the girls were unequivocal – anyone can do anything! Nevertheless, when asked their own choice of course or career, pupils' responses fell into a stereotypical gender pattern; girls wishing to enter careers in the arts and caring professions whereas the boys were more likely to choose a technical area.

The females in our study were bright, articulate, knew where they were 'going' and what they wanted. Without exception they all expected to have careers and be self-supporting. Career prospects were found to be of equal importance to females and males; however, females were significantly more likely to value being able to play a useful role in society, being in contact with other people, and enjoying their work more highly than males. Contrary to expectation, having a flexible job and being able to accommodate family commitments were found to be of significantly greater importance to males than females.

Higher education

The two studies mentioned above found support in a third Scottish study (Lightbody *et al.* 1995), this time involving first-year university students enrolled on courses which have remained male dominated, including engineering, physics and computer science, and two courses, law and medicine, on which females now outnumber males. In this instance, a questionnaire was developed to investigate why students chose the course on which they were enrolled. Results indicated that the reason women favoured law and medicine, rather than more techno-logical courses, was because the former courses were seen to be leading to work that contributes to playing a useful social role and that would allow a higher level of social contact. It was concluded that although women tend to avoid techno-logical courses this was not necessarily a negative choice, rather they positively choose courses which lead to careers with higher levels of social involvement.

Resumé

The research studies which have been reported above each endeavoured to untangle some of the issues which may be implicated in the persistence of sex-stereotyped career choice. Initially we described a study which utilised Q-methodology in order to gain a deeper understanding of sixth-year school pupils' career aspirations by developing a schematic representation of the attrib-utes that pupils associate with a 'social' or technical' role and subsequently com-paring these representations to pupils' own aspirations. The results of this research indicated that when dealing with hypothetical situations, the 'sex-stereotyping' of careers was not an issue for either male or female school pupils; nevertheless, their own career aspirations fell into a traditional, 'gendered' pattern. School pupils' schematic representations of technical and more socially oriented roles were found to be polarised at either end of a continuum which extended from 'ambition/material rewards' at one extreme to 'social/caring' at the other. Two other studies were mentioned, the first involving school pupils, and the second involving first-year university students. Both studies revealed that females tend to choose careers in which they perceive there to be a higher degree of social contact than they associate with technological courses and ensuing careers.

The implications

Research shows that although males and females report remarkably similar descriptions of their ideal job there are marked disparities between their actual career plans (Kelly 1989). Certainly we found no evidence in our research that girls were being advised to follow traditional 'female' subjects at school.

(Lightbody *et al.* 1996). Nevertheless, when asked what career or course they wished to follow, school pupils' responses fell into a stereotypical gender pattern.

It is possible that for some female school-leavers their avoidance of careers in science and technology may not be initiated at a conscious level. Sandra Bem, (1993) proposed that hidden beliefs about sex and gender roles, which she labelled 'lenses of gender', are so deeply entrenched in society that they are no longer visible, nevertheless, she claimed that their pervasive qualities permeate our entire culture. In an investigation of the issues that American university students considered important when entering courses traditionally dominated by the opposite sex, Strange and Rae (1983) found that both males and females entered courses precisely because they already shared the prevailing values of that field rather than taking on these values retrospectively. The authors concluded that although congruence of sex role and vocational choice was an important factor in career decisions it may not be considered at the same level of consciousness as other issues.

The personal self vs. the collective self

There is a considerable body of research which shows that there is a discrepancy between the characteristics associated with the large-scale social categories which make up the collective self, for example, occupation, gender or nationality, and the attributes which an individual accepts as part of their own personal identity, despite acknowledging membership of a particular group. Two examples of this phenomenon which are particularly pertinent here include research carried out by Zuckerman and Sayre (1982) who reported that subjects expressed predominantly non-stereotypic attitudes toward occupations and activities in general; nevertheless, when they chose careers for themselves, their choices were very traditional. The second example is a study carried out by Sanders (1987) who investigated female computer usage; she suggested that while girls may lack confidence in their own ability to work with computers, they do not believe that this inability generalises to females as a whole. Sanders described this phenomenon in terms of 'we can, I can't', that is, we (females in general) can, but I (personally) can't.

The potential impact of these 'other to self' comparisons, which are based on a complex, and possibly unconscious, combination of self-concept and stereotyping, can be far-reaching. We believe that it is important to harness these 'natural' modes of thinking in order to reduce the impact of gender-typing on career choice.

'We can, but do we want to?'

Despite a temptation to accept the similarity between the above examples and the findings of our Q-study, there are a number of issues which still require resolution. While males and females undoubtably derive their self-esteem from different activities and beliefs, the picture of girls in the 1990s being intimidated by boys to the extent that they can't participate in an activity they wish to follow is questionable. The possibility of 'we can, I don't want to', that is, if it is a lack of desire rather than lack of confidence which prevents girls from entering technical careers, appears not to have been given equivalent attention. It is possible that too much emphasis has been placed on differences at the expense of identifying areas of similarity.

Pragmatic choices?

Career choice research has almost exclusively focused on school pupils, perceptions of different occupations and their practitioners, rather than their understanding of these practitioners' perceptions of them. If females believe that careers in science and technology are unsympathetic to their needs they may not be willing to enter these occupations. In an American study which investigated the attitudes held by males and females towards women combining scientific careers with family roles (Lips 1992), results showed that males disagreed more often than females that women can combine scientific careers and family. With men currently holding the top scientific and technical jobs this does not bode well for female applicants and subsequent career progression, and would suggest that female avoidance of careers in science and technology could be based on a pragmatic realism of which courses and subsequent careers are likely to accommodate other commitments. Further support for the 'unsympathetic' technical workplace came from O'Connell *et al.* (1989) who proposed that there were greater penalties for working part time or taking a career break in non-traditional occupations and that childcare, rather than traditional gender beliefs, may affect career plans; they concluded that female participation in non-traditional areas and gender role liberalism will not ensure gender equality in the workplace even in the absence of discrimination.

The 'professions'

Despite the rather disheartening picture painted above, female entry to a number of the professions which were previously male dominated, including medicine, dentistry, veterinary science and law, has increased to the point where female entrants now outnumber males (see Figure 3.1). The success of females in these areas reinforces our belief that girls are exercising their right to choose their career destination, and that science and technical careers do not match their criterion.

The future

There is an urgent need for a reappraisal of the 'technical' career. Engineering and the physical sciences have changed. It may be that the public's perception of these occupations is lagging behind reality, or it may be that their perceptions are well founded. Recent advances in the theory of stereotyping (Oakes *et al.* 1994) have questioned the commonly held assumption that perceiving individuals as category members necessarily distorts reality. According to Self-Categorisation Theory, stereotypic 'exaggeration' reflects a shared perception rather than a distortion.

The importance of stereotyping in education and the labour market

The results of our research indicated that if female school-leavers do avoid careers in science and technology due to 'sex-stereotyping' this process may not be effected at a conscious level. The schematic representations relating to technical and more socially oriented occupations, collected from school pupils, may have been influenced by knowledge derived from personal experience, and expectations about the characteristics and behaviour relating to a person within a certain role. Knowledge may have been gained through work-placement or a part-time job, or it could have been based on impressions formed by contact with a parent or friend employed in that area. Irrespective of the source or quality of knowledge behind the pupils' stereotypical understanding of various careers, attitudes, once formed, are difficult to change.

Despite a general acceptance that 'stereotyping' can lead to inaccuracy and over-generalisation, the tendency, when dealing with people, to think in terms of group membership appears to be indispensable to the way we function (Oakes *et al.* 1994). Psychologists claim that the propensity to think of individuals on the basis of their group membership results in bias due to differences between groups or categories of people being exaggerated while differences within groups are minimised. Stereotypes, which can be understood as a form of role schema, are expected to share certain characteristics on the basis of category membership (Fiske and Taylor 1984; Hinton 1993), for example, a group of people could be categorised on the basis of broad socially defined categories such as sex, or occupation.

While psychologists and historians point to errors of judgement, and decisions based on limited information, insufficient cognizance is taken of the complexity with which individuals have to cope on a daily basis. Real life involves countless decisions, the majority of which are based on limited and incomplete knowledge – satisfactory rather than perfect solutions. Without cognitive short cuts or heuristics, which can be employed quickly and almost without thought or effort (Fiske and Taylor 1984) many decisions would never be made. The availability heuristic in particular is implicated in many of our judgements of the social world (Taylor 1982). In this case, distinctive or salient examples could bias judgement due to their greater availability, for example, while there are more male than female engineers, the few female examples will be more salient and hence more easily brought to mind.

Unfortunately, it is the tendency to 'anchor', or categorise, on an 'all or nothing' basis which leads to the development of schematic representations such as the 'ambitious' technical stereotype, or the 'caring' social stereotype identified in our research. Overemphasis on particular characteristics could well account for the dubious notion that fulfilling a useful role in society, and an interest in new technology, coupled with a desire for some degree of responsibility, are mutually exclusive. The challenge is to recognise the strength of stereotypical perceptions, and in turn to demonstrate that the combination of fulfilling a useful role, being interested in new technology and having a desire for some degree of responsibility are attainable. Such a combination would suggest that there is considerable scope for a reappraisal of course content in addition to improved communication between course organisers, school-leavers, and future employers.

In the remainder of this chapter we will introduce a graphic model portraying the social/technical spectrum within educational establishments, after which we will suggest a number of ways in which we believe that stereotypical modes of thinking could be channelled in order to overcome the persistent patterns of gendered career choice evident in the UK.

Career choice and the occupational possibility curve

Career choice represents the last in a series of decisions, each of which will have had an effect on the subsequent stage. Numerous issues require to be borne in mind, including financial remuneration, length of training, opportunity for advancement, flexibility to accommodate future family needs and, last but certainly not least, the likelihood of employment. The situation of every university or college applicant is unique; some will know what they want to study but will be constrained by inadequate or unsuitable qualifications. Others will have adequate qualifications but no clearly defined ambition. The significance of different aspects of career choice could be likened to the economic concept of 'opportunity cost' – the weighting accorded to each being dependent on the interaction between a potential student's self-concept and their perception of the social climate that they will subsequently enter.

The occupational possibility curve

The decision-making process undertaken by prospective students can be illustrated by an 'occupational possibility curve'. This curve shows the choices available to a student with a given level of qualifications. However, choices cannot be reduced to only a question of educational qualifications. School-leavers, and mature returners, bring with them their beliefs, values and preconceptions based on a combination of personal experience and imperfect knowledge. In real life there is an infinite number of possible combinations which could comprise an occupational possibility curve. For illustrative purposes the results of the Q-study cited earlier will be utilised.

The technical/social dichotomy

The Q-study described above was designed to investigate sixth-year school pupils' schematic representations of career areas with either a high technical content or a more social orientation. Results showed a marked dichotomy between the social stereotype which was perceived to have a strong desire to play a useful role in society and to help others (social concern), and the technical stereotype which was portrayed as having a desire for power, status and high financial remuneration (ambition). These stereotypical representations formed either end of a continuum.

The occupational possibility curve (OPC) would thus depict 'social concern' on one axis and 'ambition' on the other (see Figure 3.2). As with the economic 'production possibility curve' more of one aspect must be offset by less of another, for example, the most extreme scenario would be illustrated by the two 'stereotypes', described above, being discrete categories. In real life this would be a rare occurrence. In our research when sixth-year school pupils described their own aspirations four distinct 'career types' were identified. The four types or categories were distributed along the continuum demonstrating that both dimensions were of varying importance to them.

The shape of the curve

Different aspects of a future career or course have greater salience for some individuals than others, and this will determine their position on the OPC. In the following diagram (Figure 3.2), if 'social concern' were of considerable import-

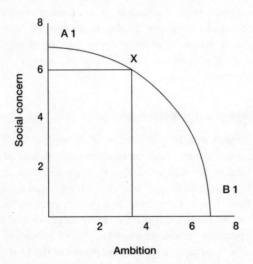

Figure 3.2 Occupational possibility curve showing the balance between 'social concern' and 'ambition'

ance to an individual their position on the curve would lie at a point (point X) where the slope of the curve would be such that the marginal substitution rate of one 'unit' of social concern, e.g. level of contact with the public, would require more than one unit of ambition, e.g. financial remuneration, to offset it. The slope becomes steeper as we move down the 'social concern' axis allowing the reverse situation to occur if an individual perceives 'ambition' to be the more important aspect.

The above simplified example serves to illustrate how an OPC could be derived. However, in the normal course of events there are many competing interests which require to be accommodated, for example, masculine/feminine; career/family; arts/science; specialisation/broad-based.

The current situation

Having explained the concept of the OPC the situation encountered in a hypothetical university will be mapped onto an OPC (see Figure 3.3a). For illustrative purposes three disciplines, social sciences, business studies, and science and technology are used. This spectrum typically encompasses a diverse range of courses which correspond to a continuum on which gender ratios, measured by female participation rates, and the technical or scientific content vary in inverse proportion to each other. The current situation is depicted by the occupational possibility curve, A1B1, in Figure 3.3a.

As mentioned earlier, government policy is to prioritise growth in science, engineering, and technology. To encourage institutions to comply with this directive funding policies have been modified such that the majority of universities now find themselves in a highly competitive market endeavouring to fill

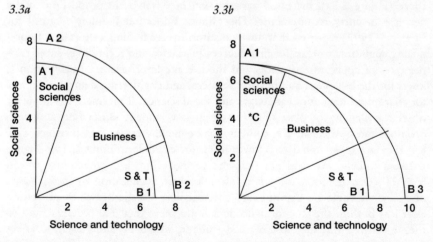

Figure 3.3 The occupational possibility curve showing the effect of intervention strategies based on entry qualifications

laboratory- or workshop-based courses which attract higher funding. Lack of female participation in these areas has been highlighted, and a number of government and professionally sponsored initiatives have been introduced, for example WISE (Women into Science and Engineering) and WiC (Women into Computing).

In order to maximise their revenue, institutions will aim to increase overall student numbers and at the same time alter the proportion in each faculty such that the largest increase is in the Faculty of Science and Technology. In order to increase participation rates either the position, or the slope, of the OPC would be required to change. The curve itself is a boundary derived from the interaction between entry requirements and demand. A fall in entry requirements designed to increase the intake equally to all courses would result in the curve moving out from A1B1 to A2B2 (see Figure 3.3a). The percentage of students, and the gender balance, in each faculty would be unaltered. If the entry criteria for only one sector, in this instance courses with a substantial IT component, were reduced the slope of the curve would change and increased recruitment to these courses would follow, the curve would move from A1B1 to A1B3 (see Figure 3.3b).

Student satisfaction

It will be recalled that the OPC depicts the possible opportunities, and that students themselves remain unchanged. The findings of our research suggested that school-leavers base their course choice on an already established self-concept, rather than deriving their identity from their chosen career. If this is the case and the growth in the faculty of science and technology is to be accomplished by reduced, or distorted, entry requirements altering the slope of the curve (Figure 3.3a), increased participation may not be in proportion to the decrease in entry requirements. The Higher Education Funding Council for England (1992) reported that 'many institutions are finding a shortage of good quality applicants to read for first degrees in science and technology subjects' – the ratio of applicants to places and the average level of entry qualification is lower for the biological and physical sciences, and engineering courses, than it is for courses in humanities, languages and social sciences. Enrolment based purely on the availability of places may result in low student satisfaction and high drop-out rates. Alternatively, students may enter the career area to which they feel they are most suited at a lower level, for example at point C (see Figure 3.3b); a student who was not prepared to move into a degree course with a high IT content might opt for a lower level of qualification in their chosen discipline. It could be hypothesised that the above scenario, which portrays a clear loss both to the student, who does not achieve their full potential, and to the university, who may lose a good student, would be more likely to affect females who are less willing to make concessions in their choice of career (Gati 1992).

The fringes

Enhanced participation on courses which are not deemed to be popular in the current climate depends upon the underlying reasons for the lack of interest being clearly established, with the ensuing revision of existing courses and the introduction of new themes. These innovations would not alter the slope of the OPC, but the boundaries between the faculties would become less pronounced, allowing students a greater degree of flexibility, for example the boundary UY1 would shift to UY2 (see Figure 3.4) encompassing a proportion of potential business students without compromising their overall career aspirations.

Students who subscribe to a less prototypical point of view in any discipline would be located on the boundaries in the areas UX1/X2 and UY1/Y2 (Figure 3.4). These are the students, currently enrolled in disciplines such as business studies where the gender balance is 50:50, who will provide a receptive audience for an intervention policy aimed at increasing participation in science and technology.

Targeting intervention – addressing the stereotypes

When investigating the duration and modification of stereotypes, Weber and Crocker (1983) found that modifications originated from changes in the relationship between groups. Three possible models of how stereotyped beliefs could change were proposed.

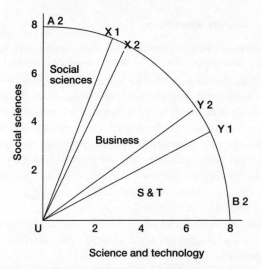

Figure 3.4 The occupational possibility curve showing the effect of intervention strategies based on course content

1　The bookkeeping model – gradual accumulation of counter-stereotypical information.
2　The conversion model – shift due to dramatic salient instance.
3　The subtyping model – counter-stereotypical information forms the basis for subtypes.

There is little doubt that there has been a shift in the relationship between males and females; the balance between the sexes has altered in all walks of life and the repercussions are likely to be felt for some time yet. The position of females in the workforce has improved markedly since the beginning of the century, and the fact that there is still some way to go should not be allowed to detract from the progress to date. High levels of unemployment and an expectation that the 'new man' will shoulder more of the domestic responsibility have undermined the 'stereotypical' vision of 'man the breadwinner'.

The three models of stereotypical change proposed by Weber and Crocker (1983) have all been employed in some form in the drive to encourage more girls to enter courses in science and technology. There has been a natural proliferation in counter-stereotypical information as women enter previously male-dominated occupations in increased numbers; 'token' women who have succeeded in non-traditional careers are photographed and displayed on school notice-boards. Female 'role-models' have arranged day-schools aimed at attracting girls to computer science and engineering; unfortunately the more positive attitudes have proved to be of limited duration (Watt *et al.* 1993). However, it is the third model, 'the sub-typing model' which appears to have the greatest chance of success.

Student mentoring

The notion that role-models have to be same-sex individuals is misguided. Students who choose their future occupation on the basis of their self-concept, or identity, rather than subsequently deriving an identity from their occupation will be influenced by like-minded individuals whom they respect regardless of their sex. The mentoring system which is currently gaining popularity is an ideal way to encourage not only increased entry to but also improve completion rates on courses with a high technical content. Campaigns designed to encourage more females, and males, to enter technical occupations must not stop the day the new recruits enrol. Increased admission rates are just the beginning of a process which must then look to drop-out rates, student satisfaction and final career destination. It is the commitment to sustain and encourage new recruits regardless of sex which is important. The mentoring system in itself will promote an increased ethos of co-operation rather than competition, a situation which is more conducive to the majority of females.

Counter-stereotypical information based on personal contact is the most promising approach to the breaking down of negative attitudes to careers in science and technology. 'Role schema' based on contact between school pupils and groups of current students, both male and female, who feel that they are realising their full potential, and graduates who have found suitable employment, must be engendered. A visit from the 'token' female will be recognised for what it is and will not have the same impact as a group approach. Stereotypes are based on category, or group membership, and it is only by introducing counter-stereotypical information on a similar scale that attitude formation will be modified. However, it must be acknowledged that role schemas, which comprise an organised set of knowledge and expectations relating to the characteristics and behaviour of a person within a particular role, must have some basis in reality, and to this end groups of satisfied students and suitably employed graduates must be available.

The market

As with any other market, supply is a function of demand; if potential students are not attracted by the product, a degree of modification will be required. It is to be hoped that the educational establishments will be more innovative than merely changing the 'wrapper' in the form of new course titles. Girls are remarkably discerning consumers and unlike their male colleagues are rarely persuaded to compromise their interests in favour of enhanced prestige (Taylor and Pryor 1985; Gati 1992).

References

Archer, J. (1992) 'Gender stereotyping of school subjects', *The Psychologist* 5: 66–9.

Archer, J. and Freedman, S. (1989) 'Gender-stereotypic perceptions of academic disciplines', *British Journal of Educational Psychology* 59 (3): 306–13.

Archer, J. and MacRae, M. (1991) 'Gender-perceptions of school subjects among 10–11-year-olds', *British Journal of Educational Psychology* 61: 99–103.

Bem, S.L. (1993) *The Lenses of Gender*, New Haven: Yale University Press.

Cockburn, C. (1985) *Machinery of Dominance: Women, Men and Technological Change*, London: Pluto Press.

Colley, A., Comber, C. and Hargreaves D.J. (1994) 'School subject preferences of pupils in single-sex and co-educational secondary schools', *Educational Studies* 20 (3): 379–85.

Culley, L. (1988) 'Option choice and careers guidance: gender and computing in secondary schools', *British Journal of Guidance and Counselling* 10 (1): 73–81.

Durndell, A. (1991) 'Paradox and practice: gender in computing and engineering in Eastern Europe' in G. Lovegrove and Segal, B. (eds) *Women into Computing: Selected Papers 1988–1990*, London: Springer Verlag.

—— (1992) 'Gender, technology and schooling: Britain and Eastern Europe', *School Science Review* 73 (265): 131–6.

Durndell, A. and Lightbody, P. (1993) 'Gender and computing: change over time?', *Computers and Education* 21: 331–6.

Durndell, A. and Thomson, K. (1997) 'Gender and computing: a decade of change?', *Computers and Education* 28 (1): 1–9.

Durndell, A., Cameron, C., Knox, A., Stocks, R. and Haag, Z. (1997) 'Gender and computing: West and East Europe', *Computers in Human Behaviour* 13 (2): 269–80.

Fiske, S.T. and Taylor, S.E. (1984) *Social Cognition*, New York: Random House.

Fuller, A. (1991) 'There's more to science and skills shortages than demography and economics: attitudes to science and technology degrees and careers', *Studies in Higher Education* 16 (3): 333–41.

Gardner, P.L. (1974) 'Sex differences in achievement, attitudes and personality of science students: a review', *Science Education: Research (ASERA)*: 232–58.

—— (1975) 'Attitudes to science: a review', *Studies in Science Education* 2: 1–41.

Garza, R.T. and Herringer, L.G. (1987) 'Social identity: a multidimensional approach', *Journal of Social Psychology* 127 (3): 299–308.

Gati, I. (1992) 'Gender differences in readiness to accept career compromise'. Presented at 25th International Congress of Psychology, Brussels.

Goodwin, A.J., Hardiman, B. and Rees, V. (1981) 'An investigation of the attitudes to school, science and science lessons of 10–13-year-old children', Report, Manchester Polytechnic, England.

Griffin, B.L. and Holder, J.R. (1987) 'Sex and ethnicity as factors in children's career choices', *TACD Journal* 15 (2): 145–9.

Griffin, C. (1985) *Typical Girls?: Young Women from School to the Labour Market*, London: Routledge and Kegan Paul.

Higher Education Funding Council for England (1992) Cabinet Office News Release of 18 December 1992 (OPSS 65/92)

Hinton, P.R. (1993) *The Psychology of Interpersonal Perception*, London: Routledge.

Kelly, A. (1989) 'When I grow up I want to be . . . A longitudinal study of the development of career preferences', *British Journal of Guidance and Counselling* 17 (2): 179–200.

Lightbody, P. (1993) 'The persistence of sex stereotyped career choice', *Proceedings of the British Psychological Society* 1, 52.

Lightbody, P. and Durndell, A. (1996a) 'The masculine image of careers in science and technology: fact or fantasy?', *British Journal of Educational Psychology* 66 (2): 231–46.

—— (1996b) 'Girls on the fringe: using stereotypes to dispel negative perceptions of careers in science and technology'. Unpublished manuscript, Glasgow Caledonian University.

Lightbody, P., Siann, G. and Walsh, D. (1995) 'Macho male or nouveau neutral: careers that attract women'. Presented at the Scottish Gender and Education Research Network Annual Conference, Stirling.

Lightbody, P., Siann, G., Stocks, R. and Walsh, D. (1996a) 'Motivation and attribution at secondary school: the role of gender', *Educational Studies* 22 (1): 13–25.

Lightbody, P., Siann, G., Tait, L. and Walsh, D. (1996b) 'Gendered career paths: channelled or chosen? The role of advice and decisions in secondary schools' in G. Lloyd (ed.) *Knitting Progress Unsatisfactory: Gender and Special Issues in Education*, Edinburgh: Moray House Institute of Education.

Lips, H.M. (1992) 'Gender and science related attitudes as predictors of college students' academic choices', *Journal of Vocational Behaviour* 40 (1): 62–81.

McTeer, J.H. (1986) 'Gender differences in relationship to likes and dislikes of four subject areas', *High School Journal,* 69 (4): 260–3.

Newton, P. (1986) 'Female engineers: femininity re-defined?' in J. Harding (ed.) *Perspectives in Gender and Science,* Brighton: Falmer Press.

Oakes, P.J., Haslam, S.A. and Turner, J.C. (1994) *Stereotyping and Social Reality,* Oxford: Blackwell Publishers.

O'Connell, L., Betz, M. and Kurth, S. (1989) 'Plans for balancing work and family life: do women pursuing non-traditional and traditional occupations differ?', *Sex Roles* 20 (1/2): 35–45.

Pratt, J., Bloomfield, J. and Seale, C. (1984) *Option Choice: A Question of Equal Opportunity,* Windsor: NFER-Nelson.

Radford, J. and Holdstock, L. (1995) 'Gender differences in Higher Education aims between computing and psychology students', *Research in Science and Technological Education* 13: 163—76.

Robertson, I.J. and Stark, R. (1992) 'Performance in science: is gender an issue?'. Presented at Gender and Education in Scotland: creating a research network seminar, University of Dundee.

Sanders, J. (1987) 'Closing the computer gender gap in school' in J.Z. Daniels and J.B. Kahle (eds) *Contributions to the 4th GASAT Conference,* University of Michigan: National Science Foundation.

School Leavers Destination Report: 1992–93 Cohort (1994) Strathclyde Careers Service.

Shemesh, M. (1990) 'Gender-related differences in reasoning skills and learning interests of junior high-school students', *Journal of Research in Science Teaching* 27 (1): 27–34.

Strange, C.C. and Rea, J.S. (1983) 'Career choice considerations and sex role self-concept of male and female undergraduates in non-traditional majors', *Journal of Vocational Behaviour* 23: 219–26.

Super, D.E. (1957) *The Psychology of Careers,* New York: Harper and Row.

Taber, K.S. (1992) 'Science-relatedness and gender-appropriateness of careers: some pupil perceptions', *Research in Science and Technological Education* 10 (1): 105–15.

Tajfel, H. (1981) *Human Groups and Social Categories: Studies in the Social Psychology,* Cambridge: Cambridge Press.

Taylor, N.B. and Pryor, R.G. (1985) 'Exploring the process of compromise in career decision making', *Journal of Vocational Behavior* 27: 171–90.

Taylor, S.E. (1982) 'The availability bias in social perception and interaction' in D. Kahneman, P. Slovic and A. Tversky (eds) *Judgement under Uncertainty: Heuristics and Biases,* New York: Cambridge University Press.

Turner, J.C. (1985) 'Social categorisation and the self-concept: a social cognitive theory of group behaviour' in E.J. Lawler (ed.) *Advances in Group Processes* (Vol. 2), Greenwich, CT: JAI Press.

—— (1987) *Rediscovering the Social Group: A Self-Categorization Theory,* Oxford and New York: Blackwell.

UCAS Annual Report 1995 Entry (1995) Universities and Colleges Admissions Service, Mansfield: Linneys ESL Ltd.

UCCA Statistical Supplement (1971) Cheltenham: The Universities Central Council on Admissions.

—— (1979) Cheltenham: The Universities Central Council on Admissions.

Walford, G. (1983) 'Science education and sexism in the Soviet Union', *School Science Review* 65 (23): 213–24.

Watt, H., Durndell, A. and Lightbody, P. (1993) 'A follow-up of girls visiting a girls only computing workshop', *School Science Review* 75: 93–7.

Weber, R. and Crocker, J. (1983) 'Cognitive processes in the revision of stereotypic beliefs', *Journal of Personality and Social Psychology* 45 (5): 961–77.

White Paper (1993) *Realising our Potential: A strategy for Science, Engineering and Technology*, London: HMSO.

Whyte, J. (1986) *Girls into Science and Technology*, London: Routledge and Kegan Paul.

Zuckerman, D.M. and Sayre, D.H. (1982) 'Cultural sex-role expectations and children's sex-role concepts', *Sex Roles* 8 (8): 853–62.

4

THE RATIO OF MALE TO FEMALE UNDERGRADUATES

Leonard Holdstock

In most countries with well-developed systems of Higher Education, rather more women than men enter it. This point was reached in the UK only in 1993. However, wherever the system is sampled, there are marked differences in entry to the various subjects of study, and these differences seem to persist over at least several decades, despite quite vigorous attempts to modify them in one way or another. Leonard Holdstock first of all seeks to establish the actual facts, which are not always appreciated, then asks whether there are theoretical reasons which might account for the differences, and finally raises the question as to whether the current situation can be altered by social or political initiatives, and if so how.

Introduction

This chapter is about sex segregation among undergraduate students in any given academic subject, measured for each subject as the ratio of male students to female students. The approach is statistical, although the treatments will be elementary. The data is Western European, mostly from the United Kingdom, but the findings seem to be much the same for many other countries from which data has been reported and which are economically, socially and politically similar, including the United States (Ransom 1990) and Australia. Nothing is implied about any individual person, the study is essentially about statistical groups of students. In more detail the following points will be discussed:

1   How large are the sex segregation ratios? How well do students and others making decisions about them know the facts about these ratios?
2   Can theoretical treatments help to explain why the ratios may be large?
3   Can the ratios be reduced by social or political initiatives and, if so, how?

To avoid unnecessary repetition, sex-segregation ratio will often be denoted by R in what follows.

Sex *and* Gender *conventions*

In this chapter, the usages of the terms *sex, sex related* and *gender* will closely follow that of Halpern (1992: 18–19) or Eagly (1995: 145). The need for these usages is simply the avoidance of confusion. The term *sex* will be used to mean the dichotomous label applied to almost all persons at birth (or soon afterwards). The decision is officially documented and retained unchanged through the person's lifetime. The classification, by medical persons attending the birth, is made on simple visual inspection and is recorded on a birth certificate, and has a limited relevance to that person's later optimum occupational behaviour. Official records about that person form an unbroken chain through primary school, secondary school, university and employers, and are officially kept by the registrar-general, the inland revenue, the social services ministry and perhaps the employment ministry. The two categories of official labelling are *male* and *female*. This use of the terms sex, male and female does not differ from its everyday usage, including public use and discussion in the national press, or on radio or television. Another reason for using the term sex rather than gender is that much information comes from questionnaires, and a respondent will be asked what his or her sex is rather than what his or her gender is.

Sex-related property or *behaviour* will be used to refer to behavioural variables which are, in the present study, continuous dimensions or statistical distributions and are discovered by psychologically satisfactory empirical procedures. They include the descriptive variables ability, personality and interest (and perhaps cognitive style) and also the wide behavioural variables of academic subject choice and occupational choice. The terms *masculine* and *feminine* will be used to mark the extremes or poles of such variables. Thus any given male or female is more or less *masculine–feminine* when measured on any relevant variable; very few are at either extreme. Behaviour is *sex related* because males will tend to be biased, at least statistically, towards the *masculine pole* of any behaviour under study and females biased towards the *feminine pole*. It is quite possible for any individual male or female to be masculine on one variable and feminine on another. Govier (Chapter 1) has shown that some females work in 'male' (i.e. masculine, or numerically and often behaviourally male-dominated) jobs and some males work in 'female' (i.e. feminine, or numerically and often behaviourally female-dominated) jobs, and that the choice may be more related to individual and objectively measurable psychological characteristics which are statistically sex related than to their biological sex.

One important representation of a given behaviour, a frequency distribution, is a two-dimensional graph, the horizontal scale of which is a continuous dimension, representing some property of psychological interest (such as an ability), the vertical scale is *frequency* for finite variables and *relative frequency* for infinite variables (the latter as in the use of a normal distribution). Such a graph makes no statement about any individual person, except in a probabilistic sense, given no other information. The two sexes, male and female, or men and women, or boys and girls, are represented by separate, overlapping distributions. If there were no connection between sex and behaviour, there would be no purpose in this book, in any purely psychological interest in sex or, indeed, in this chapter. But that is not to say that at the present time we know much about what these relationships are nor their magnitude, as it is hoped this study will bring out.

Since the chapter is concerned with whether and how the behaviour of a person, in this case the choice of academic subject or occupation, may be changed, either as a result of the customary practices of a society or social group, or by deliberate action taken by parents, peers or teachers, *encouragement* is another major construct, since it will be used to describe these practices or actions. For example, various campaigns carried out by the Engineering Council and other bodies *encourage* girls and young women to take up science, technology and engineering. Some psychologists would like to *encourage* more boys to take an interest in psychology. Encouragement as a construct is rather like *reinforcement* in learning theory, referring to the actions involved, the numerical results, and to any limitations in behavioural modification. The term is already in general usage and seems to meet what is required quite well, and is sufficiently suggestive of the notion that a basic need is to remedy a lack of confidence on the part of girls if they would like to do more advanced mathematics, or go along with their own preferences rather than follow their peers if they are boys finding an interest in psychology.

Gender will have a restricted use in this chapter. It will be used in parallel with sex related property, the difference being that gender variables are not information elicited by a satisfactory empirical procedure but are the beliefs or opinions the person has about him or herself, may be learned perhaps under various kinds of encouragement by parents, peers or teachers, and strongly govern that person's behaviour, and will include *gender roles* and *gender stereotypes*. Thus, gender, on the few occasions of use in this chapter will refer to a coherent bundle of behavioural properties which are socially induced by parents, ethnic contacts, peers and teachers and sustained by the beliefs and practices of employers. Although gender is of the greatest importance and interest, the present study has little information about the first set of influences and is not concerned with the second.

A masculine feminine dimension

Gender stereotypes

By means of questionnaires, Radford and Holdstock (1993–5) conducted a number of studies into the aims of Higher Education. Most of them contained the following item:

Some subjects are chosen much more frequently by female students, and some by males, while others attract both equally. In your opinion, are some subjects more suitable for women and others for men?

Fifteen subjects were presented in alphabetical order, to give a fair representation of most of the major areas that could be taken for a first degree at university. Respondents had to rate each of the fifteen subjects by choosing one integer from 1–5. One study was of 580 A level students in which they expressed their opinions on a number of characteristics of the fifteen subjects; a second study was of the views of 193 students just beginning their degrees at various universities and polytechnics on the aims of Higher Education; a third study was of the parents of university students, some of whom were in the United Kingdom and others in Portugal.

The studies yielded two quite distinct gender stereotypes. The first could perhaps be called 'an equity stereotype', since the mid-value 3 was chosen for every one of the fifteen subjects. The other might be called 'a differentiated stereotype', since the response to at least one of the subjects differed from the mid-value of 3. If the response differed from the equity stereotype it was usually distinctly different. It is as though respondents had both stereotypes available, and often wanted to signal which of them he or she had adopted and which rejected, a point which would be interesting to test experimentally. In the present study there were sometimes unsolicited comments; another response was to put a single elongated ring round all the 3s. Of the fifteen subjects, the one which differed most in mean rating, and most frequently, was engineering. Table 4.1 gives the frequencies of each stereotype by study and nationality of parent. The sex of the respondent (not shown) was not significantly related to the stereotype.

Table 4.1 Gender stereotypes of students and parents

Stereotype	A level students	Aims students	UK parents	Portuguese parents
Equity	235	103	40	28
Differentiated	345	85	40	46

In each study, the mean ratings were calculated for each subject, and then placed in rank order. The inclusion of the equity responses in the analysis of the ratings did not affect the rank order, since it added a constant value to each mean rating. The ranked orders are shown in Table 4.2, in columns to the right of the subject name. In Table 4.2, the subjects themselves are ordered by their 'male dominance', that is the percentage of male university students in each of the

Table 4.2 Gender and main academic subjects

% Males	Subject area	A level study	Aims study	UK parents	Portuguese parents
90[a]	Engineering	15	15	15	15
86	Computer studies	13	13	12	10
83	Physics	14	14	13	14
70	Economics	10	10	11	13
66	Mathematics	12	12	14	9
55	Business studies	11	8	9.5	12
54	History	7	6	7.5	5
53	Medicine	8	9	7.5	8
49	Law	9	11	9.5	11
42	Biology	6	7	6	7
32[b]	English language	2	4	4.5	4
31	Sociology	3	1	1	6
27	Psychology	5	3	3	2
26[c]	Foreign languages	4	5	4.5	1
17[d]	Education	1	2	2	3
correlation with % males r =		0.95	0.90	0.92	0.88
significance one-tail p =		0.001	0.001	0.001	0.001

Notes:
a An average of several branches of engineering, USR data (1992–3).
b Or Portuguese, as appropriate.
c An average of French, German and Hispanic.
d Teacher training.

subjects, and that percentage is shown to the left of the subject name. By inspection, the different groups of respondents agree among themselves quite strongly. Of perhaps greater interest is the good agreement between the respondents' differentiated stereotypes and the facts concerning these proportions. The differential stereotypes are therefore quite realistic. The equity stereotype might be said to represent the respondents' opinions as to what ought to be on some unexpressed and unsolicited criterion, the differentiated stereotype represents what actually is.

Discussion of results

These results confirm previous findings, in so far as comparable individual subjects are concerned, for example, studies of sex differences in the academic choices of children and students made by Weinreich-Haste (1981) and Archer (1992). The order in which these subjects are listed can perhaps be seen as a *'masculine–feminine'* dimension of academic and occupational choice. The dimension is continuous, since any position on the scale can be occupied. Many academic subjects are highly segregated by sex; engineering and physics are male dominated, and education and psychology are female dominated. The relationship holds equally well if all subjects taught at university are represented, about eighty may be distinguished. In the longer list, subjects tend to occur in clusters, there is a cluster near the top of the list of different branches of engineering, a cluster of physical sciences a little lower down, a cluster in the middle of the list of biological sciences, also in the middle comes a cluster of studies ancillary to medicine, slightly lower down a cluster of languages, lower still a cluster of social sciences, and near the bottom are female-dominated subjects, such as nursing, textiles and domestic science. Each cluster has its own masculine–feminine dimension, e.g. it is of interest that chemical engineering is more *feminine* than mechanical engineering. These clusters are of course, interlaced. R tends to vary for different subjects within each cluster, for example, R is higher for electronic engineering than for chemical engineering.

Summing up this section, on the evidence we have at present, there is the possibility that there is something psychologically fundamental about the masculine–feminine dimension, not only for social and developmental psychology, but for cognitive psychology as well, especially as it relates to the choice of academic subject and occupation. For any individual person, the masculine–feminine dimension may well be a more important determinant of occupational choice than biological sex. It is only necessary to show that some females make competent and happy engineers, and some males are competent and happy at counselling.

An elementary statistical treatment of sex segregation ratio

Student selection

Following the conventions which have grown up in the study of sex differences, in the present study by *ability* is usually meant one of a number of components of intelligence, the subdivisions of verbal ability, numerical ability and visual spatial ability. The reported differences between male mean scores and female mean scores nowadays tend to be quite small and rarely larger than about half a standard deviation (Halpern 1992), so why are sex segregation ratios so large? There is only one really impressive sex difference, in visuo-spatial ability. One set of reasons is that, subject by subject, undergraduate students are not chosen randomly to be representative males or females, but have to pass entrance tests which are common to both sexes, that is to say, that a candidate will only be accepted if his or her performance is above a set criterion, although the judgement may not be very formal in these days of mass university education. The chosen criterion is often related to attainment on that subject, perhaps at A level, on a related subject (e.g. performance on biology for a medical degree applicant) or to some important critical subject like mathematics. Selection means using the tails of a statistical distribution rather than the distribution as a whole, usually having the effect of magnifying the difference between the means of the male and female distributions, as follows:

1   The placing of the cut-off which expresses the criterion of selection. The higher the cut-off, the smaller the absolute number of each sex accepted, but the larger (as we shall see) will be the sex ratio. A simple corollary, *in so far as we are dealing with cognitive abilities and not other main determinants such as interest in the subject*, is that one way for a government to reduce sex segregation would be to enlarge the post-primary education programme by reducing standards of attainment and test performance, particularly those features that students find difficult such as mathematics and first language.

2   Although differences in means may be small, differences in variances may be larger (Feingold 1992). A larger variance for one sex means a greater proportion of that sex will be above any given criterion. Again this will be illustrated by an elementary statistical treatment.

3   Mean and variance combine in their effects. If the sex with the higher mean also has the higher variance, the sex ratio can be further magnified.

4   We must remember what each distribution means. Both distributions relate to the relative frequencies with which an ability having a particular strength is possessed. But the absolute frequencies of the two distributions are likely to be very different in reality. This consideration might well outweigh all others in any particular case.

Assumption of normality

According to Feingold (1995), ability variables can be treated as being normally distributed. In this chapter that assumption will not be pressed too far, since there is a great deal of evidence that although the distributions may approximate to normal near the means, the real data deviates from the normal distribution in the tails, and can only be case-studied individual by individual (Radford 1990).

Moreover, most of the data is from the analysis of intelligence test results, and could be somewhat artefactual in the tails. Abilities are usually taken to be the various components of intelligence. Following the recommendations of Cohen (1977), the convention is to measure mean sex differences as d, the actual difference in means divided by the pooled standard deviation, and it is widely accepted that d = 0.20 is small, d = 0.50 is medium and d = 0.80 is large.

An elementary treatment of the cut-off magnification

Suppose people can be divided into two mutually exclusive groups, or sexes, A and B (Figure 4.1), and that they possess some behavioural property critical to an academic course or particular employment, which is normally distributed for each group. Suppose sex B possesses, on average, more of this property than sex A. Sexes A and B (here supposedly of equal numbers) can be represented by two overlapping normal distributions, which apart from a difference in means d (here treated as a z-score) are statistically identical. Suppose there is a cut-off value of

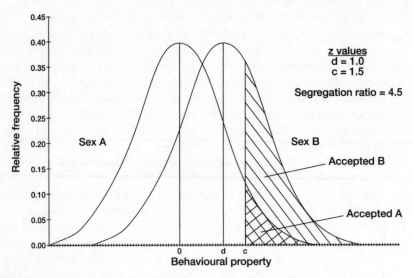

Figure 4.1 Sex segregation ratio (effect of cut-off)

the behavioural property, c, which must be exceeded for the candidate to be accepted. The proportions of each sex accepted can be calculated by reference to a table of the normal distribution, and each proportion will be represented by the proportionate area in the tail of the respective distribution to the right of the cut-off value, shown hatched in Figure 4.1. Figure 4.1 illustrates d = 1, c = 1.5, for which the sex segregation ratio would be 4.5. The cut-off value, c, can lie anywhere along the continuum and can be positive or negative, depending on the academic course or employment requirement.

The farther c lies to the right, the greater the ratio of sex B accepted to sex A. We can try out various values of d and c, including the terms 'small', 'medium' and 'large' as recommended by Cohen (1977), see Table 4.3.

Although the difference in the means of the two groups may not be large, the existence of a cut-off will tend to magnify the sex segregation ratio. The stricter the criteria for acceptance, the higher the cut-off and the greater the sex segregation ratio.

An elementary treatment of the variance difference magnification

Typically, for abilities, the two group distributions will differ in variance, and this could well have more effect on the sex segregation ratio than the mean difference (Feingold 1995). A similar diagram (Figure 4.2) is used as for the equal variance case, for simplicity the numbers in each distribution will be supposed equal. The diagram this time shows raw scores measured from the mean of sex A, with unit

Table 4.3 Variable cut-off and sex segregation ratio

	Equal variances						
	d = inter-sex difference in behavioural property						
c = cut-off	0.0	0.2	0.5	0.8	1.0	1.5	2.0
−1.0	1.00	1.05	1.11	1.12	1.16	1.18	1.19
−0.5	1.00	1.10	1.22	1.31	1.35	1.41	1.44
−0.2	1.00	1.13	1.31	1.45	1.53	1.65	1.70
0.0	1.00	1.16	1.38	1.58	1.68	1.87	1.95
0.2	1.00	1.19	1.48	1.72	1.88	2.14	2.28
0.5	1.00	1.23	1.61	1.99	2.23	2.71	3.01
1.0	1.00	1.33	1.94	2.63	3.13	4.31	5.25
1.5	1.00	1.45	2.39	3.61	4.63	7.46	10.30
2.0	1.00	1.56	2.91	4.90	6.96	13.48	17.80

Source: Compiled from Table 1: Lindley & Miller (1966)
Notes: d and c values are in z-scores.

variance for sex A. Sex B will be shown as having the higher variance as well as the higher mean, which indicates that even more of the candidates of sex B will be in the tails. Inspection alone may show that R will be greater for the greater variance, but some examples will also be calculated. The main difference from the previous calculation is that as each of the two distributions has its own variance and hence its own z-score, and if the variance for sex A is taken to be 1, then the

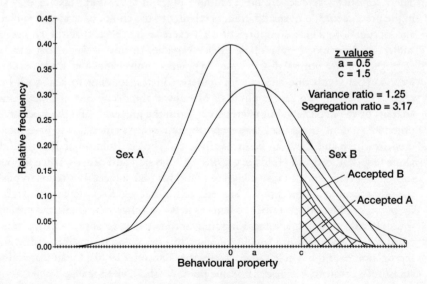

Figure 4.2 Sex segregation ratio (effect of unequal variances)

distribution for sex B will have to be rescaled (divided by the standard deviation which is the square root of F, the variance ratio) resulting in comparable z-scores. Since the mean of the B distribution is shifted to the right, taking the variance into account is like making an addition to the mean of the B distribution.

Table 4.4 shows the effect of a range of likely variance ratios.

Table 4.4 Unequal variances and sex segregation ratio

Mean (B) = a	z(A) = c	SD	z(B) = (c − a)/SD	p(A)	p(B)	R
0.2	1.0	1.0	0.80	0.159	0.212	1.33
0.2	1.0	1.1	0.73	0.159	0.237	1.49
0.2	1.0	1.2	0.67	0.159	0.251	1.58
0.5	1.0	1.0	0.50	0.159	0.308	1.94
0.5	1.0	1.1	0.45	0.159	0.326	2.05
0.5	1.0	1.2	0.42	0.159	0.337	2.12
0.8	1.0	1.0	0.20	0.159	0.421	2.65
0.8	1.0	1.1	0.18	0.159	0.429	2.70
0.8	1.0	1.2	0.17	0.159	0.432	2.72

Notes:
a is the difference between the two means (not a z-score).
SD is the square root of F, the variance ratio.
z(B) is the position of the cut-off related to the adjusted mean of B.
R is the sex segregation ratio.

A framework for the study of R

These statistical exercises are quite illuminating, but really don't take us very far in the present study – of sex differences relating to the choice of academic subject and occupation. The assumption of each exercise has been that the choice of subject is determined by a single ability variable, or any package that can be aggregated into a normal distribution. In practice, universities and academic subjects compete with one another for undergraduates, tending to lead to lower criteria (a well-known case is physics). Moreover, the decision is not made unilaterally by the university, but bilaterally by both the university and the student. A potential student, highly satisfactory on the university's criteria, may have interests elsewhere and they can easily override the choice made on ability grounds alone (e.g. Radford and Holdstock 1993). A high standard of acceptance for one subject not only tends to give a high sex ratio for that subject, but tends to push the other sex into a subject highly segregated for that sex. Every female who takes up physics reduces the number of females in some other subject. At the present time (1995), although United Kingdom universities have approximately equal numbers of both male and female students, this has by no means diminished sex segregation over the whole range of subjects. Ransom (1990), by an interesting statistical treatment, has made the same point for the United States.

What determines the choice of field of study and occupation has long been the concern of occupational psychology, and is not only determined by a package of abilities, but of other variables also, and the other variables may be dominant. One example of a systematic scheme for determining the optimum choice of occupation was the *Seven-Point Plan*, due originally to Alec Rodger (Rawling 1985). As Radford and Holdstock continued their study of sex segregation, so more and more did the variables of interest which emerged map congruently onto the Seven-Point Plan. Small differences arising would seem to be due to the much narrower range of interests of the present study, which is of A level and degree students, whereas the Seven-Point Plan was intended for all ages from primary school to university, and for both craft and academic employments. It is becoming clear that study of sex segregation, particularly its causes and any possible means of reduction, is in its infancy. It is interesting therefore, to look at the Seven-Point Plan to see the possible shape of a framework for the study in relation to the present study (Table 4.5).

Table 4.5 Seven-Point Plan and main variables of the present study

Seven-Point Plan name	Present study name	Of interest to present study	Comments
Circumstances	Opportunity	Yes	Circumstances were the psychological and material support given by parents. Opportunity is the numbers of current university recruits for each subject
Physical make-up		No	Not used by universities
Attainments	Attainments	Yes	GCSE, A level and other usable assessments
General intelligence	Abilities	Yes	Term in general usage in the literature
Special aptitudes	Talents	No	Requires case studies of rare individuals
Interests	Interests	Yes	Potentially the strongest variable in the study of sex segregation
Disposition	Personality	Yes	Administration of personality inventories in study

Summing up this section, it is clear that the sex segregation ratio is a very complex function of a number of variables, some purely statistical like the cut-off due to the university's selection policy and unequal variances and the different absolute frequencies of the populations from which the students are selected, others due to major psychological variables like relevant abilities, interests and personality. In relation to the complexity of the problem, the progress made so far has been small and most of the social and political effort has gone into 'blanket' policies which tend to view young people as undifferentiated aggregates of males and females and do not have much concern for individual differences, like those of the Engineering Council.

The persistence of sex segregation

Changes in UK Higher Education 1980–95

The period 1980–95 has probably witnessed the biggest changes in UK Higher Education that have ever occurred. The number of students has vastly increased: by 1995 more than one-third of school leavers were going into full-time Higher Education, over one quarter of school-leavers entered university as undergraduates (Department for Education 1995). New ways of qualifying for university entrance had developed; in addition to the standard A level, BTec, Access courses and General National Vocational Qualifications (GNVQs) had become widely accepted. Former polytechnics and some colleges of Higher Education were upgraded to universities in 1992. By the end of the period almost half the students were female. And yet at the end of the period sex segregation remained high, and in some cases (e.g. psychology) had even increased.

Experience in the United States was similar. Summing up, Meece and Eccles (1993) say:

> there has only been a slight reduction in the amount of sex segregation found in courses of study selected by women. Women continue to dominate many traditionally female fields, such as education, library science and foreign languages. The most significant changes have occurred in law, medicine, business and architecture. Women have also made significant advances in science, mathematics and engineering, but are concentrated heavily in life sciences, social sciences and psychology.

This was despite the achievement in overall parity in the total number of graduates.

In the United Kingdom, changes were patchy, subject by subject. In general the subjects which increased in student numbers most rapidly were those which were not intellectually too demanding, and provided good employment prospects, not only in level of remuneration but also in the probability of gaining and keeping employment (Radford and Holdstock 1995b). Three subjects of great interest for attention were computer studies, psychology and engineering. Computer studies and psychology in many ways seemed mirror images of each other (Durndell 1991) although there were also interesting differences on closer acquaintance, and the removal or substantial reduction of the sex segregation ratio in engineering seems to be the supreme challenge to those who like to conduct sociopolitical experiments.

Computer studies

The world has undergone a computer revolution, and taken it so much in its stride that computers today are hardly noticed pieces of essential equipment. Factories, businesses and companies have them in great quantities, and almost every professional, probably most readers of this book, has one on his or her desk, if only to serve as a word processor and store of essential information.

Not surprisingly, this has affected university teaching. Almost every university has a computer studies degree course, with an intake of up to perhaps 100 per year, providing bread and butter for every university operating on a tight budget. Yet few members of universities, or the public generally, have a clear idea of what is taught in a Department of Computer Studies. That is, they have the wrong stereotype, and this has been true, almost to an extent which is comical, of several authors who have contributed to research journals in experimental psychology. Over the last two decades, computer studies has changed radically, but the stereotype has not caught up; the stereotype is of a subject which is highly mathematical, consisting of electronics and engineering skills; but the true picture of computer studies is almost the opposite. Most degrees in computer studies require applicants to have almost no mathematics, no electronics, no physics and no engineering. This is even more true of the courses given by the newer universities, those which were polytechnics or institutes of Higher Education up to 1992. There are, in the older universities, some courses which contain artificial intelligence, and some joint degrees where the computer part of the degree takes on the character of whatever is in the other part. In mathematics and computer science, the computer part would be highly mathematical; in engineering and computer science the computer part would have much to do with computer-aided design, and so on. Also of interest is that the A level syllabus in computing run by the Associated Examining Board expressly excludes mathematics, electronics and engineering. This may be one more example of what Kolb (1981) noted: one department in a university is often totally ignorant of what another is doing. The Universities' Statistical Record had not caught up with the change by 1994, continuing to classify computer studies as a 'mathematical science'.

The standard computer studies course (as accredited by the British Computer Society) is essentially about programming business software, is 80 per cent male dominated and growing rapidly in student numbers. The total output of graduates in computer studies from all universities (including the former polytechnics and institutes of Higher Education) is about 5,000 per annum, with every sign of continued growth. It must be popular with universities, since little equipment is needed apart from the computers and a good library of software, and the computers are available anyway as PCs or in the use of the university mainframe. Every university has a large computer department providing services to every other department. To a large extent, therefore, teaching a computer studies degree is a by-product. In the former polytechnics, the degree itself is highly standardised, comparing syllabuses. At the present time there are very good employment prospects for the graduates, some of whom are mature students upgrading their computer attainments; many of the new entrants to computing take four-year sandwich courses.

Of the greatest interest for the present study is that despite the rapid expansion in absolute numbers of computer studies students, the sex segregation ratio for computer studies has remained remarkably constant, although we have to plot this by a different kind of degree and institution, as is shown by Figure 4.3. Why the sex ratio should be so high is a mystery. There is nothing obviously *masculine* about present day computer studies syllabuses, and it would seem ideally suited to females – plenty of opportunity for a graduate to be with people. A graduate would usually be engaged in finding out the needs of clients by personal interview. It is a myth that most of the hours of work would be spent in front of a VDU, that chore would be for the less qualified, and even for those less qualified than Higher National Diploma (HND). There is the possibility that the subject is *unfeminine* in that it (being mainly programming) requires analytical rather than holistic abilities, it is certainly very formal and highly disciplined, requiring precise application of inflexible rules; all programming needs strict adherence to a linear sequence of precise operations. But we really don't know enough to say

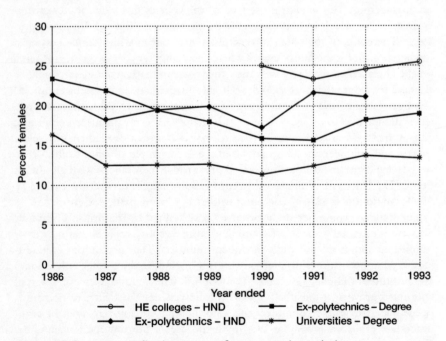

Figure 4.3 Computer studies (constancy of sex segregation ratios)

that it is a matter of ability or interest differences, or whether it is a matter of girls lacking confidence again, and hence responding more slowly than boys to new opportunities. It is likely to be all these causes working together.

It is clear that many students don't like computing (Radford and Holdstock 1993; Brosnan and Davidson 1994). But those commentators who describe the avoidance as a phobia seem to have misread the statistics and have the wrong stereotype. Nevertheless, Radford and Holdstock (1995b) showed that female computing students tended to be more *masculine* than the average for all female students in their Aims (and their Aims will, of course, be related to their interests). A further study (unpublished) supplementing the Aims questionnaire with the NEO Personality Inventory showed that computer studies students differed from Psychology students in a number of *facets* (this is the NEO name for traits). This compares with the Wilson and Jackson (1994) finding that physicists, both male and female, differ from the general population on a number of personality traits, using the Eysenck Personality Profiler (EPP) which seems to be much more sensitive to sex differences than the NEO. In line with the general findings reported in the present chapter, female physicists were more *masculine* in their personality on several traits than the averages for females in the population.

Psychology

Psychology, 75 per cent female dominated, is another of the rapid growth subjects for universities, both old and new, with a graduate output of United Kingdom universities approaching 5,000 per annum, and there is every sign of continued growth. It is also popular at GCSE level (about 20,000 entries per annum, 80 per cent female dominated), but may have passed its peak at this level. A level psychology in 1994 reached nearly 15,000 passes, is 75 per cent female dominated, has doubled every four years for the past sixteen years, and no downturn is yet in sight. Like all statistical time series there must at sometime be saturation, and one can only speculate on when that might be. It will be interesting to see if the maximum in the time series for one sex is reached before the other sex, which would, of course, change R.

Psychology wasn't always female dominated; in the 1950s, when it was so much concerned with learning theory, there were about equal numbers of males and females. What is true for the United Kingdom is largely also true for the United States, Western Europe and Australia.

In a study of student objectives, Radford and Holdstock (1993) asked respondents to rate twelve different areas of knowledge taught in a degree in psychology according to their importance. When the mean ratings were ranked, the following order was produced:

1 Emotion and motivation
2 Mental and behavioural disorders
3 Cognitive processes

4   Social and group processes
5   Development, birth to old-age
6   The physiological basis of behaviour
7   Experimental design and methods
8   Psychometrics, psychological tests
9   Cross-cultural studies
10 Use of computers
11 Statistical analysis
12 Historical and theoretical issues

This list might, perhaps, be interpreted as a *feminine* order of importance. The order seems to be mainly determined by the personality trait *caring for the individual* (compare the EPP trait *manipulative-empathy*). Among the first five items there is only one intruder, *cognitive processes*, not really surprising when the immense progress in cognitive psychology over the last thirty years is taken into account. Five of the last six items are technical, the intruder *cross-cultural studies* is to do with people, but people in groups. (In this respect students of psychology tend to be sharply differentiated from students of sociology.) There was no difference in the study between the two sexes of the respondents, i.e. all the students of psychology, whether male or female, were *equally feminine* in relation to what they found important about their chosen subject of study. A little development of this line of thinking makes psychology a very feminine subject, since the earliest items in the list might be thought of as the core items of psychology. The others are either peripheral, ancillary or means to ends. The study provides another example of the theme of this chapter, a feminine subject attracts young people with *feminine academic interests*, whether they are *male* or *female*, and hence a low value of R is to be expected.

Confirmation of this finding came from the Aims study (Radford and Holdstock 1995b). Complementary to the finding quoted for computer studies students, mentioned above, male psychology students were more feminine than the average for all male students in their Aims. In line with Govier's findings for a number of professions (this volume), and as with computer studies, the *sex related* variable is a better guide to subject choice than a person's *biological sex*.

Some teachers of psychology feel concern about the level of female domination of the subject, although this may have levelled off at about 75 per cent (Radford and Holdstock 1995b). It is becoming increasingly difficult to include the items lowest in the list given above, and hence teach a comprehensive degree in psychology, and this will be increasingly the case as degrees become more modular. There is a danger that many psychology students will want to specialise in counselling (largely emotional and motivational problems) and therapy to the exclusion of experimental design, statistical analysis and historical and theoretical issues. How could more boys be encouraged to take up psychology? There would seem to be two approaches, one to emphasise any possible *masculine* interest in the subject (perhaps psychology as a science) or to identify and encourage the more *feminine males*. But at what age should that take place? Edmunds (1992) has shown the importance of catching students for psychology when quite young. But at quite what age and with what material is not clear. The content of GCSE examinations (a limited syllabus that is mainly developmental) is not very helpful from this viewpoint. The public stereotype of psychology, and the general confusion over the several related terms psychology, psychotherapy and psychiatry, is another barrier to progress. It is interesting to note that the encouragement of boys with *more feminine interests* will have no effect on current trends in the teaching of psychology, since the courses provided would remain equally *feminine*.

Engineering

THE ENGINEERING COUNCIL: ORIGINS AND FUNCTIONS

The Engineering Council was created by Royal Charter in 1981 following the Finniston Report, and so has a history covering the same period of time as the present study. The purpose of the Engineering Council was 'to advance education in engineering, and to promote the science and practice of engineering for the public benefit and thereby to promote industry and commerce'. More specifically it supervises the engineering profession in the United Kingdom, seeking the views of employers of engineers, maintaining a register of 290,000 chartered engineers, incorporated engineers and engineering technicians, co-ordinates the working of forty-four engineering institutes, sets the standards for the registration of individuals and accreditation of academic courses in universities and colleges, and speaks for the profession of engineering to the government.

The interest of this study is in the measures the Engineering Council has taken to recruit more young people into engineering and, specifically, to increase the proportion of females. So far, it has come up with three schemes: Neighbourhood Engineers, the Integrated Engineering Degree and the Women into Science and Engineering initiative (WISE).

Neighbourhood Engineers Neighbourhood Engineers uses practising members of the profession to make contact with teachers and encourage children at school to take an interest in engineering and to consider engineering as a possible career. They 'adopt' local schools in small teams of about four members per team, help with project work, arrange visits to engineering companies, advise on the acquisition and use of equipment, and give advice on careers. By 1993, 2,100 schools were involved in the scheme and 9,000 engineers. The target is to involve all post-primary schools in the United Kingdom and 24,000 engineers. To put this in perspective, the total annual intake of engineering degree students in the UK is a little under 20,000, combining those from the older and newer universities; so, if all the efforts of each professional engineer recruited one extra university student, the university degree student intake would double.

The Integrated Engineering Degree   Previously, engineering degrees had been specialised to the various branches of engineering, civil, chemical, mechanical, aeronautical, manufacturing, electrical, electronic and production. The Integrated Engineering Degree, an honours degree resulting in BEng. or MEng., was intended for those who wanted a good engineering background (perhaps for a management or technical sales job) but less than a design capability in a specific branch of engineering. Graduates would become fully qualified engineers, and be able to register for the standard professional designation, Chartered Engineer. Entry requirements to the degree would normally include A level mathematics, but the other two A level subjects might be, say, economics and geography. More recently, with the rapid expansion of university courses in the United Kingdom, many other qualifications are acceptable, including BTec and Access. Six universities in the United Kingdom run accredited Integrated Engineering Degree courses: the Universities of Durham, Southampton, Wales (Cardiff), Strathclyde, Portsmouth, Nottingham Trent and Sheffield Hallam.

The Women into Science and Engineering (WISE) initiative   The WISE initiative was launched in 1984 jointly by the Engineering Council and the Equal Opportunities Commission 'to help change the attitudes of young people, parents and the general public to the value of engineering and its suitability as a career open equally to both men and women'.

The measures taken include the use of five WISE vehicles (four large adapted coaches and one articulated vehicle) equipped as mobile teaching and exhibition centres which can tour secondary schools and provide practical experience of engineering and technology to help girls develop greater confidence.

The Engineering Council has issued a series of guidance booklets targeted at parents, staff in primary schools, secondary schools and colleges of Further Education (the sources of potential students which provide the encouragement) and to colleges of Higher Education and universities (their destinations which provide advice and create the circumstances for the success of the scheme). The series is called 'Education Equals' and lists key factors to encourage women into science and engineering, provides examples of good practice and gives a check-list to action. Other measures include a directory of awards, courses and visits, videos, an A3 poster for schools and a Young Engineers for Britain competition, with two WISE awards for the best projects entered by a girl or a team of girls.

The Engineering Council claims that as a result of the WISE initiative, the proportion of female engineering students has risen from 7 per cent in 1984 to more than 15 per cent in 1994.

APPRAISAL OF THE ENGINEERING COUNCIL SCHEMES

In common with technology and physics, engineering has not been a growth area for universities. Over the period 1980–94 (about half a generation, which is an appreciable length of time for social and economic change), the number of male engineering graduates from the older universities increased from 7,142 to only 8,406, male technology graduates remained at about 500, the number of physics graduates increased from only 1,789 to 1,832. Compare these numbers to frequently expressed political ambitions to turn the United Kingdom into an advanced technological economy (thirty years ago Harold Wilson 'planned' to have a 'white hot technological revolution', which resulted in little apart from Concorde). Engineering, technology and physics are not popular subjects with young people of either sex in the UK, and of the three areas, the growth in engineering has been the least. Table 4.6 shows three years, one at the beginning of the period, one in the middle and one at the end, for the seven branches of engineering shown in USR and UCAS data. Particular consideration should be given to two facts which emerge: the absolute increase in numbers of females since 1981 was 873; and since 1987 was 569.

Table 4.6 New graduates in engineering from the older universities

	Year ending								
	1981			*1987*			*1993*		
Branch	*Male*	*Female*	*% F*	*Male*	*Female*	*% F*	*Male*	*Female*	*% F*
Aeronautical	294	14	4.5	319	18	5.3	451	36	7.4
Chemical	769	65	7.8	686	127	15.6	628	206	24.7
Civil	1,923	91	4.5	1,340	157	10.5	1,261	214	14.5
Electrical and electronic	2,248	84	3.6	1,644	107	6.1	3,158	283	8.2
Mechanical	1,714	38	2.2	1,471	86	5.5	1,696	172	9.2
Production	194	14	6.7	185	24	11.5	541	113	17.3
General	—	—		486	91	15.8	671	155	18.8
Total	7,142	306	4.1	6,131	610	9.0	8,406	1,179	12.3

Figure 4.4 shows the growth for each year over the period 1981–93 in the proportion of female graduates in these seven branches of engineering. The rate of growth does not deviate much from a straight line; in other words the rate of growth after the introduction of the WISE initiative was much the same as it had been for seven years before the initiative could have an effect. Much the same is true for technology and physics data (not shown). So far as engineering is concerned, it is difficult to fit the figures claimed by the Engineering Council to the data. They claim a rise from 7 per cent to 15 per cent. Even if their campaigns had any effect, the maximum claim would be an increase from the 9 per cent of 1987 to the 12 per cent of 1993.

The absolute numbers of females recruited to engineering, technology and the physical sciences by the campaign taken as a whole by the Engineering Council (there was also some action by the Institute of Physics) must therefore be small,

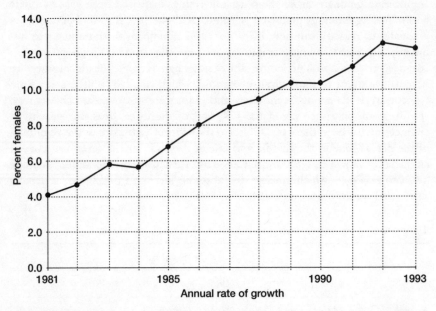

Figure 4.4 New graduates in engineering (percentage of female to total graduates)

very small or even zero, despite the magnitude of the campaign. Looking at the WISE initiative separately, it began in 1984 and could not therefore have affected the numbers of graduates until 1987, approximately the mid-point of the present data. The *extreme* claim would therefore be that all these campaigns taken together have so far recruited an additional 569 females per annum to engineering, 102 to technology and 516 to physical sciences. Even this extreme claim, if correct, could hardly have made much of a contribution towards making British society fairer to females, if fairness is interpreted as a removal of occupational sex segregation.

A lesson for sex segregation?

Occupational psychologists can regard the recruitment campaigns of the Engineering Council as an interesting set of experiments on the encouragement of young people to take up one kind of career rather than another. The Engineering Council took many of what should have been the effective actions. Girls were encouraged directly (if they read the literature), by their parents and by their teachers to believe that engineering was a suitable career for women. Girls were provided with the necessary information, including examples of women who had been successful at engineering, including some that were publicly well-known. And nobody could question the magnitude of the effort made.

The WISE initiative took place at a most favourable time and under a most favourable set of circumstances to the recruitment of females to engineering:

1 There should have been some effect from the increased absolute numbers and proportions of females admitted to all subjects by universities over the period; between 1980 and 1994 the proportion of females increased from 40 per cent to 46 per cent.

2 Engineering graduates probably now go into a greater number of jobs rather than engineering design or engineering research, for example, technical sales and comprehensive schoolteaching. Later in the period under consideration, the recession from 1990–4 may have affected decisions about careers. By why should it have differentially affected engineering, technology and physics when other subjects grew so fast?

3 The decline in heavy engineering in the United Kingdom, especially shipbuilding and mining, which would seem to make the remainder of engineering less 'masculine'.

4 There has been a progressive softening of education standards in the United Kingdom which has affected many branches of engineering: the Engineering Council is concerned about standards in mathematics following the changes made to the GCSE following the Cockcroft report and about to be made to A level. As a result of educational softening, there is a general tendency for 'first degrees' to become an MEng. or MSc. These matters have been the subject of a special report commissioned by the Engineering Council itself (Sutherland and Pozzi 1995).

5 Public attitudes about which careers are most suitable to females are now much more favourable. Our own surveys, mentioned earlier, show that an 'equity' stereotype is held by about half the undergraduates and half the parents surveyed. It is, it must be allowed, true that in the 'differential' stereotype engineering was rated least suitable for women.

The biggest reductions in the sex segregation ratio for branches of engineering occurred in those branches which have long been least segregated, civil engineering, chemical engineering and production engineering. The new branch of engineering served by the Integrated Engineering Degree introduced by the Engineering Council, shown in USR records and here as 'general engineering' seems to have got off to a good start, but that could be viewed as part of the general tendency to offer softer degrees.

Comparison of United States experience

For the United States, Meece and Eccles (1993) conclude that:

During the first half of the 1980s, many programs emerged to increase the proportion of women in engineering and the physical sciences. Between 1976 and 1986, we saw a 29 per cent increase in the number of women earning bachelor's degrees in science and engineering (National Science Foundation 1990). The success of these programs clearly demonstrates that it is possible to recruit more women into technical fields. Unfortunately, funding for such programs has decreased over the last 8 years. Not surprisingly, the number of women enrolling in, and completing, bachelor degree programs also has decreased. At present, women earn only 14 per cent of the bachelor's degrees awarded in engineering (NSF 1990). This decline suggests that women continue to avoid programs in engineering and physical sciences unless they are exposed to active recruitment efforts. Why?

Perhaps not enough time has been given to change the attitudes and practices of centuries. Alternatively, that girls *taken as a whole* are just as suited to all branches of engineering as boys remains a hypothesis.

Conclusion

Experiences in the United Kingdom and the United States show that the sex segregation ratio can be highly resistant to any attempt at socially induced change. Although for various reasons the ratio may change without social manipulation, for example the ratio for seven branches of engineering changed at a fairly constant rate from about 4 per cent in 1980 to about 12 per cent in 1994, it is possible that each change converges towards a limit, as may be the case for psychology, and if the experience of the United States is a guide, these seven branches of engineering, as an average, may have a limit not much above the present value.

It is necessary to make even finer distinctions, drawing an illustration again from engineering, the branches that deal with making machines of one kind or another may converge to a limit appreciably below 10 per cent. For some reason where materials or textiles are concerned rather than vehicles or other machines, there seems to be much less male domination. Chemical engineering has a lower sex segregation ratio, and if we had included metallurgy and other materials technologies the point would have been made more strongly. The author knows of no psychological discussion of why these differences exist between different branches of engineering, nor between engineering, technology and the physical sciences. It is not the most 'macho' branches of engineering that have the highest male domination, since the ratio for electronic engineering (where the work is light, done in comfortable offices and air-conditioned laboratories) is much higher than that for civil engineering (which makes large fixed structures and where some work must be done in the open air and involves clambering over rough sites and wearing some protective clothing and headgear). Again the facts of what occupations are suitable to males and females seem to be very different from the popular stereotype.

A number of psychological studies of quite different kinds (Govier, this volume; Radford and Holdstock 1993, 1995b) have shown that an individual's score on a *masculine–feminine dimension* seems to be a more important determinant of field of study and occupational choice than that person's bio-logical sex. From this arises a statistical distribution into the various academic subjects, and since the masculine–feminine dimension is sex related, sex segregation ratios will necessarily arise for different academic subjects. An optimum choice of field of study is *sex related, not sex determined*. Some females will become happy and competent engineers and some males will become happy and competent nurses, but it is very likely that more engineers will be male than female and more nurses will be female than male for the foreseeable future. For engineering then, the lesson would seem to be to identify the girls with a tendency to *masculine academic interests*.

A high sex segregation ratio is not necessarily evidence that something is wrong but that the characteristic demands of individual fields of study and consequent occupations have to be matched to the characteristics of the supply of young people, and we do not, at the present time, know very much about either, except that much more psychologically is involved than any package of abilities. The scientific exploration of academic and occupational sex segregation must therefore be very important for human welfare.

There is another important point that needs to be properly brought out. Initiatives like WISE are attempts to encourage *categories* of young people to take up a specific occupation as a profession after undergoing a long and specific education. All these initiatives seem to have been pursued with enthusiasm rather than any knowledge of psychology. All occupational psychologists know that *selection must be by the individual and a balance achieved among several kinds of information*. That principle has been embodied in all selection schemes, and the Seven-Point Plan used as an illustration goes back to 1930. To discuss the success or otherwise of the WISE campaign purely in terms of equal numbers in categories could be irresponsibly naïve. Suppose some young people are persuaded to take up a particular profession, by hypothesis outside the normal range of their experience, especially when it is done by glamourised examples, and then find they have made the wrong choice? That would seem to argue for restraint on the part of individual professions and reform of the educational system, particularly at the primary level. To put on show a nationally known female astronomer proves that some females will be good at astronomy. But not all females will take to astronomy and neither will all males. The problem is to make early, continuous and accurate assessment of individual abilities, interests and personality, and to give good information and advice based on that assessment. There seems to be a very narrow 'window of opportunity' since the encouragement could easily be given too early, the case seems to be strongly made for keeping children open minded until they are properly informed and know as individuals clearly what they want. On the other hand, it may be too late if delayed until teaching is broken down by subject divisions, and there are more subjects than teaching time per pupil. There is also the danger, as we have seen with computer studies, that children at school and young persons will be given a totally wrong stereotype by teachers and professional institutions.

References

Archer, J. (1992) 'Gender stereotyping of school subjects', *The Psychologist* 5: 66–9.

Brosnan, M.J. and Davidson, M.J. (1994) 'Computerphobia – is it a particularly female phenomenon?', *The Psychologist* 7: 73–8.

Cohen, J. (1977) *Statistical Power Analysis for the Behavioral Sciences* (Revised edition), San Diego, CA: Academic Press.

Department for Education (1995) *Education Statistics for the United Kingdom* (1994 edition), London: HMSO.

Durndell, A. (1990) 'Why do female students avoid computer studies?', *Research in Science and Technological Education* 8: 163–70.

—— (1991) 'Gender, psychology and technology: a mirror image' in J. Radford (ed.) *The Choice of Psychology*, Occasional Papers of the Group of Teachers of Psychology of the British Psychological Society Vol. 12.

Eagly, A.H. (1995) 'The science and politics of comparing women and men', *American Psychologist* 50: 145–58.

Edmunds, A. (1992) 'The gender imbalance in undergraduate psychology: a navigation through sources of influence'. Unpublished undergraduate project. Warwick, England: University of Warwick.

Feingold, A. (1992) 'Sex differences in variability in intellectual abilities: a new look at an old controversy', *Review of Educational Research* 62: 61–84.

—— (1995) 'The additive effects of differences in central tendency and variability are important in comparisons between groups', *American Psychologist* 50: 5–13.

Halpern, D.F. (1992) *Sex Differences in Cognitive Abilities* (2nd edition), Hillsdale, NJ: Erlbaum.

Kolb, D.A. (1981) 'Learning styles and disciplinary differences' in A.W. Chickering (ed.) *The Modern American College*, San Francisco: Jossey-Bass.

Lightbody, P. and Durndell, A. (1993) 'Senior school pupils' career aspirations: is gender an issue?'. Paper presented at the British Psychological Society London Conference, December 1993.

Lindley, D.V. and Miller, J.C.P. (1966) *Cambridge Elementary Statistical Tables*, Cambridge: Cambridge University Press.

Meece, J.L. and Eccles, J.S. (1993) 'Introduction: recent trends in research on gender and education', *Educational Psychologist* 28: 313–19.

Morris, P.E., Cheng, D. and Smith, H. (1992) 'How and why applicants choose to study psychology at a university', *The Psychologist* 5: 247–51.

Radford, J. (1990) *Child Prodigies and Exceptional Early Achievers*, Hemel Hempstead: Harvester Wheatsheaf.

—— (1991) 'First-year honours students' choice of psychology' in J. Radford (ed.) *The Choice of Psychology*. Occasional Papers of the Group of Teachers of Psychology of the British Psychological Society Vol. 12.

Radford, J. and Holdstock, L. (1993) 'What students want: objectives of first-year psychology students in Ireland, Norway, Portugal, Spain and the United Kingdom', *Psychology Teaching Review* 2: 39–49.

—— (1995a) 'Does psychology need more boy appeal?', *The Psychologist* 8: 21–4.

—— (1995b) 'Gender differences in higher education aims between computing and psychology students', *Research in Science and Technological Education* 13: 163–76.

Ransom, M.R. (1990) ' Gender segregation by field in higher education' , *Research in Higher Education* 31: 477–94.

Rawling, K. (1985) *The Seven-Point Plan by Alec Rodger. New perspectives fifty years on*, Windsor: NFER/Nelson.

Sutherland, R. and Pozzi, S. (1995) *The Changing Mathematical Background of Undergraduate Engineers*, London, The Engineering Council.

Weinreich-Haste, H. (1981) 'The image of science' in: A. Kelly (ed.) *The Missing Half: Girls and Science Education*, Manchester, England: Manchester University Press.

Wilson, G. and Jackson, C. (1994) 'The personality of physicists', *Personality and Individual Differences* 16: 187–9.

Institutions and other bodies for statistical data
(T = telephone; F = fax)

Associated Examining Board (AEB), Stag Hill House, Guildford, Surrey, GU2 5XJ. T = 01483 506506; F = 01483 300152.

British Computer Society (BCS), 1 Sanford Street, Swindon, SN1 1HJ. T = 0793 417417; F = 0793 480270.

British Psychological Society (BPS), St. Andrews House, 48 Princess Road East, Leicester, LE1 7DR. T = 0116 254 9568; F = 0116 247 0787.

Business and Technology Education Council (BTec), Central House, Upper Woburn Place, London, WC1H 0HH. T = 0171 413 8400; F = 0171 413 8430. (Now part of EDEXCEL Foundation.)

Careers Services Unit (CSU), Armstrong House, Oxford Road, Manchester, M1 7ED. T = 0161 236 8677; F = 0161 236 8541. Contact – Colin Lawton. (Formerly Central Services Unit.)

Committee of Vice-Chancellors and Principals (CVCP), Woburn House, 20 Tavistock Square, London, WC1H 9HY. T = 0171 419 4111; F = 0171 383 5766.

Department for Education (DfE), Mowden Hall, Staindrop Road, Darlington, Co. Durham, DL3 9BG. T = 01325 460155; F = 01325 392695. (Now DfEE.)

Engineering Council, 10 Maltravers Street, London, WC2R 3ER. T = 0171 240 7891; F = 0171 240 7517.

Higher Education Statistics Agency (HESA), 18 Royal Crescent, Cheltenham, GL50 3DA. T= 01242 255577; F = 01242 232648.

Universities and Colleges Admissions Service (UCAS), Fulton House, Jessop Avenue, Cheltenham, Gloucs GL50 3SH. T = 01242 225924; F = 01242 221622. Contact – Richard Dennis. (Combines previous UCCA and PCAS.)

Universities' Statistical Record (USR), PO Box 130, Cheltenham, GL50 3SE. T = 01242 225906; F = 01242 221622. Contact – Cynthia Holme. (Ceased to exist in 1995 – Publications still available from HESA Services Ltd, address as above.)

5

ENTERING HIGHER EDUCATION: OLDER STUDENTS' CONSTRUCTIONS OF SELF AS LEARNERS

Estelle King

Whatever the genetic, physiological and social factors that influence choice, it remains an individual matter. Estelle King has studied individuals in detail to try to understand how the process appears to them. She has concentrated on older women partly because this group may have special problems; but this also means that they show up such problems, which may in fact be very common, in greater relief. How students see themselves is undoubtedly a crucial part of the complex equation that results in a particular pattern of choices. As suggested in the final chapter, individuals appear, not very surprisingly, to seek a match between the way they see themselves and the way they see the various possibilities before them.

Introduction

In Chapter 2, Ann Colley examined gender differences in school subjects at secondary level. In this chapter, I focus on the first phase of a longitudinal study of older students, predominantly female, and their narratives of struggle and reward involved from childhood onwards, in constructing new roles for themselves as learners, and the conflict that this often seemed to provoke. In spite of the considerable increase in the number of older students entering Higher Education (that is, those over the age of twenty-one), the current situation does not appear to have changed much since Osborne *et al.*'s 1984 study, which demonstrates that research on older students in the United Kingdom generally involves those who are white and middle class. The study discussed here is one attempt to redress this balance.

I start the chapter by outlining my personal interest in this area, and then emphasise the difference in feminist as opposed to traditional models of student

84

learning, making a case for examining the qualitative experiences of this student group. Unlike most other studies of older students, nearly all the participants in the current study left school with minimum, if any, qualifications and over half identified themselves as coming from a working-class background. All but two in my study describe how their early sense of self was affected by conflict or trauma during childhood, and I discuss how this is related to their fragile learner identity, which often seems to permeate to the present. Discussion focuses on predominant themes and central issues constructed from the narratives, with the emphasis placed on potential differences and the influence of the social structure on individuals' lives. These are organised under the headings of the path to becoming an older student, in which the notion of the 'right time' becomes important, and the first impressions of Higher Education. Finally, the chapter concludes with some suggestions as to how this may become a nurturing environment, one which recognises diversity of culture and background.

Background to my study

Access to Higher Education courses flourished during the late 1980s, so that by 1990 more than 500 Further Education colleges had become experienced in catering for this minority group (Melling and Stanton 1990). Access courses aim to equip their students with the confidence, study skills and techniques to enter Higher Education with the same degree of credibility and success as those students who enter by traditional routes.

My interest in the area of older students entering Higher Education stems from having designed and implemented such a course over a three-year period. The recruitment philosophy was to target individuals not well-represented in Higher Education. Through working closely with those on the scheme, I was given intimate access to their narratives of the pain, excitement, struggles and rewards involved in constructing new roles for themselves as adult learners and how they attempted to resolve or accommodate the conflict that this often seemed to provoke. Some of these narratives resonated deeply with my own earlier experiences and associated fragmented, somewhat negative, sense of myself as a learner. Although I had moved on very considerably from a learning position similar to those I was tutoring, I knew how echoes from my own past could still come to haunt me. My commitment to carrying out research in this area is therefore bound up with my own past (dislocated from my working-class roots by virtue of my education), my professional role as a teacher/lecturer and my status as an older research student. As a feminist, it also reflects my political commitment to all those engaged in emancipatory struggles against oppression, although this, of course, is not without its own difficulties.

Traditional and feminist models of student learning

Perry's model (1970, 1981) of students progressing through nine intellectual stages has been very influential in the field of student learning, and was proposed as a global account of student intellectual and ethical development, with disorientation and struggle being very much a part of the personal growth involved in one's intellectual development. However, it was devised on the basis of a predominantly male sample with no separate consideration of female students. In the 1980s, in an attempt to counteract this, several investigations were carried out, using rigorous qualitative methodology, into the experiences of women students, and the general conclusion was that intellectual development in female students usually proceeds along parallel, but different, development schemes from that identified by Perry with regard to male students (see, for example, Baxter-Magolda 1988, 1992; Belenky *et al.* 1986; Clinchy and Zimmerman 1982). Therefore, for example, while Belenky *et al.*'s style of writing is refreshingly vital and they emphasise that women's engagement with their levels of knowing is not static, their theoretical proposal is not totally dissimilar from that promoted by Perry. Such an approach which emphasises 'women's ways of knowing' is problematic for other reasons too, for, as in this instance, the researcher's role in editing and control can be obscured, and can result in an 'intellectual paralysis' which does not acknowledge multiple, contradictory social positions (Bhavnani 1998).

What most models of student learning, largely originating from cognitive psychology, have failed to do is to take account of individual experiences of learning and to account for, or address, intra- and inter-individual variations. Learning needs to be regarded as an holistic process, yet until recently, most of the literature about learning neither reflected the experiences of the individuals concerned, nor acknowledged that ideas cannot be separated from experience. Accessing life experiences involves using qualitative methods that operate within a phenomenographic 'new paradigm' or poststructuralist approach. Typically, interviews, diaries or focus groups have been used. However, where qualitative studies have been used, broadly speaking they can be summarised as being of one of two types. The first is aligned with a more realist, empirical view of the world (see Baxter-Magolda 1992; Elsey 1982). The second, which adopts a phenomenographic or experiential approach to student learning, can be viewed as resting on individualistic assumptions. Perry's work comes under this category, other examples are Entwistle and Marton (1994) and Morgan *et al.* (1982). Exceptions to this are addressed below.

As a whole, this non-traditional group have offered varying reasons for wishing to enter Higher Education. While many may have clear vocational aims, they may also have personal goals not shared by younger students. Marshall and Nicolson (1991) have summarised these as a desire to enhance self-confidence as well as to open up professional and intellectual opportunities. But it is important to stress here that older students are not an homogeneous group. For instance, Thacker and Novak (1991) found that women students aged 35–44 wanted to gain a degree, achieve independence, acquire new skills and vocational achievement, whereas those aged 45–64 wanted an intellectual challenge.

Much of the debate on access to Higher Education focuses on identifying, preparing and admitting students, as if the functions and purposes of Higher Education are clear and the system presupposes an unproblematic learning context for older adults and their needs (Tuckett 1990). Given their diversity as a group, any consideration of adult students and their needs must therefore take into account a multiplicity of factors and not give credence to unsubstantiated, simplistic or reductionist notions.

In general, approaches to adult learning and adult development are too descriptive, and they do not consider the many factors impinging on a student's life and the complex interrelationship between them and the learning experience for that individual. While there are some studies, such as Perry's, that are longitudinal, they generally do not include students who have entered Higher Education without standard qualifications, and who consider themselves as coming from, or belonging to, the working classes. In the case of those studies that have examined this older, non-traditional group, they are either not longitudinal nor are they conducted from a feminist standpoint within a social constructionist perspective. Exceptions to this have informed my own study and are addressed below.

A language of experience about student learning?

Traditional models of intellectual development have attempted to accommodate women, as well as men, within pre-existing theoretical frameworks in which age, gender, social and ethnic background have usually been ignored as social constituents. Furthermore, despite the trend in access populism, until recently most of what has been published about adult learning neither reflects the experiences of those concerned nor analyses the power relationship between learner identity and the educational institution. Weil and Edwards are two notable, feminist exceptions.

In her study of undergraduate and postgraduate students, Weil (1988, 1989a, 1989b) enriched the theory of adult learning by exposing a language of genuine, lived experience, and analysed her data around the key emergent themes of 'disjunction' and 'integration' with formal learning at school. Looking at the 'why' and the 'how' rather than simply the 'what' can facilitate the intellectual processes of interpretation, conceptualisation and analysis by recognising that alternative experiences and views may be equally valid and rational. However, while Weil (1989a) does pay attention to researcher reflexivity, for instance by writing in two voices, and acknowledges some areas of contradiction in her participants' accounts, she does not really align herself with a social constructionist perspective in her analysis, one which postulates multiple, fragmented identities. This latter positioning is not consonant with being able to represent 'genuine, lived experience'.

Edwards (1993), in her study *Mature Women Students*, draws on in-depth interviews with mother–students, to examine whether these women separate or connect their public and private worlds. Her thematic analysis, while lacking

methodological rigour as far as psychology is concerned, results in her constructing 'an overall typology and continuum of the ways in which education and
family can coexist in women's lives', that is, how they interact and impinge, with
particular implications for women's positioning (Edwards 1993: 128). What is of
particular relevance to my study is her consideration of power in both domestic
and educational spheres, and how her participants' shifting patterns and identities
relate to this.

The present study is fundamentally different from others in this area in a number of ways. Principally, all individuals approached to participate in the study
were already known to me in a tutorial or small-group teaching situation, with a
previously established level of rapport, although this of course was not without its
problems of power and control, albeit rather subtly imposed in the interview
context. However, it was an attempt to span boundaries and reduce conflicting
perceptions, to get closer to presenting and analysing the complex dimensions of
lived experience, of trying to 'hear the voice' (Merriam, 1988), if not to actually
'get close to the bone' (Rennie *et al.* 1988). Additionally, I was able to collect my
data for the duration of my participants' degree course.

My aim has been not to obtain the 'truth' about the experiences of older
students, but to collect and explore the variety of accounts constructed within
the restricted social context of the interview. The initial cycle of my study
involved life-story interviews with twenty-one women and four men, aged from
22–55, who were interviewed close to the end of their first term in Higher
Education. Out of these, four self-identified as black, five as being born outside
the United Kingdom, and thirteen felt they came from a working-class
background.

Viewed as a joint social interaction, factual background information was
collected before proceeding to the life-story interview (see King 1994 for
details). Emphasis was placed on gaining access to participants' understanding of
their experiences and conceptions of themselves as a learner from their own frame
of reference. This autobiographical material may be viewed as a reconstruction of
the past from the present, structured, selected and edited as the person sees fit
and 'influenced by fallible memories' (Kitzinger 1987). My attempt to span
boundaries, combined with the in-depth nature of the interview was not
unproblematic, and the resulting sticky web of power relations has led me to
reconsider the interviewing skills required in such situations and to make a
comparison between research and counselling interviews (King 1996).

Discontinuity/conflict in childhood

In contrast to the findings of Woodley *et al.* (1987) about the status of deferred-
entry students, nearly all the participants in my study had been neither
educationally nor socially advantaged, and the majority, eighteen, left school
with minimum, if any, qualifications. Eighteen had come directly from an Access
course. The core category emerging from these narratives affected all but two of

the participants' early sense of self, and may be summarised as discontinuity or conflict in childhood. This is indicated by a number of constituents relating to parental characteristics, personal and family trauma and environmental and/or cultural changes as follows:

Table 5.1 Discontinuity/conflict indicators in childhood

Family stress	Changes in	Parental	Personal
separation	school	age	trauma
death	address	culture	sexual abuse
mental illness/handicap	culture	language	illness
violence	country	education	pressure
	language	income	

Some individuals were affected by a number of these constituents, and participants' accounts offer meaningful interpretations and examples of how these constituents were inextricably bound up with the educational system and their learner identity as part of their developing self-conception. Loss through separation, death or divorce affected ten of my study during their primary schooling. Often they talked about how the effects lasted until the present:

CARL: In the first two years of secondary school I pushed myself quite a lot, at home I was pressurised as well, doing my homework, looking after my siblings and keeping an eye on Mum . . . I remember sitting and praying and wishing Dad was here, I still didn't ever come to terms with my father's death. Educationally, I think I miss him.

This extract clearly indicates the profound psychological and practical effects endured as a result of Carl's father dying when Carl was 10, which seem to permeate into the present. In the interviews, conflict arising between parent and child, particularly with the onset of adolescence, frequently arose. The divergence of parent–child attitudes or educational standard attained was often articulated. To continue the case of Carl, at the age of 13 he approached his mother about his wish to go to university:

CARL: Mother said she couldn't cope if I went to university, which had a dramatic effect on me. I had lost my goal, my target, there was nothing to aim for. I felt bitter. Learning seemed pointless, there seemed nothing really to go for.

This sense of loss of inner drive and ambition, of needing to have something to aim for, or not realising that there *was* anything to aim for, was stressed by a number of participants, relating both to the past and the present. Furthermore, a number voiced strongly that they had been thwarted or disadvantaged or discriminated against while at school. This was usually when they changed schools, or transferred to a secondary school outside their local area.

SALLY: When I went to the school in Kent, I didn't have any friends at all, because I had this awful [Glaswegian] accent, and no one could understand me. So I got badly bullied. I'd missed a lot of school so I was quite behind a lot of them . . . And I think they [the teachers] saw me as not being an achiever and having a funny accent and sort of, uh, I don't know.

The number of schools attended was usually either three or four, although five individuals had attended between six and ten schools. Only for these five did the number of schools attended seem to be related to negative learning experiences while at school, although a number of other interviewees did talk about how unhappy they were upon moving to a secondary school outside their immediate area.

LOUISE: But now, I think [about having moved from many schools], it's, um, I never sort of had anything, not in the material sense, but I never quite knew where I was. Because I feel that I just, I didn't have the backbone. You know I've always given up. It's like my, look at my O levels, I gave up. And I just feel that if they [parents and teachers] would've turned round and said, 'No, you've got to do it', I would've done it. And I think I would've been a stronger person.

This quote from Louise's interview may be interpreted in a number of ways. However, she seems to be blaming her weakness, her propensity to give up, on both her teachers and her parents, and the fact that she moved schools 'about eight times, more often than I can actually say' for her lack of qualifications. She is not accepting responsibility for her part in this, and is an example of one of several participants who adopted a 'victim syndrome', who, at the time of their first interview with me, felt retrospectively that they had had no control over their lives, and often blamed others for their low self-esteem and lack of achievement.

A number of those interviewed reported discrimination on the part of teachers between children, as Pat put it: 'you know, there were the brainy ones and the ones that weren't so brainy, and we were sort of separated and treated differently by the teachers'. In cases where levels of attainment were reported as having dropped, the school's response and its timing (relating to teachers and occasionally pupils) may be construed as crucial contributors to the individual's sense of self and resultant learner identity. In the majority of instances, it was most apparent that participants felt they had lacked appropriate guidance from both educators and parents or carers.

TED: I would have wanted someone to have told me how good or how bad I was . . . Because it was an average, wasn't it, in the end [of the school year]? You were good at something, and not so good at something else, but in the end it was an average ... I would have liked somebody to explain, 'well, you're good at this, you're good at that'.

When ambition and hopes went unfulfilled, the frustration experienced was described as having been immense. Some felt their attempts to do well were not rewarded and this was often linked to 'giving up' at school around adolescence as an act of rebellion against parental pressure of unrealistic expectations of high educational attainment.

ENID: And I remember on one occasion, I got 100 out of 100 for geography and history, and came bounding home, only to be sort of stopped dead in my tracks by my father, saying, 'But you should've got 101 out of 100'. And that was my childhood, whatever I did, I could've always done better. I was doing my best, it was never enough, there was never any praise. At all.

Parental attitude towards learning, compounded by a feeling of alienation from the (white) middle-class educational system sometimes resulted in a strong disjunction between life in and outside of school, with the two being treated as contrasting worlds. Others did not feel alienated until they reached adolescence, when life outside school was exciting:

ANN: I just stopped studying because of my husband. That's why I stopped studying, I started going out with him ... So, if I could change anything, it would have been that, putting that right.
ESTELLE: Why, why do you think that affected you so greatly?
ANN: Because I felt I had failed everybody. Failed myself, failed my parents, um, my sister, when I was playing truant ... And, er, because of at home. My father was adding to that grief.

Ann was certainly not alone in voicing her sense of failure regarding her schooling.

In contrast to the core category described above, two accounts were given of happy, non-stressful childhoods. Emily described herself as 'having come from a delightful, stable family' and had proceeded from school to university. The other exception to the above was Joy:

JOY: And I had really caring parents ... my mother, she was always there. And I think I had a really good childhood ... You know, we were sort of like one big happy community in [junior] school.

For her, strong identification with her chosen peer group at the age of 13, which involved breaking school rules regarding the wearing of uniform, make-up and smoking, led her to look back on those years and say:

91

JOY: I think I would have liked to, as well as be in the peer group, to have taken more charge of my own learning, I think. I think being in those groups, um, in a way led me not to think about my education so much. I mean I didn't look to the future . . . I missed the basics of understanding subjects and things . . . By then, I started to feel that, um, I was sort of lacking, sort of a bit of a failure, because I left . . . I left everything too late.

In this sense, Joy was like most others interviewed, for whom the second and third years at senior school were described as pivotal-turning points where formal education was rejected, and school grades started to fall. This is described in most developmental text books, but for those in my study there was no returning to study while of school age. In other instances, where individuals were not happy at school, they described how they did not fit in at school, and how there was a high price to pay for not identifying with one's peer group:

LIZ: And we were talking about music at the end of some lesson with the teacher. And I happened to say I like ballet music, I like ballet, I like classical music. Pheweet [whistles], everybody disappeared. I was an untouchable.

However, in contrast with this, a number of people did talk about enjoying school, although they were not without their criticisms. For a number, when they approached adolescence, their enjoyment of school was for social rather than educational reasons:

RACHEL: I mean, I remember the particular thing that stayed with me, was that I, you know, after the first-year exams, I was actually third in the class. When I left, I was twenty-third. I mean, I'm not, yes, I just wasn't motivated. I was, erm, very sociable. I wasn't interested in doing it [schoolwork] . . . You know, Mum was never there at home anyway . . . Oh, my school life was very important, very important.

This account appears quite disjointed. Although the extract has been severely edited, the narrative did not flow as smoothly as most of the other interviews. Interwoven with enjoying school, there are several other themes being mentioned here: Rachel's falling level of attainment appears to be associated with her mother not being at home, but out at work, and Rachel being required to do a lot of housework from an early age. Alongside this in her narrative runs a strong sense of negativity about homelife.

Several other interviewees talked about the roles they assumed in and out of school, and rather than describe *themselves* as failures, they talked about having been labelled as failures or low achievers. Holt (1964) writes that children who rely heavily on adult approval may come to decide that if they are unable to attain total success, the next best thing is total failure. Perhaps this is too simplistic a view, but Lorraine described how she had assumed the position of class joker, and although altered, this identity was obviously still important to her:

LORRAINE: Well, even through the PCSE [Further Education course] I was very much the joker anyway, of the class . . . But I learnt to work as well. And I still feel it is for me, I'm not sure why, part of my identity . . . I think I've learned to take it out of the classroom, and into the refectory, canteen, outside . . . I'm learning you can still get respected by other people for being the comic, you know, one for having a laugh.

It seems Lorraine had assumed this role in the past, when she had been labelled as a failure at school, as a way of gaining respect from her peers, if not from her teachers. However, the majority of the sample saw adolescence as a period fraught with inner and/or outer turmoil, and often damaging to their vulnerable self-identity. This, and alienation from the formal educational system, was often related to a desire to leave school at the earliest opportunity. Where participants told of teachers having recognised hidden potential, it had proved too late, the individual had disengaged from learning. For instance, Enid describes how 'the maths teacher tried to salvage my maths, but it was too late. I read and tested myself on a number of things, but no one was to know about it, I did it in private.'

To sum up, all but two narratives may be organised around the emergent theme of disjunction with formal education. This may well be related to the fact that having a fragmented and vulnerable sense of learner identity, most participants chose to prepare for Higher Education via an Access course.

The path to becoming an older student and the notion of the 'right time'

Many themes, identities and positions interweave to provide a complex picture of interrelated and overlapping processes and experiences associated with an often gradual, tentative and painful sense of considering and negotiating a move towards further formal education.

TED: I used to, I used to look at, and think, well you know, I must start learning, but the thought of the long haul from nothing, because I had no qualifications, and I used to think, and then, oh, give it up, it'll take too long, and I've got to work.

Here, a notion of lost time is indicated, and Ted was deterred from trying to acquire qualifications thinking it would take too long, presumably, to study while working full time. While learning assumed a variety of meanings for those interviewed, a gradual dawning of a need to assume control, a desire to radically alter one's learning identity was often expressed. Discovery experiences, often related to issues of class, gender and race, were frequently, but not always, expressed as increasing awareness, of gradually promoting a positive sense of self, a sense of empowerment. Such experiences were also related to the present:

KATE: I suppose I brought my gender to college anyway, so I've probably noticed things that substantiate what I thought a bit more anyway. I'm still finding out more about it . . . and I've got all the opinions and views I had before, and still there, even stronger. They are just either supplemented in different ways, or supplemented more strongly by things going on.

Occasionally, participants linked such experiences with their decision to enter Higher Education. Learning outside formal education, including the experience of childrearing, was viewed as being qualitatively and quantitatively different from formal learning, and was not positively related to self-achievement and success. Applying to Higher Education and gaining access to it were seen as very large obstacles to hopefully be overcome.

RACHEL: Oh I felt, oh my God, you know, I'm gonna have to do a very good interview here [laughs], and I was not, I felt absolutely sick, I just felt oh my God, and I, I just felt it wasn't a very good interview, because, I actually, I actually really wanted to do it. I thought, what am I gonna do now [if I don't get in], my whole life's gonna, you know, and, um, and I kept saying to myself that this is where I really want to be . . . You know, but it was very important.

This is but one example of many from my interviews where the stakes seemed to be very high, obtaining university entrance was seen as extremely important. Having made the decision to apply to Higher Education, there seemed to be no going back.

In anticipating and making the move to Higher Education, determination and commitment to succeed often seems to have been related to a desire to realise one's own intellectual potential, moreover, to prove oneself to oneself. However, echoes from the past, relating to prior learning, were often voiced as interfering with the struggle to reach out for an altered learner identity.

ENID: So as a result, certainly academically, it has spread to other aspects of my life, I've got a very low opinion of my capabilities, which is why, even now, I still sort of have a tendency to pinch myself that I'm actually on the law course.

A gradual dawning of the need to assume control or responsibility for one's own learning and development was often expressed, sometimes through the use of extended metaphor.

CARL: I really saw Access as my last chance, I had a feeling it could be a door [shut] new in my face again. Probably a door I was gradually closing on myself, rather than someone else. I needed to push and to motivate myself rather than expect or need someone else to do it for me.

Here, there is a sense of time running out, from Carl's perspective, if he did not walk through the Access gateway, he would not be able to have a fulfilling future. Inherent in this appears to be a fear of potential avenues or possibilities being closed off for Carl, with a recognition that he had a central role to play in whether or not this would be so. For some others who had also had negative experiences at school, it seems that they did not even dare to consider the possibility of their entering Higher Education:

CHARLOTTE: It was really good for me to get going on a [Access] course like this, because I kind of don't know where I am in life . . . But I first thought you might not even want me. No, I mean, I had to come for an interview and things, and you think, well, you might even be turned down or something. I mean I have been kind of sitting at home for 20 years. I don't know, you have all these feelings, but I wasn't planning to go to the poly . . . It was way too difficult to my mind.

This extract, and the one above from Ted's interview, convey something of how complicated and daunting even contemplating entering formal learning can be. With a multitude of contrasting feelings, it seems to be difficult to assemble them to describe them in the narrative. At the pre-Access stage, Charlotte did not seem to be able to, or want to, assume responsibility for her learning, and in the interview she describes herself as having a very passive role, with my showing her the direction that she ought to perhaps follow. Her learning identity, so under-developed by a very restrictive childhood in which her family constantly made her aware that she was not as bright as her sister, had led her to believe that not only would Higher Education be too difficult for her, but that she might be refused entry onto the Access course for which she was being interviewed. Being a housewife for twenty years also seems to have contributed to her lack of confidence, highlighted by her talking about her children's attitude towards her:

CHARLOTTE: And I've told you that before . . . one of them actually told me, 'You haven't got brains, you can't do anything'. That's what they used to tell me.

Gillian gives another impression of what the Access course had to offer:

ESTELLE: Is there anything else about you, that you've not yet mentioned, that you remember as having changed during the Access course?
GILLIAN: I think I've got more confident. I can walk into a classroom now

without getting the jitters . . . we've been taught to go the right way about Higher Education learning . . . Some of the others [on my course] wish they'd had more general experience . . . The Access course has got me over that fear [of using computers], and I'm saying, well I'd like to get on and do a bit of graphics on the computers. Um, I'm not frightened of doing essays now . . . I haven't got that fear now, because I've already done it [written two and three thousand-word essays] . . . A lot of things like that. Taking notes, I find it easy to take notes . . . I've gained a lot out of it.

Gillian certainly was not alone in talking about getting a lot from an Access course. Lesley adds to this by explaining how the Access course was for her a test of her aptitude, again like an obstacle to be gotten over, yet it did not quite succeed in preparing her for Higher Education:

ESTELLE: What meaning did learning have for you then, what did you see it [the Access course] as giving you?
LESLEY: Um, well basically it was going to give me an entrance into polytechnic. That's what I wanted. And also sort of confidence in my, in the fact that I could learn, achieve, something I had to get over. Or, setting myself a test almost. I wanted to try and see if I could pass, not the actual test or exam, just doing the Access course. That's how it seemed to me.

Ann expressed similar sentiments, but relates her position in Higher Education by comparing herself to her 18-year-old counterparts:

ESTELLE: Could you have been better prepared for starting the present course?
ANN: No, I don't think so. I don't think there's any way because everybody sees it differently. I think what was done practically was OK . . . Academically, that brings us into the realm of not having the same qualifications as the 18 year olds. That can be, I found that can be a bit of a disadvantage. Uh, like particularly like with maths.

Ann was the only student in my study who was on a science degree, and had found the transition into the level of Higher Education maths rather difficult. While the Access course had offered a lot to those who had pursued one, Ann was not alone in expressing a sense of loss or inadequacy when comparing herself to school-leavers, who were thought to have had consistency in their education. This quote by Ann is but one example of the implications of loss of chronological age in learning, when related to present circumstances, and relates very closely to the regret expressed about not utilising compulsory education to the full.

In nearly all the interviews, age-related learning was a feature. There was a notion of 'the right time' for obtaining qualifications, which referred both to the past and to the present, this was usually expressed as a sense of loss, alongside in some cases a sense of failure, at not having done well or better at school. This is clearly expressed in two of the quotes given above. The concept of 'the right time' relates to the present in a number of ways. Not having obtained appropriate qualifications for Higher Education entry while of school age can be construed as having to make up for lost time. In doing so, the price to pay for this was considerable, and appears to be related to a lack of self-esteem, low self-confidence and a need to prove oneself to oneself, that is, in such instances it was only possible to partially make up the time. This seems to be why a number of students in my study compared themselves unfavourably with their 18-year-old counterparts and felt such a strong need to now assume control over their lives.

Those three, Emma, Dick and Nick, who had obtained qualifications appropriate for Higher Education entry while at school, did not compare themselves unfavourably to younger students, nor did they talk either about a lack of confidence or lost time. For them, the issue was one of uncertainty. Emma had already obtained a degree in Ireland, and initially was uncertain about how well she would do now, in her mid-forties, at undergraduate level. Dick's position was also one of uncertainty, but only in so far as the fact that at the start of his degree he obtained very high grades for minimum input, and he could not understand why this was so. There was an implication here that he was not earning his university place as he had expected to do. This sentiment was also clearly expressed by Nick.

First impressions of Higher Education and managing oneself

Eighteen of those I interviewed entered Higher Education via an Access course, although the small-scale supportive environment of such courses did not necessarily prepare individuals for induction into Higher Education, which was often expressed as impersonal and chaotic.

ANN: It [the degree course] was pretty awful to begin with, but the start of the second semester wasn't so bad. With, er, just culture shock . . . I don't think any Access course can actually prepare you for that. I think you all have to go through it.

Individuals gave a number of reasons for pursuing a degree course:

ROXANNE: Coming here is coming back to this subjectivity and objectivity. I wanna know about black people and my, that part of me, and I'm British-born and if I don't learn it here and I don't find it, who's gonna teach me? Do you understand me, that's how I feel?

While Roxanne's reason is specific to her, what can be generalised from this to many of the other interviews was that the decision to enter Higher Education was often linked to intrinsic goals, to a strong desire to find oneself, or to prove oneself to oneself, despite the hurdles.

However, to compare the above quote from Roxanne's interview with the one below from Sarah's, there seem to be subtly different qualities between the two, that is, between a desire to find oneself and the desire to prove oneself:

SARAH: I'm doing it for maybe emotionally selfish reasons . . . It's actually developing myself. And you get a degree at the end of it, fine, that's a bit of paper. But it's, it's actually just learning and coping with what's put in front of you.

This is a very gendered connection, why should it be selfish to fulfil one's emotional needs? Sarah refers again in the interview to her putting herself first as selfish, to balance her need to feel in control with her family responsibilities:

SARAH: I think, um, my goal is [to be] in control again, of work . . . So anyway, it is really just basically just trying to get myself, find myself enough time without doing damage to the family life. Um, to be selfish, and to be able to say, 'Look, I've got study to do, I've got to fit this in'.

Here, her conflict is evident. Sarah is struggling to find enough time for her studies and her family, and the implication is that when she feels able to balance the two, she will be in control of her working life. A number of women in my study expressed this conflict, even if, as in Sarah's case, they had been in full-time employment prior to becoming a student. Studying requires finding time outside of ordinary working hours and is a major part of the transition into becoming a full-time student. This is in direct opposition to Nick's experience:

ESTELLE: Do you see yourself as undergoing a process of change?
NICK: Yes, very much. I'm not sure whether it's a continuous thing, or whether I've actually done it . . . I'm not sure how much is actually coming from the, uh, university, or how much has just come from me . . . I see you know, myself, family and, you know, the world at large in sort of slightly different terms than I used to . . . Um, but I see now my time with them [my family] as being far more important than that which I was, um doing, or providing, previously . . . And by being at university, I've got a lot more time than I ever would've done in the normal course of events . . . Um, you know, I'm actually a lot more involved now.

In contrast to Sarah, Nick found himself to have far more quality time with his family as a result of his becoming a student, and from his perspective this was very much tied up with his having changed. He talked about taking his two children to and from school, pursuing interests with them, but made no reference to his position with regard to domestic work. For the female mother–students, although there were some alterations to childcare arrangements, domestic roles did not appear to have changed much, nor did they express that they felt they should.

Accounts of participants' positions at the time of the interview varied considerably. Many indicated a high level of self-awareness and were fired with enthusiasm and determination to succeed:

LIZ: I mean I can see where all my problems with studying lie. I know they're there. And I know why they're there. I mean, OK I've intellectualised them. But I don't feel we can feel anything about them unless you do, and I know that I can't deal with all of that at once. I mean, it's got to be, bits of it have got to be put right in stages . . . Um, I've just got to break those things gradually and it's a long process, because to change, it does take a long time . . . I know it's possible and I'm going to do it. I am going to do it and that's that.

It is worth noting from Liz's narrative that her sense of imbalance, of struggle, was perhaps higher than most. Others did not report as high a level of determination to succeed, but like Liz articulated a sense of struggle, of being an outsider, as they had also experienced their position in compulsory education. Six reported having used the counselling service. At the follow-up interview, another three mentioned having used this as a resource.

All those I interviewed had experienced a mixture of anxiety, apprehension and excitement at commencing their Higher Education course, the induction period often being experienced as impersonal and chaotic. Many felt at a disadvantage to their younger counterparts:

GRACE: I was a bit nervous, yeah, 'cos of going, and I was going with all these A level students, you know, they were fresh and all that. Well I was panicking, I wasn't looking forward to September . . . at all. And I said, 'Will I be able to cope?'

Early integration appears to be strongly related to the quality of the interpersonal interface between students and staff. However, when high anxiety was voiced during the interview about one's potential, this did not appear to have been markedly reduced by supportive tutoring and high-grade attainment on the Access course.

ESTELLE: Do you see anything as having changed in you, since finishing the Access course in June?
ANDREA: Intellectually, I'm aware of my ability, but emotionally that doesn't matter . . . Apart from the fact that I felt I had gained confidence [on the Access course] and that now seems to have left me, not really. It's almost as if sort of all the same fears or similar fears that I've had at every most [sic] stages

of my education are there, but in a sense they're bigger because this is a higher course, do you know what I mean?

ESTELLE: Mmm, there's more at stake I suppose?

ANDREA: Mmm, yeah. What happens if I can't achieve this and, you know, these sort of exams?

At this early stage, Andrea is expressing a need to regain control, having lost it at the point of entering Higher Education, along with expressing a high level of anxiety over exams some five months away. Previous support and positive feedback were not successful in enabling her to overcome the negative learner identity she was articulating. While her expressed anxiety was higher than most, this example demonstrates how vulnerable learner identity can be, having acquired considerable self-confidence while on the Access course this appears to have been lost upon entering Higher Education. In other instances, where the interpersonal element between the institution and the individual was lacking, support and encouragement from one's peers were crucial in gradually fostering a more positive learner identity.

All students, including those three who did not talk about lacking confidence, considered themselves to be undergoing a period of transition. Often, an imbalance was implied:

LIZ: You know I have these real intense times. I mean, if I do some work, if I've worked really hard and really got hold of some concept or other, I'm up here, and really high, and I drive everybody mad . . . I sometimes think, 'why am I doing this, this is so hard, this is such a struggle?' And then, when you get through it, I am in such, I'm right at the top, it gives me more satisfaction than any relationship now. I'd rather have that.

This is an extreme example from those I interviewed, but nevertheless, generalising to other narratives, it does indicate something of the difficulties encountered when accommodating Higher Education into one's life. On the one hand, there can be very significant gains to be had from studying, while on the other, certainly close to the start of a Higher Education course, it is a struggle to obtain these.

Other negative experiences were narrated in varying ways. The power of the institution and inequality of experience (and feeling oneself to be disadvantaged or discriminated against) were voiced by some in terms of gender, age, race or class.

LESLEY: They are *very* I find unsympathetic towards anything to do with needs of the children . . . It's a question of, 'Well, you made the choice to come here, deal with the problems when they come, if you can't cope with it, then it's your problem' . . . you just get, you hit a blank [*sic*] wall really.

Thus, the experiences and skills of older students (interestingly, not for those on social science courses) were not necessarily seen as 'valuable assets' by the institution. In this example, being a mother–student is seen as a considerable disadvantage, but one for which those representing the institution are not prepared to make any allowance. This last extract also indicates something of the complex position of a female student with a family, which was echoed throughout my interviews with mother–students. In several interviews, the role of student was not assimilated into the interviewee's lifestyle, with the inference that one can only be a 'real' student when not hampered by the responsibility assumed for carrying out housework, or attending to family needs.

Concluding remarks

In the study represented here, the effects of the interaction of gender with other variables such as age and ethnic background are very complex and it has not been possible to make sweeping generalisations from such a small sample. However, it is not by chance that most older students entering Higher Education are female, and this is especially the case with those who enter via an Access course. Interestingly, such individuals tend to opt for social science and humanities or arts subjects, perpetuating even further the stereotype of distribution found in their younger counterparts. This complies with Thomas's (1990) proposal that ideas about degree subjects and ideas about gender largely reinforce one another. While a woman may theoretically be able to choose either typically masculine or typically feminine subjects, the effects of social pressures and the subtleties of social conditioning and constructions, including those associated with former schooling, may then become internalised and are likely to affect her choice. Higher Education does not necessarily actively discriminate against women, yet it does seem to employ culturally available ideas in such a way that women may be marginalised and sometimes alienated. In this chapter, this is most obvious in the contrasting and pervasive gender difference between mother–students and father–students.

There are powerful pressures promulgating for change and wider access opportunities, but the powerful set of resistances operating have resulted in there being little evidence of a more comprehensive and open system of Higher Education (see Fulton and Ellwood 1989). Yet, those represented in this study had not experienced difficulty in obtaining a place in Higher Education. Rather, the difficulties encountered were very much related to how they had felt about themselves as learners, and their associated feelings of self-worth, both prior to entry and during their Higher Education course. For the women in my study, this often seemed to be an impediment to their progress, in the different ways in which this was construed by them.

There are clearly many consequences to be faced as a result of the recent overall increase in the student population, a number of which may be specific to the needs of older and other non-traditional.students. In this context there is a lot more that institutions of Higher Education can do to improve the situation for older students, particularly older women students. For instance, more research is needed into the dynamics of staff–student interactions, alongside serious attention to be paid to implementing creative induction programmes, as well as allocating resources to staff development to be aimed at encouraging teaching staff to examine their attitudes towards older female students, and how this relates to their teaching duties.

If wider access to Higher Education is to be implemented successfully, it is crucial to listen closely to non-traditional students' accounts of the processes, boundaries and struggles involved in developing a positive sense of learner identity. While some disciplines obviously lend themselves more readily to this suggestion than others, inter-relating life experience with formal learning contexts could well be part of a process which would add richness to what should, after all, be part of an enabling, empowering experience.

References

Baxter-Magolda, M.B. (1988) 'Measuring gender differences in intellectual development: a comparison of assessment methods', *Journal of College Student Development* 28: 443–8.

—— (1992) *Knowing and Reasoning in College: Gender-related Patterns in Students' Intellectual Development*, San Francisco: Jossey-Bass.

Belenky, M.F., Clinchy, B.M., Goldberger, M. and Tarule, J.M. (1986) *Women's Ways of Knowing*, New York: Basic Books.

Bhavnani, K.-K. (1998) 'The "giving of voice" within feminist standpoint theory: a study of incarcerated women', in K. Henwood, C. Griffin and A. Phoenix (eds) *Standpoints and Differences: Essays in the Practice of Feminist Psychology*, London: Sage.

Clinchy, B.M. and Zimmerman, C. (1982) 'Epistemology and agency in the development of undergraduate women', in P. Perun (ed.) *The Undergraduate Women: Issues in Educational Equity*, Lexington, Mass.: D.C. Heath.

Edwards, R. (1993) *Mature Women Students: Separating or Connecting Family and Education*, London: Taylor and Francis.

Elsey, B. (1982) 'Mature student experience of university', *Studies in Adult Education* 14: 69–72.

Entwistle, N.J. and Marton, F. (1994) 'Knowledge objects: understandings constituted through intensive academic study', *British Journal of Educational Psychology* 64: 161–78.

Fulton, O. and Ellwood, S. (1989) 'Admissions, access and institutional change', in O. Fulton (ed.) *Access and Institutional Change*, Milton Keynes: Open University Press.

Holt, J. (1964) *How Children Fail*, Surrey: Pitman.

King, E. (1994) 'An investigation into the learning experiences of mature students entering higher education', in G. Gibbs (ed.) *Improving Student Learning*, Oxford: Oxford Centre for Staff Development.

—— (1996) 'The use of the self in qualitative research', in J.T.E. Richardson (ed.)

Handbook of Qualitative Research Methods for Psychology and the Social Sciences, Leicester: B.P.S. Books.

Kitzinger, C. (1987) *The Social Construction of Lesbianism*, London: Sage.

Marshall, J. and Nicolson, P. (1991) 'Why choose psychology? Mature and other students' accounts at graduation', in J. Radford (ed.) *The Choice of Psychology*. Occasional Papers of the Group of Teachers of the British Psychological Society, Vol. 12.

Melling, G. and Stanton, G. (1990) 'Access to and through further education', in G. Parry and C. Wake (eds) *Access and Alternative Futures for Higher Education*, Sevenoaks: Hodder and Stoughton.

Merriam, S.J. (1988) *Case Study Research in Education: A Qualitative Approach*, San Francisco: Jossey-Bass.

Morgan, A., Taylor, E. and Gibbs, G. (1982) 'Variations in students, approaches to studying', *British Journal of Educational Technology* 13: 107–13.

Osborn, M., Charnley, A. and Withnall, A. (1984) *Mature Students. Review of Existing Research in Adult and Continuing Education*, Leicester: National Institute of Adult and Continuing Education (England and Wales).

Perry, W.G., Jun. (1970) *Forms of Intellectual and Ethical Development in the College Years: A Scheme*, New York: Holt, Rinehart and Winston.

—— (1981) 'Cognitive and ethical growth: the making of meaning', in A.W. Chickering and Associates, *The Modern American College: Responding to the New Realities of Diverse Students and a Changing Society*, San Francisco: Jossey-Bass.

Rennie, D.L., Phillips, J.R. and Quartaro, G.K. (1988) 'Grounded theory: a promising approach to conceptualization in psychology?', *Canadian Psychology* 29: 139–50.

Thacker, C. and Novak, M. (1991) 'Student role supports for younger and older middle-aged women: application of a life event model', *Canadian Journal of Higher Education* 21: 13–36.

Thomas, K. (1990) *Gender and Subject in Higher Education*, Buckingham: Society for Research into Higher Education and Open University Press.

Tuckett, A. (1990) 'A higher education system fit for adult learners', in G. Parry and C. Wake (eds) *Access and Alternative Futures for Higher Education*, Sevenoaks: Hodder and Stoughton.

Weil, S.W. (1988) 'From a language of observation to a language of experience: studying the perspectives of diverse adults in higher education', *Journal of Access Studies* 1: 17–43.

—— (1989a) 'Influences on lifelong learning on adults' expectations and experiences of returning to formal learning contexts', unpublished Ph.D. thesis, University of London.

—— (1989b) 'Access: towards education or miseducation? Adults imagine the future', in O. Fulton (ed.) *Access and Institutional Change*, Milton Keynes: Open University and Society for Research into Higher Education.

Woodley, A., Wagner, L., Slowey, M., Hamilton, M. and Fulton, O. (1987) *Choosing to Learn: Adults in Education*, Milton Keynes: Society for Research into Higher Education and Open University Press.

6

GENDER ISSUES IN EMPLOYMENT SELECTION

Neil Scott and Paul Creighton

Individuals choose occupations, but occupations also choose individuals, formally through selection procedures. In the UK, legislation makes it normally illegal to select on the basis of the individual being a man or a woman. Although this was only introduced in the 1970s, it is more or less taken for granted, and it is surprising to see job advertisements in, for example, the People's Republic of China, which specifically rule out one sex or the other. Neil Scott and Paul Creighton show that, despite legislation and an undoubted change in practice, gender factors can still influence selection. In so far as this means that some section of the population is thus excluded from consideration, it is unproductive, and further steps need to be taken towards a fairer system.

Introduction

Considered in the time frame of the development of modern human society, the move towards equality in employment between the sexes is an extremely recent phenomenon. It was only in 1970 that an act was passed in Britain requiring employers to pay male and female employees equitably, and only in 1975 that the act came into effect and that a second act was passed to have both employees and job applicants treated on an equal basis. While the passing of such acts may reflect changes, or the desire for change, in the values and perceptions of a nation, it also takes time for those values to filter into the normal practice and attitudes of the people.

There is no denying that huge changes in attitudes and practice have occurred since 1970, or indeed that change has occurred throughout the twentieth century brought about through women's suffrage, industrialisation and the changes in women's roles in the two world wars. One only has to look at films or television programmes from the 1950s to note the stark contrast between the then images of women as objects or homemakers with how women are considered in society today. Nevertheless, there is still a very long way to go before the ideas behind the Equal Opportunities legislation are translated into real and fundamental changes in attitude and practice in the recruitment and employment of women. No doubt, in a further forty years time, we will look back in horror at the ways things are today as reflected in the recorded culture.

In this chapter, we wish to consider gender issues in the selection process (covering both recruitment and promotion); to consider whether and how women are being unfairly treated and what should be done to improve matters. We will consider women's current position in the world of work and current appointment methods and practices. In particular, we will be concerned with whether current practices are fair and with the extent to which fairness can ever be properly assessed in a situation where ideas about women's roles and the nature of how work is organised reflect fundamental inequalities.

Current position of women in the workplace

While the legal requirement is for equitable treatment, it is inevitable that many of the assumptions that have lasted for centuries about the occupational roles of men and women, and which are embedded in our culture, will take time to be replaced. An employer who viewed himself (and it probably was a him) as being fair might well express that fairness by not requiring a female employee to take on onerous managerial responsibilities for which he believes she would not be suited by virtue of her sex. We may have had a woman Prime Minister, but women still only accounted for 9.2 per cent of MPs in 1992. Women make up 80 per cent of clerical workers but only about 22 per cent of managers (Cassel and Walsh 1993). Even in the British Civil Service, where the revolutionary Northcote-Trevallyn reforms outlawed patronage and instituted the principle of 'fair and open competition on merit' over a century ago, there is a significant mismatch between female representation at the junior and senior grades. Women now account for over 50 per cent of the total Civil Service workforce, yet while they make up almost 70 per cent of the most junior clerical grades (administrative assistants) only 12 per cent of those in the top five grades (the 'mandarin' category) are women (Civil Service Data Summary 1995). This picture, while bleak, represents a strong continuing trend of improvement for female representation in the Civil Service, an organisation which is still a leader in equal opportunities in employment.

While more and more women have found employment and have worked their way into senior and professional positions, the progress has been slow. Only 12 per cent of solicitors are women, and 16 per cent of secondary school headteachers (see Cassel and Walsh 1993). Furthermore, women's earnings are, on average, around 75 per cent of those of men, and this is true across all levels of jobs including the highest levels. For example, women directors are paid on average almost £10,000 less than men (National Management Salary Survey 1996). While some of this has been due to society's failure, or refusal, to equip women adequately for many jobs (how can we hope to have successful female physicists if schools used to suggest that this was a subject more appropriate for male pupils?), it is also due to the way women are perceived by employers both in terms of their abilities and in terms of how employment relates to their lives outside work.

The difference between the historical occupational position of women and the current situation is that now there is less conscious exclusion of women from senior, managerial and professional posts. Current legislation forbids the explicit refusal to consider or appoint women for the full range of jobs with relatively few exceptions (e.g. frontline combat duties in the armed forces). What remains, though, is an approach to the selection and promotion of women that was developed in the context of a male-based workforce where most jobs were 'gendered'. This is aggravated by the belief, still tenaciously held in some quarters, that women are fundamentally ill-equipped for the more senior or traditionally male roles and are better equipped than men for the more menial and traditionally female roles. Curran (1986) has shown that many jobs remain 'gendered' and that recruiters are strongly affected by these stereotypes in their selection decisions. Such stereotypes affect job seekers as well as recruiters and these are reflected in the choices of male and female job seekers.

The Sex Discrimination Act of 1975 was introduced to address these issues.

The Sex Discrimination Act (1975)

The Sex Discrimination Act (1975) identifies two types of discrimination, direct and indirect, both of which legislate against discrimination on grounds of sex or marital status.

Direct discrimination refers to the situation in which a person is treated less favourably than another specifically on the grounds of their sex (or marital status).

Indirect discrimination relates to practices which require people to comply with a condition, which, while in theory is equitable and is applied to both men and women, is such that there is a difference in the proportion of each sex who can comply with it. For example, a minimum height requirement applied equally to male and female applicants would work against women as they are typically shorter than men.

A very important aspect of the Sex Discrimination Act is that indirect discrimination is considered lawful if the employer can demonstrate that the discriminating condition is justified. We will return to this issue when considering the validity of the recruitment process, the nature of jobs and the way in which criteria for recruitment and promotion are established.

The effects of the 1975 Sex Discrimination Act

Research suggests that the act has had surprisingly little effect in preventing discrimination in employment. Curran (1986) concluded that 'ten years after its appearance on the Statute Book . . . the Act is a law which is little understood and frequently broken by those involved in recruiting people to jobs . . . it appears that recruiters believe that their contraventions may be justified by recourse to commonsense stereotypes of roles of gender and parenthood and to the practical requirements of their businesses'. Fletcher and Williams (1992) note that 'The disappointing impact of the Sex Discrimination Act leads to the conclusion that the law itself is only a partial solution to the problem of discrimination.'

It seems that while some employers have worked hard to remove sex discrimination from their workplaces, others have maintained entrenched attitudes in which jobs are 'gendered' and in which men and women are thought to be better suited to particular jobs because of their (assumed) characteristics and because of the (assumed) constraints of other factors (e.g. family commitments).

One of the factors which has led to so few prosecutions being brought under the Act is that it is very difficult to prove the existence of discrimination. Curran (1986) notes that 'employers gave considerable emphasis to subjective factors such as personality, manner and appearance, assessments of which are susceptible to gender stereotyping and sufficiently indeterminate to obscure the operation of more direct discrimination'.

It is interesting to note that over the last decade there has been a much greater use of more objective assessment methods in recruitment, such as cognitive ability tests (Shackleton and Newell 1991). These have the advantage of being more reliable and therefore of being more measurably related to performance in the job. They are also, potentially, fairer because they do not allow subjective, unconscious and discriminatory attitudes on the part of the recruiter to come into play. However, there is a danger that such objective assessments may fall into disuse because of their very objectivity. Such assessments provide hard data on which sex discrimination cases may be based, and recruiters may prefer to use more subjective and probably discriminatory assessment methods such as interviews rather than risk prosecution.

We believe that this would be a backward step and that observed differences between applicant groups on an objective occupational assessment may not necessarily reflect a bias in the instrument. The operation of bias in employment should be a much wider consideration and the forsaking of objective assessment methods in selection because of apparent differences in performance between the sexes may be a case of 'shooting the messenger'.

This proposed wider examination of the issues will entail a consideration and recognition of whatever gender differences exist in the people being assessed (or potentially being assessed) at all stages of employment selection (from the entire population through to the final shortlist) and a full consideration and recognition of the operation of gender stereotypes and biases in the processes that result in the rejection and selection of people at those stages.

Sources of gender bias in the employment selection process

While the operation of the Sex Discrimination Act is necessarily at the level of particular selection decisions, the causes of gender bias are extremely wide-ranging, including such factors as parental expectations of children, education, the advertising of vacancies, self-perceptions of potential job applicants, the nature of the assessment methods, the attitudes and assumptions of the assessors and the way that selection criteria are established. Curran (1986) notes that 'segregation and gender bias in the labour market result both from the supply side (e.g. education and self-selection) and from the demand side (e.g. employer discrimination)', and Fletcher and Williams (1992) have noted that barriers to change in the position of women in employment include systematic barriers in organisations' policies, attitudes of management and the attitudes of women themselves.

We will consider possible gender discrimination in employment selection by taking as wide a view as possible of the sources of gender differences and gender discrimination, and will then consider how fairness within the process can be assessed. The employment selection process and the factors influencing it can be conceptualised as shown in Figure 6.1.

The pool of potential applicants is reduced to the actual applicant pool by the 'decision to apply' and the applicant pool is reduced to the successful candidates by a 'selection process'. Both of these processes, resulting in the successive reduction in the number of applicants or potential applicants, are influenced by a number of factors, many of which have implications for sex discrimination. We have highlighted 'job definition' as being an important factor and have labelled it as

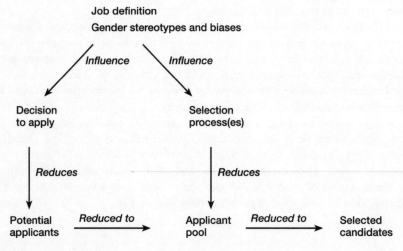

Figure 6.1 The employment selection process

being distinct from 'gender stereotypes and biases' because we believe that it is one of the few factors in sex discrimination which is under our direct and relatively immediate control. Job definitions themselves are, of course, influenced by gender stereotypes and biases. Nevertheless, we will argue that, through the application of 'gender aware' job analysis techniques and the resultant effects on job advertisement and the design of assessment and selection methods, it will be possible to encourage women to apply for positions they might not otherwise have applied for and to reduce the operation of sex discrimination in the selection process.

The characteristics of, and factors influencing, each of these groups of people and processes in the model are now discussed.

Potential applicants

We will consider just about anyone as a potential applicant for the purposes of the model and will not narrow the group down by factors such as age since any such factor may not be a reasonable selection factor and may itself be a source of discrimination. We will suppose that the potential applicants have characteristics relevant to the selection process and that these characteristics can themselves be influenced by several factors. Thus potential applicants have the following characteristics:

- Attitudes relating to the particular position
- Attitudes relating to their career
- Qualifications
- Experiences
- Job relevant knowledge, skills, abilities and personal characteristics
- Self-perceptions

These will be (variously) influenced by:

- Heredity
- Socialisation
- Formal education
- Work and work-related experiences

Because there are gender differences in all of these influencing factors, it is likely that there are gender differences in the characteristics of the potential applicants (e.g. males tend to be taller than females; females are more likely to study psychology at university than males).

Applicant pool

The applicant pool is that subset of the potential applicants which decided to apply for the position. Therefore any gender differences that exist within this group will reflect the gender differences that exist in the potential applicant group plus the modifying effects of any gender differences in the decision to apply.

The decision to apply

There are many factors which influence the decision to apply for a position and many of these are themselves likely to have differential gender implications. Such factors are as follows.

Awareness of the vacancy

This in turn will depend on such factors as where the vacancy was publicised. It may be through informal contacts or through public advertising, both of which have clear gender implications. Readerships of different publications differ by gender and the power of the 'old-boy network' in getting on in employment is infamous.

The content of the advertisement

This will depend crucially on what the requirements of the job are considered to be (and we will argue that there are unrecognised gender biases in the identification of job requirements). Many advertisements will have person requirements which are indirectly discriminatory, but which are there because the recruiter believes that they can be justified in terms of eventual performance on the job. There are also considerations of the relative attractiveness of the advertisements to men and women, and of the advertiser's ability to correctly target the identified audience.

Perceived fit of own abilities and career desires to job requirements and characteristics

This in turn will depend on what the potential applicants' abilities are (and how they perceive them to be) and what the requirements of the job are perceived to be. For example, a recruiter may take extreme care in avoiding gender-typing in order to attract females to apply for a traditionally male job, but the male-gendered nature of the job, in the minds of the female potential applicants, may nevertheless lead them to not apply.

There is an increasing use of 'self-selection questionnaires' to help potential applicants decide if the job would interest them and match their skills. While this is welcome as an empowering tool for the applicant and a way of reducing inappropriate applications, if it is designed without an awareness of gender issues and without monitoring the impact on different groups it could prove to be a further source of bias against women.

Confidence to apply

Different people may need to feel more certain about the relative level of their abilities before making job applications. For example, men may be more likely to 'have a go' than women, who may tend to apply only when they are well qualified for the position.

Selection process

The selection process will typically be a set of assessments of the applicant pool. The assessment methods should (ideally) be designed to discriminate between candidates who do and do not have the knowledge, skills, abilities and personal characteristics which have been identified as being necessary for good perform- ance on the job. These assessments may include eligibility sifts, application form sifts, biodata, educational qualifications, interviews, cognitive ability tests, per- sonality assessments, work sample tests, achievement records, group discussions or formal presentations.

On the other hand, recruitment and promotion may be a matter of decisions behind closed doors through informal contacts. Indeed, even when jobs are advertised and selection processes are designed to be formal, Curran (1986) noted 'these studies of actual recruitment decisions emphasise the distinctions between formal, and apparently rigid, recruitment and selection policies and the indeterminacy and flexibility of actual recruitment decision making.'

It is at this selection process stage that most gender discrimination attention is focused, and in terms of the Sex Discrimination Act, it is the job requirements which have to be demonstrated to be either unbiased or justifiable, and the assessments of the abilities to fulfil those requirements in the applicants which have to be shown to be fair (or at least have to avoid being shown to be unfair, which is not the same thing). The job definition will determine what the selection methods should be designed to measure, and there may be sex differences in those measures, and gender stereotypes and biases may operate within the application of the methods to cause biases in measurement.

This wide-ranging model of the possible sources of gender discrimination in the employment selection process has been proposed in order to provide a con- text for the following discussion of the assessment of fairness in the selection process. We believe that the current focusing of anti-discrimination effort only at the point of selection ('selection process' in the model) without taking into account other wider considerations may result in misleading and ultimately unhelpful conclusions.

The operation of gender bias in the employment selection process

Gender bias and sex discrimination in employment selection is driven by conscious and unconscious stereotypes and overgeneralisations about the 'gendered' nature of jobs and about the actual or supposed differences between men and women.

Thus, while patronage, interviews and application forms remained the mainstay of assessment technology when deciding who should be appointed, the erroneous conscious and unconscious assumptions of the appointer would inevitably have a major impact on female representation in the workforce. Such subjective assessment methods would be likely to perpetuate gender and employment stereotypes and, by their nature, be relatively inaccessible to investigation and the control of law.

We can see how these assumptions can lead to gender bias by consideration of the model (see Figure 6.1). Women may not apply for 'male' jobs because they have been socialised not to desire such jobs, or because they have been socialised to think that they would not perform well in the job for whatever reason, or because they perceive themselves not to have the qualities which have been stated to be necessary or are assumed to be necessary for the job, or because they believe they would suffer discrimination in the job, or because they (probably correctly) believe that their application would not be treated fairly by the recruiter.

Preferential appointment or promotion decisions in favour of men can be based on direct or indirect discrimination, but are often based on assumptions about the skills men and women differentially possess. It is popularly accepted that, for example, men are more competitive and aggressive than women and that women are more emotional and less confrontational. Personality scales support these perceptions, and differences between males and females are often found on measures of these attributes. For example, significant gender differences are found on twenty-one of the thirty Occupational Personality Questionnaire (OPQ) scales (Parker 1994). These differences concur with male and female stereotypes; males scoring higher on factors relating to persuasiveness, control, independence, tough-mindedness, competitiveness and achieving behaviours, while women score higher on scales of affiliative, democratic and caring interpersonal styles. Similarly, the *Handbook for the 16PF* reports differences in male and female scores across the range of scales which indicate women are warmer, more tender-hearted and more affected by emotions, while men are more assertive and confident (Cattell *et al.* 1970).

Suppose that a job specification demands a 'dominant personality'. If women are automatically discounted from the competition for the job because they are women and 'women are not dominant types' then direct discrimination has occurred. Indirect discrimination would occur if the assessment of dominance was part of the selection procedure as fewer women will obtain high scores on 'dominance' than men. Such indirect discrimination would be defensible under the Act if it can be shown that dominance is really required for the job. However, we will argue below that it is not sufficient simply to show that dominant people have carried out the job in the past (which may just reflect that that area of work has been male dominated), or that dominant people are successful. Rather, we should consider that there may be many ways to achieve successful outcomes in a job, and recognise that many of them may not yet have been tried.

Such beliefs need not be consciously, or actively, held for an assessment to be biased. The psychological literature is replete with studies on the effects that subjective perceptions and bias can have in the process of assessment. The sex of the assessee and the interaction with the sex of the assessor can both add unwelcome variance into the process. For example, the attractiveness of a candidate can impact on the way they are seen. Attractive people are perceived to be more effective in their senior roles unless the role is not associated with that person's gender. However, if a woman is attractive and successful, her beauty is assumed to be part of the reason for her success (Heilman and Stopeck 1985a and b). Gender cues that are completely unrelated to the job, such as dress or the wearing of perfume or aftershave, can lead to different assessments depending on the sex of the assessor and assessee (see Herriot's 1987 review). In the absence of information, or with only irrelevant information, about a candidate, assessors will revert to assumptions based on the group the person is a member of (Nieva and Gutek 1980). If the group does not match the job then the candidate's chances of success will necessarily be reduced. In almost all of these cases the effect works against women, although it need not be assumed that it is only men whose selection assessments are influenced by gender. The evidence suggests that women assessors also show sex bias (e.g. Swim *et al.* 1989; Top 1991).

It was for these reasons that the use of more objective and thorough procedures such as cognitive and personality tests, assessment exercises, assessment centres, etc. were promoted. In the past few years we have seen a steady growth in the use of these tools. A study by Sneath, Thakur and Madjuck carried out in 1976, suggested only marginal use of tests. A follow-up study of companies with 1,000+ employees reported by Mabey (1989) reported that 66 per cent had used cognitive tests on at least ten people in the preceding twelve months and 47 per cent had used personality tests. This latter figure had risen to 57 per cent by 1992 (Mabey 1992). Smaller organisations also use such tests. A more recent survey of organisations of 200+ employees found 59 per cent having used occupational tests, with 47 per cent of the total doing so currently (Baker and Cooper 1995). Shackleton and Newell (1991) reported a threefold increase in the use of personality tests between 1984 and 1989 (from 12 per cent to 37 per cent) and an even greater increase in the use of cognitive tests (from 9 per cent to 41 per cent in the same period).

This increase in the use of objective measures of ability should have positive effects; people will tend to be selected on the basis of their ability rather than on the basis of assumptions and subjective impressions. Unfortunately, as we will explain, the interpretation of 'objective' measures of ability is not at all straightforward. Furthermore, although the sources of gender bias in employment selection are, as we have shown, extremely wide and far-reaching, the way that equal opportunities initiatives have tended to operate has been to focus on the point of selection in a very narrow way. If a reliable and objective measure shows a significant difference between the men and women who are assessed at a particular stage of the selection assessment, then 'adverse impact' is said to have been demonstrated. Assuming for the moment that the measure is an accurate reflection of the underlying quality it is being used to assess, such adverse impact may reflect the fact that there are underlying sex differences in the entire population, or that there are sex differences in the population from which the job applicants are drawn (e.g. university graduates), or that there are no sex differences in the whole population but that there are sex differences in the men and women who apply for the job. In each of these cases, the measure is functioning as it should do. However, the existence of adverse impact is often considered to be a bad thing regardless of the reasons for it. Indeed, a measure which showed no adverse impact at the point of selection would tend to be viewed favourably, even if there was a true underlying difference in favour of one sex which the instrument had failed to detect.

We will discuss all of these gender issues in the application of selection instruments with specific reference to the use of cognitive ability tests, although many of the points raised will apply equally well to any assessment method. Cognitive tests are considered in detail here because they are objective measures of ability, and therefore not subject to the added confounding effect of subjective influences, and because there is plentiful data on cognitive tests, therefore the issues can be more clearly examined and demonstrated. Also, there is a great deal more data available for study for cognitive tests than for other assessment methods.

With regard to gender effects in the use of cognitive tests for employment selection, the concerns we present here are fivefold. First, that women tend to do less well on cognitive tests, and because of the way these tests are used, can have significant effects on their chances of getting jobs and promotion. Second, the distributions of women's scores on tests are consistently narrower than men's, which has a major implication for the proportion of males and females who get through the sift stages of the more popular and prestigious jobs. Third, the not uncommon use of tests in isolation can further exacerbate inaccuracies in the selection process. Fourth, the most commonly used procedures for assessing the fairness of selection procedures may be hopelessly inappropriate.

Finally, we believe that the very way in which we identify the requirements of the job and design our assessment procedures may be unjust to women. However, we also believe that the development of 'gender-aware' job analysis methodologies provides the most direct path to changing women's lot in the workplace and, via that, to changing the very stereotypes which are the underlying cause of the problems. It is this final point that is most fundamental and where we believe that attention should be ultimately focused.

Gender differences in the level and range of cognitive test performance

There has been much debate recently on the relative abilities of boys and girls as reflected in school examinations. Until very recently, boys tended to outperform girls in all subjects and also tended to show a wider range of performance. These data were widely accepted as reflecting fundamental differences between the sexes, though theoretical explanations for them ranged right across the nature–nurture debate. However, recent examination results in the UK, in which girls have overtaken boys in virtually all subjects, cast serious doubt on any theory proposing innate sex differences as an explanation of the data.

Cognitive tests are standardised objective assessments of reasoning ability. They differ in their format depending upon their level and the area or areas of ability they are seeking to measure. They also differ in style depending on author and publisher. While performance in academic examinations is clearly affected by a huge range of factors, cognitive tests are designed to assess underlying cognitive ability, reasoning ability or even 'intelligence'. The assumption is that such underlying ability cannot be taught. With strong cognitive ability, one is likely to do well academically, but not doing well academically does not necessarily demonstrate a lack of cognitive ability. The supposition then, is that cognitive test performance should reflect, in a relatively fundamental way, the underlying cognitive abilities of men and women. Specific tests will normally be measuring this ability in a crystallised form, that is, they will measure it in the context of a learned form such as reading, writing, or mathematical ability. However, they will typically be investigating the underlying ability, whether it be crystallised or potential.

The authors carried out a review of several sets of test data to examine the level of difference between male and female candidates for tests taken between 1994 and 1996. A wide range of tests was used from a number of test producers in a range of selection contexts. In most cases the samples were not pre-selected except by eligibility for the job (e.g. having the appropriate qualifications or, in the case of some public sector employers, by nationality). The sample sizes ranged from 84 to 11,184. Tests were categorised as 'verbal', 'numerical', 'reasoning' or 'other'.

The verbal tests were designed to measure the ability to understand or present verbal information clearly and accurately. These include tests such as the GMA (verbal), the AV2/EV2 – verbal organisation tests (RAS Ltd), and SHL's VMG2 – verbal reasoning test. The numerical tests required candidates to interpret tables of data, identify numerical relationships and sequences, compute figures involving addition, subtraction, multiplication, division, percentage and ratio calculations and occasionally the use of square or square root figures. This category includes tests such as the NMG2 – numerical reasoning, and NIT2 – number series (SHL), the AN5 and EN5 – data interpretation tests (RAS Ltd) and the GMA (numerical). The reasoning category covers a range of tests that involve abstract or unfamiliar problem-solving, identifying non-numerical sequences or manipulating (verbally presented) information to find logical conclusions. This category includes, for example, Ravens' SPM and APM, and RAS Ltd's AR3 – analysis of information test and AN4 – dominoes.

Tables 6.1–4 show the relative performance of male and female samples

Table 6.1 Verbal tests

Test description	Higher mean	Difference between means	Greater range	Range difference	Sample size
Ai) Management level for scientists	m	.018	m	.124	512
Bi) Supervisor level	m	.173	m	.167*	154
Ci) Management level	m	.197*	m	.041	442
Di) Supervisor level	f	.335	f	.063	132
Ei) Supervisor level	m	.112*	m	.078*	3686
Eii) Supervisor level	f	.028	m	.031	3686
F) Supervisor level for IT personnel	m	.050	m	.030	182
Hi) Management level	m	.210*	m	.063	1524
Ji) Management level	m	.053	m	.047*	5406
Ki) Management level	f	.104*	m	.020	5592
Kii) Management level	m	.075*	m	.026	5592
Kiii) Management level	m	.085	f	.028*	5592

Table 6.2 Numerical tests

Test description	Higher mean	Mean difference	Greater range	Range difference	Sample size
Aii) Management level for scientists	m	.699*	m	.081	512
Bii) Supervisor level	m	.510*	m	.278*	112
Cii) Management level	m	.615*	m	.210*	442
Dii) Supervisor level	m	.349*	m	.099	158
Ei) Supervisor level	m	.471*	m	.129*	3686
Eii) Supervisor level	m	.749*	m	.124*	3686
Fii) Supervisor level for IT personnel	m	.533*	m	.127	182
Hii) Management level	m	.622*	m	.121*	1524
Hiii) Management level	m	.537*	m	.120*	1524
Hiv) Management level	m	.554*	m	.110*	1524
Jii) Management level	m	.131*	m	.032	5406
Kiv) Management level	m	.548*	m	.064*	5592
Li) Management level	m	.567*	m	.169	5592

Table 6.3 Reasoning tests

Test description	Higher mean	Mean difference	Greater range	Range difference	Sample size
Aiii) Management level for scientists	m	.028	m	.136	512
Aiv) Management level for scientists	f	.049	f	.053	512
Bii) Supervisor level	m	.510*	m	.278*	112
Hv) Management level	m	.202*	m	.048	1524
Ii) Management level	m	.128*	m	.049*	4852
Iii) Management level	m	.124*	f	.008	4852
Mi) Management level	m	.016	f	.002	520
Mii) Management level	m	.241	m	.079	42

Table 6.4 Other tests

Test description	Higher mean	Mean difference	Greater range	Range difference	Sample size
Diii) Spatial test	f	.098	f	.041	142
Div) Mechanical test	m	.508*	f	.011	98
Fiii) Spatial test	f	.101	m	.043	182
Gi) Spatial test	m	.343*	m	.049	192
Gii) Spatial test (alternate form of Gi)	m	.308*	f	.075	192

on these tests. Figures are quoted which reflect the difference in performance levels between the sexes, and also the difference in the range of performance observed in male and female samples. The code letters under the 'test description' column denote different samples. The data are presented separately for 'verbal', 'numerical', 'reasoning' and 'other' cognitive tests.

The 'difference between means' is expressed as the difference between the mean scores of the male and female groups divided by the standard deviation of all of the individual male and female scores. The difference between the ranges of male and female scores is expressed as the difference between the z-score standard deviations of male and female groups. This allows tests to be compared with each other on the extent to which they show adverse impact (i.e. differences between groups) and range differences. Differences which are significantly different at the $p < .05$ level (2-tailed) are marked by an asterisk.

Differences in level of performance between the sexes

These data support the generally accepted view that women score far less well than men on tests of numerical, visual, spatial and mechanical reasoning and differ from the view that they score slightly better than men on tests of verbal reasoning.

Of the twelve verbal tests, nine favoured male candidates (four of the nine differences reaching statistical significance) and three favoured female candidates (only one of the three differences reaching statistical significance). Mean differences were weighted by sample size and the overall difference between male and female performance was only 0.04 standard deviations greater for men. The figure should be treated with some caution as neither the samples nor the tests are fully independent, although it provides a useful indicator.

Of the numerical tests, all thirteen showed significant differences in favour of male candidates. The mean weighted difference is .497 standard deviations in favour of men.

Seven of the reasoning tests favoured males, four of the seven differences reaching statistical significance, and only one favoured females with a small non-significant difference. The weighted mean again favours men, this time by .123 SDs.

Of the 'other' tests, three spatial and mechanical tests favoured males significantly and two favoured females (both non-significantly). The sample here is much smaller but produces a mean weighted difference of .178 in favour of men.

Overall, thirty-one tests showed males performing better than females (twenty-five of them significantly) and six showed females performing better than males (only one difference being significant).

Differences in the range of performance between the sexes

These data support the generally accepted view that the range of performance on cognitive tests is greater for males than for females.

Of the twelve verbal tests, male candidates had a greater range than females in ten cases, three of the ten differences reaching statistical significance, and female candidates had a greater range than males in two cases, one of the two differences reaching statistical significance.

For the numerical tests, male candidates had a greater range than females in all cases (eight of the thirteen differences reaching statistical significance).

There were eight reasoning tests with male candidates having a greater range than females in five cases (two of the five differences reaching statistical significance) and female candidates had a greater range than males in three cases (none of the differences reaching statistical significance).

Of the five 'other' tests, male candidates had a greater range than females in two cases and female candidates had a greater range than males in three cases, none of the differences reaching statistical significance.

Overall, thirty tests showed a greater range of performance for males than for females (thirteen of them significantly) and seven a greater range of performance for females than for males (only one difference being significant).

The general effect is that males, on average, tend to perform better than females on cognitive tests and they tend to have a wider range of performance than females. This seems to be particularly pronounced for numerical tests.

The implications of the sex differences in cognitive test performance for job applicants.

Clearly, the first and major implication is that females are less likely to be appointed if cognitive tests are used in selection than if assessment instruments which do not show adverse impact against women are used. Equally, any group which suffers adverse impact on any assessment method will be less likely to be appointed if the impacting assessment method is used in selection. This does not necessarily mean that adversely impacting assessment methods are unfair, as will be shown in the discussion of validity below.

The extent to which the lower scoring group will be adversely affected as regards their chances of being appointed (or of passing to the next stage in a selection process) depends on the following two main factors.

The size of the adverse impact effect

Clearly if there was a very large difference in performance between male and female candidates it would be very unlikely for a female candidate to be success-ful. If there was only a very small difference in the average performances of men and women, then the chances of selection for women may only be slightly less than for men.

Where the cut-off for selection is set

This is most relevant in the 'sift' part of a selection procedure where a large number of candidates are assessed and where a certain percentage of them (or those who exceed a predetermined pass mark) are selected for the next stage in the selection process. It is a statistical fact that, for any given difference in the average performance of two groups, the ratio of the two groups in the successful candidates will vary with the level of pass mark chosen. The relationship between pass mark and the representation of the adversely impacted group is that the higher the pass mark the smaller the ratio of the lesser performing group in the successful candidates. To put it simply, if women in general perform less well than men in a test, then the ratio of women to men will be smaller the higher the pass mark. This effect can be extreme if very high pass marks are set; the effect could be that it is highly unlikely that there will be any successful women even though there is only a relatively small difference in average performance between the sexes. The most extreme case of a high cut-off is the case where there is only one job on offer and that position will go to the highest performing candidate.

Since the practical effect on women will depend on how the test is used as well as the extent to which women perform less well in it than men, an index of 'fairness' in the application of tests has evolved called the 'four-fifths rule'. This rule is a heuristic which grew out of litigation in the United States, and simply states that if the pass rate for one group (e.g. women) is less than four-fifths that of another group (men) then the application of the test is 'unfair'. The test itself, independently of how it is used, might be considered to be 'unfair' to the extent to which there are significant differences between the average performances of the sexes in the test. We will argue that these criteria take too narrow a view of the selection process.

The fact that male performance tends to be more widely ranging than female performance will also lead to less females being selected *even if there is no difference in the average performance of males and females*. This will be true if the pass mark is set higher than the average mark, which is usually the case in selection sifts, although if the pass mark is less than the average mark, then the proportion of females amongst the successes will be greater than that of the males. As with the effect of differences in average performance, the negative effect on the ratio of female to male successes will increase as the pass mark increases. To put it simply, the greater the range of male performance means that there will be more higher and more lower scoring males than females and more average scoring females than males. Since success in a test depends on achieving a high score, it follows that there will be a greater proportion of males in the high scores than females (even if there is no difference in average score between the sexes).

The smaller female standard deviation is not restricted to tests. A study by Pema and Scott (1996) found that ratings of women in a series of assessment centres were consistently more homogeneous than those of men. These included exercise ratings, test scores, summary ratings over up to ten different intellectual, interpersonal or personal dimensions and overall ratings. In every case the standard deviation for females was narrower than for males.

The main question raised by these findings is 'is it justifiable to use assessment instruments which lead to one group having less chance of success than another group?' This in turn raises many further questions. The following discussion hinges on the questions of whether gender differences in performance in such assessment instruments reflect differences in the ability to perform well in the job (which would be a justification, under the Sex Discrimination Act, for using the instrument), and what differences between the sexes cognitive test performance might actually reflect. We will argue that both of these questions are difficult if not impossible to answer unequivocally in practice, but that, nevertheless, clear guidelines can be proposed for the development and application of assessment instruments in selection.

The validity of assessment instruments

The whole point of using assessment instruments in selection is to be able to predict which candidates are likely to perform best in the job. The idea is that high performers on the assessment should be likely to be high performers if appointed to the job in question. Validity (especially predictive validity) refers to the extent to which performance in the assessment predicts eventual performance in the job. High validity means good prediction. We will refer to cognitive tests throughout this section, but wish to emphasise that the points made are equally valid for any assessment method.

The way that the concept of validity relates to the question of the differences in performance between men and women can best be illustrated graphically.

Figure 6.2 illustrates good predictive validity. Low scores in the test correspond to poor job performance and high scores in the test correspond to good job performance. It should however be noted that the use of single narrow lines in the graphs is illustrative of a 'perfect' relationship between test and job performance. There are many factors other than cognitive ability that determine level of job performance (e.g. motivation, personal circumstances, work environment), so in practice even the best psychometric predictors of job performance would be imprecise. Since job performance is dependent on a number of factors in addition to the ability the test is measuring, there will be a range of job performance scores for any particular test score. This is illustrated in Figure 6.3 which shows a scattergram of the relationship between a number of people's test scores and job performance.

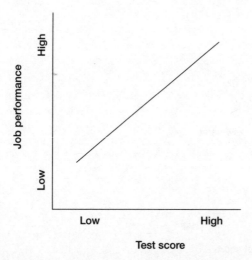

Figure 6.2 Example of good predictive validity

Figure 6.4 illustrates an ideal unbiased test. The relationship between test and job performance is drawn separately for men and women and is identical for both groups. There is no difference in average scores in the test between the sexes and the test is equally predictive of job performance for the two groups. For the job in question the difficulty of men and women being differentially able at the job does not arise.

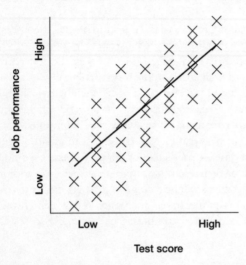

Figure 6.3 Relationship between test score and job performance

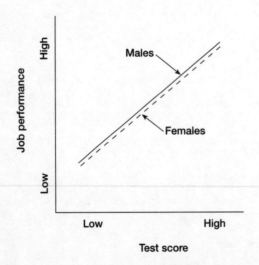

Figure 6.4 Example of an ideal unbiased test

One way in which a test might be considered unfair would be if the validity of the test were different for men and women. In the extreme, such a test may have no predictive power for women while being predictive for men. This situation is illustrated in Figure 6.5. Here the test scores of women bear no relation to their job performance. Logically, this situation could arise if men and women carried out the job in different ways using different abilities. It would not mean that the test was not effective in measuring the underlying ability, but rather that the application of the test would be inappropriate. Even if the test were predictive for both sexes, it might be the case that it is more strongly predictive for one sex than the other. This case is illustrated in Figure 6.6.

This differential validity or slope bias, known as the Cleary model after Cleary (1968), was widely used to identify unfairness in tests during the 1960s and 1970s. If the test was valid for one group but not for another it was concluded that the test was biased. Or, by extension, if there is a significant difference in the slopes of the two groups, then the test could be considered to be unfair. However, if numbers are small in one group (as is often the case when ethnic groups are under consideration) a test might show the same slope for both groups, but, because of the difference in sample size, the test might be considered valid for one but not for the other, using the .05 significance level favoured by convention.

Another way in which unfairness can be introduced through differing relationships between test and job performance for two groups is known as 'intercept bias'. This is illustrated in Figure 6.7. In this case, the average test scores are the same for both sexes. However, the test is underpredicting the performance of women in this illustration. A woman with a score of 50 (say) in the test would be expected to perform better on the job than a man with a score of 50

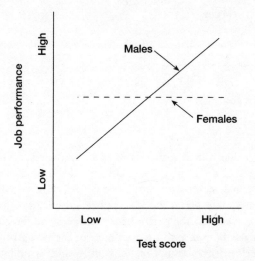

Figure 6.5 Differential validity for men and women: predictive for men only

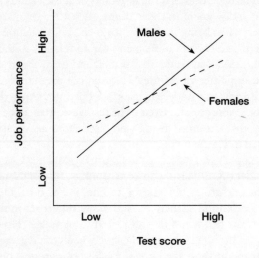

Figure 6.6 Differential validity for men and women: predictive for both sexes

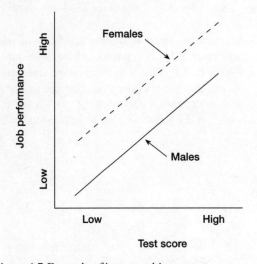

Figure 6.7 Example of intercept bias

on the test (and probably better than a man with a score of 55 on the test). This situation is clearly unfair, and either differential pass-marks for the two sexes or the addition of points to the female test scores would be necessary to remedy the situation. However, by all simple and generally applied criteria, the test seems fair; there is no difference between the performance of males and females in the test and there would be no difference in the pass rates of the two groups (assuming equal ranges of performance) thus the 'four-fifths rule' would be satisfied.

The current general approach in the industry, and of equal opportunities monitors, is to first determine if there is any difference between groups in their test performance. If there is no difference, the test is considered to be fair and unbiased and no further action need be taken. If there is a difference (say that women perform less well than men), then the test is considered to be probably unfair, and it is then up to the test user to justify the use of the test by proving that men and women with equal scores on the test will be likely to perform equally well on the job. If that can be established, then the test would be considered unbiased and we would conclude that women were simply less able in that area.

Figure 6.8 illustrates the above case, where the test is equally predictive of job performance for men and women but where there is a difference in average test score between the sexes. Such a test would, at least initially, come under heavy scrutiny from equal opportunities monitors whereas the test illustrated in Figure 6.6 would not.

If it were possible to reliably determine which of these possible relationships between test and job performance holds in any case, then we should be able to come to a reasonable view on the fairness of that application of the test. Unfortunately, this is rarely done. Employers undertake to monitor test results, but such monitoring is typically basic and often misses the point. A review of test users by Baker and Cooper (1995) found that 49 per cent did not monitor their tests for adverse impact and only 16 per cent carried out systematic monitoring. Of the three common aspects of a test that are assessed to give an index of how fair the test is: adverse impact, differential validity (or slope bias) and differential prediction or intercept bias, only adverse impact is normally assessed.

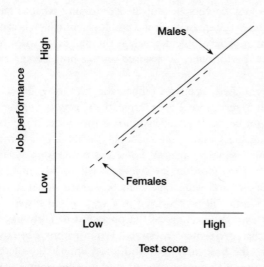

Figure 6.8 Differences between men and women in test score and job performance

In mitigation, there are real practical problems with carrying out such research into predictive validity. First, there will need to be relatively large numbers of people appointed from each of the groups in question in order for the analysis to be reliable, and this requirement will be met by only the largest of employers. Second, only the highest scoring candidates will be appointed which means that the predictive validity of the test across the whole range of scores can only be estimated, and third, there will be a considerable time gap between the original testing and the assessment of job performance. Finally, these assessments of job performance may be equally biased (see below).

One way round some of these problems is to conduct concurrent validity studies in which the job performance and test performance of current staff can be related. Test designers will try to validate their tests in this way for as many jobs as possible before and during the published life of a test. However, few employers are prepared to commit the considerable resources necessary to carry out concurrent validity studies for the particular jobs for which they are using the tests. Test publishers endeavour to show that their tests are widely valid and employers tend to justify their use on the basis of the designers' avowal of validity.

Therefore, in any particular case, there is unlikely to be any differential validity data available and it may prove impossible to gather it (often because the numbers are too small, or even that the job does not yet exist or is expected to change). Recourse is often made to meta-analyses of the validity of assessment methods in general across a wide range of jobs. For example, Schmidt and Hunter (1977) showed that cognitive tests are generally very valid predictors of job performance. But such studies rarely consider differential prediction for the sexes.

However, we will argue that even if there were a great deal of differential validity data available, it may not be very helpful in determining what is fair, unfair, biased or unbiased within a system of work and employment which is itself fundamentally biased and unfair. The problem arises in the nature of work, in how jobs are defined, in how performance is assessed and in how people are assessed in employment selection.

If the whole system were biased against women, the bias may be self-perpetuating and very difficult to recognise. For example, the selection interview, as an assessment method, might be validated against job performance. If the job performance measure is a manager's rating, the (probably) male manager may exercise his bias (possibly unconsciously) against women as workers by giving lower ratings than deserved. The selection interviewers will be like-minded people (or even the same people) and will similarly mark women down in the interview. Thus, very high validity will be observed in a very biased system of recruitment. This is a rather extreme example of the operation of fairly naked bias. However, we will argue that, even where assessment is transparent, objective and reliable, and people have the best intentions and good knowledge of the potential pitfalls, the very nature of the way that work and jobs are defined can still lead to bias against women in selection that will never be reflected in studies of differential validity and adverse impact in assessment methods.

Job definition

We have already touched on the issue of the appropriateness of criteria measures. Initially there is the relatively simple issue of how accurate the performance ratings are. All of the evidence cited above relating to the extraneous factors affecting the way that women are rated by men and women alike will apply equally to their job performance as to their selection assessment performance. The dynamics of the organisation will further confound the scores and their interpretation. If it is easier for a man to get promotion than it is for a woman then the junior women may be far more able than the junior men (able men getting promoted, able women staying junior). As such, the ratings of junior workers may make women seem a more able group than they are.

The situation is much complicated, however, by the very definition of the job. In as much as most organisations have developed in a male context and senior and power-based jobs have been performed by men, the accepted way of carrying out the job will have been a 'male' method. The assumption is often that this is the way the job is done and it may well be that males are better able to do the job in this way than women. The fact that a woman might still be able to do the job better, albeit in a different way, is not considered and may be hard to support empirically.

A paper by Smith, Gregg and Andrews (1989) describes a much cited example of this. A minimum height requirement was set for a US police force, based on a job analysis. The requirement was defined as the height necessary to be able to shoot a pistol over the roof of a police car, using the car for cover. This naturally impacted against women officers. The requirement was defended by the common practice in the force of using this kind of cover, but had the force been predominantly women it might well have been that the bonnet of the car would have been used for cover. Here is a clear example of the traditional 'male' approach to a task being defined as a requirement of the job.

A study by Sparrow and Rigg (1993) produced separate job analyses using the open 'repertory grid' approach. One job profile was created from male incumbents of the post and another from female incumbents. Both profiles broke down into five categories: working style, decision-making approach, interpersonal relationships with own team, interpersonal relationships with clients and job priorities. However, in each case the content of the category was fundamentally different, with the content of each category reflecting the traditional stereotypes. For example, under working style, the women identified people orientation, working through people and using a measured and participative approach as being attributes to be sought from applicants, whereas men saw being political, forceful, high profile, flamboyant, confident, aware of external events and paternalistic as being the desirable attributes.

The suggestion from this research is that in defining the job a 'gender-blind' or 'androcentric' approach is potentially dangerous (Burrell and Hearn 1989). This is because the approach that assumes no gender difference assumes that the current way a job is done is similarly unaffected by gender. As the existing jobs and organisations derive from a male oriented culture in which power positions were historically held and defined by males, and within which 'maleness' is a valued attribute, the analysis of the current job is actually of a male approach (Morgan 1986). Successful women are those who adopt a male style and so the job may still be done in a male way (Franklin 1985). Assuming that there is no gender impact on the job accepts the current way of doing the job as equally appropriate for males and females (or, perversely for a supposedly gender-blind approach, accepts the results as evidence that women really are not suited to some jobs). In short, a gender-blind approach accepts the male approach.

Possible sources of gender differences in cognitive test performance

While we have argued that assessments of validity may never, on their own, shed light on the underlying factors in sex discrimination in employment selection, and while we have also argued that the sources of sex bias are very wide-ranging, we have shown that there are consistent differences between the performances of men and women in cognitive tests which will have a negative effect on women's prospect of selection.

The differences have historically favoured men, but the size of the effect has tended to diminish over the years. Although a full discussion of the nature of cognitive differences between the sexes is beyond the scope of this chapter, the issue of the possible sources does bear directly on the issue of assessment for employment selection and promotion, and deserves consideration.

Differences in cognitive test performance could reflect any or all of the following factors which are discussed below:

- Innate cognitive sex differences
- Sex differences in socialisation and schooling leading to differences in learning opportunities, expectations and preferences
- The effects of sampling
- The way that ability is assessed
- Sex differences in test-taking style
- The extent to which a test has been designed to manipulate sex differences

Innate cognitive sex differences

If cognitive test score differences between the sexes reflected underlying innate sex differences, then it would clearly be wrong to reject the use of a test simply because it showed adverse impact (i.e. that it measured the underlying differences which exist). However, cognitive ability is never measured in a completely uncrystallised form. Assessment is always of something which has been learned, but which is supposed to rely on the underlying ability. For this reason, and for others discussed below, it is extremely difficult to determine the extent to which cognitive test performances reflect innate sex differences. Moreover, for the purposes of valid employment selection, there seems little reason to want to measure uncrystallised ability.

Sex differences in socialisation and schooling

Another source of sex differences in cognitive test performance might be differences in exposure to the dimensions concerned. For example, most mechanical reasoning tests depict people (mainly men) performing mechanical tasks such as rotating one of a series of cogs or pushing levers. The candidate is required to identify in which direction the final cog would move, where the maximum amount of leverage would be obtained, etc. Traditionally, males would have been more exposed to these situations than would females. From the mechanical toys that tended to be reserved for male children via the predominantly male interest in cars and motorbikes through to the almost exclusively male occupations of mechanic or engineer, it was males who were exposed to these dimensions. The same arguments can, to some extent, be made about computers in recent times.

Furthermore, in as much as males were traditionally associated with these domains, social pressure was against women being involved. Girls were socialised not to play with mechanical toys and tinkering with bikes and cars or seeking training and a career in engineering were considered unusual for women. In viewing such activities as 'unfeminine' women may well have been actively discouraged from such activities. This creates a situation where a woman is not only less exposed to mechanics but is also encouraged to have less interest in the area. Its male association also sends the signal that this is an area that men are more suited to than women, so confidence levels amongst women might well be lower when approaching such tasks.

When a lack of exposure to mechanics is combined with a discouragement to be interested in it along with a lack of confidence in one's ability in the area, it is far from surprising that women fared less well on mechanical reasoning tests. Add to this the likelihood that impressive scores on the test from men are likely to be more highly rewarded than such scores for women (due to it being seen as an inappropriate area for women), and the cycle is complete.

A similar pattern can be discerned in numerical ability, albeit to less of an extreme. In numeracy, however, considered as it is to be a fundamental skill, there is a great deal more interest in the aetiology of the differences.

Generally there are no significant differences identified in the numerical ability of male and female infants; males only gradually attaining a lead as they grow older. This can again be explained by maths being identified as a 'male' discipline. Even here, though, the evidence is far from clear. Some studies demonstrate that girls are still better than boys at some numerical tasks (e.g. on computational, logical and abstract problems) while boys fare better on spatial relations and 'story' problems (Marshall 1984; Pattison and Grieve 1984).

The issues of the interaction between ability, interest, exposure and social pressure have been more closely mapped here. US studies in the 1980s showed that male and female numerical performance was equivalent as long as courses remained compulsory. As soon as they became optional females tended to drop out of the courses. This may reflect perceptions that maths was a 'male' subject or a relatively greater interest in alternative subjects, for whatever reason. Either way, it meant that females tended not to develop their numerical abilities, with the consequent result that less took up numerical careers and so occupational gender stereotypes are maintained. When similar numbers of maths courses are taken the differences between male and female performance are greatly diminished or disappear (Fennema and Sherman 1977), though it seems that highest performers are normally males (Benbow and Stanley 1980, 1983; Kolata 1980).

Equally, there is evidence to suggest that the style of teaching mathematics has an impact. Kolata's study revealed that in schools with similar profiles for boys and girls, there tended to be a pattern of teaching wherein the teachers were from numerate backgrounds, taught the higher-level students in mixed groups and emphasised the reasoning component. Peterson and Fenema (1985) found that males benefited from competitive approaches and girls from co-operative ones. It seems inevitable that as long as a subject is perceived as being the domain of one or other gender, racial or other group, the standards, approaches and style of that group is likely to predominate in its teaching.

Clearly then, if sex differences in test performance reflect real sex differences in socialisation and schooling, the tests should not be rejected as being unfair simply because they exhibit adverse impact. Indeed, the reduction in sex differences in cognitive test performance may well be related to the continuing reduction in sex differences in scholastic performance. Thus, when the current cohort of schoolchildren, in which the girls outperform the boys, reach the age of employment, the cognitive tests which currently show adverse impact against women may well switch to showing adverse impact against men.

It is not clear why the differences in range of performance exist. Higher vulnerability to pre- and post-natal trauma for males means that there are more males at the low extreme of the population IQ, but this does not explain why amongst the managerial, professional and graduate groups the lowest scores are obtained by males.

Social psychology studies have shown that good performances are rated higher if they are attributed to males than to females while poor performance will be rated higher if attributed to females than to males (e.g. Deux and Taynor 1973; Nieva and Gutek 1980; Top 1991). This process of attribution may well explain the narrower spread of scores for women on the more subjective assessor ratings, but not for objectively scored cognitive tests. The answer may be found in the reasons why people decide to apply for certain jobs and the way they are selected for taking cognitive tests, but convincing explanatory mechanisms are not obvious.

The effects of sampling

Data on performance of people in tests of cognitive ability used in employment selection are typically from adult populations who have applied for jobs or are in jobs (as are the data presented in this chapter). They therefore constitute a highly selected sample.

Consideration of the proposed model of the employment selection process shows that there are many factors which can influence whether or not an individual will apply for a job, resulting in different 'application behaviours' for different groups. Samples of people who are tested will be biased to the extent to which men and women are differentially influenced by these factors and thus have different application behaviours. Therefore, it is possible that there is no difference in the overall population in a particular cognitive ability, but that the more able of one sex apply for a particular type of job compared to the other sex. The cognitive test results produced by an unbiased test would then reflect this difference in application behaviour.

Again, it would seem unreasonable to reject such a test simply on the grounds that it exhibited adverse impact. We need to trace back the relative ability levels of men and women in the various selected populations. For example, test performance for applicants for a graduate job will reflect the sampling effect of application behaviour which modifies whatever differences exist in the graduate population, which itself will reflect the sampling effect of factors which determine who goes to university to study which courses and how they are affected by their experiences there.

The way that cognitive ability is assessed

A cognitive test is usually conducted in a pressured competitive context. People's livelihood will often be affected by the result, direct competitors for limited positions are often completing the tests in the same room and tests are generally heavily time-pressured. It is possible that this style of assessment may suit one sex more than the other, just as the move away from examinations towards more project-based assessment at schools may account, at least in part, for the recent relative improvements in girls' scholastic performance.

It has been argued that numerical tests, and some would argue tests in general (e.g. Alban-Metcalfe 1987) are designed to measure the abilities as carried out by males. They are validated against the performance of males or of a mixed group performing the job in a way dictated by an occupational culture, style and practice that has been both designed and carried out by men. As such, the tests measure the male approach to the problem and require males and females alike to use this approach, to the disadvantage of women.

For example, in any numerical task there is normally a trade-off between speed and accuracy; all things being equal the faster you go the greater the possibility of making a mistake. As males are perceived to be more likely to take risks and females are perceived to be more conscientious, it is possible that men might work faster but that they would make more mistakes. Most numerical or data-checking jobs put a premium on accuracy; speed is totally irrelevant to an accountant or engineer if 25 per cent of his or her calculations are wrong. Even if the more conscientious accountant or engineer only produces one quarter of the amount produced by their speedier colleague, if their accuracy rate is 100 per cent their work is of far more worth. The faster worker may produce three times as much accurate work, but you don't know which of their projects are accurate. They may be of equal worth if the faster worker checks all of his or her work four times to ensure its accuracy and then achieves a 100 per cent level of precision.

In this example, because numerical tests generally put a much greater emphasis on speed than on accuracy, they would benefit the faster, but less accurate of the two workers. The tests are normally rigorously timed and designed so that there is too little time to comfortably spend on all of the questions. Even the best candidate should feel under pressure. As such, a very conscientious approach may be detrimental. Our conscientious worker might complete 25 per cent of the questions, getting them all right and scoring 25 out of 100. Our faster worker can complete all of the questions and get 75 per cent right, massively outperforming his or her colleague. The test has rewarded speed over accuracy taking no account of the critical nature of a wrong answer for many of the professions for which such tests are used as selection tools.

The different ways that men and women approach taking a timed test may explain the fact that males tend to have a greater range of scores than females. Females are perceived to be more conscientious and less risk-taking. A conscientious and safe strategy to taking a timed test would be to focus on accuracy at the expense of speed thus reducing the likelihood of obtaining a very low score or a very high score. A (male) risk-taking strategy might well involve more questions being attempted with a less conscientious approach to each question. The less able may get none right, the most able might get them all right, but the effect for the group will be a broader spread of scores. This effect may be amplified by the traditionally more competitive male approach to things, with a greater desire to excel than female candidates who may be more content to simply do well.

The extent to which a test has been designed to manipulate sex differences

As suggested in the above discussion, it is impossible to measure cognitive ability in a 'pure' way. The way that it is measured will always affect the results. For example, how could one decide whether a timed or an untimed test is the 'true' measure of cognitive ability, especially if sex differences changed depending on the measure. In fact sex differences are, to some extent, under the control of the test developer.

Most commercially available scales have been designed to minimise the differences between male and female scores, and so might underestimate the differences between the groups. Because it is in the test constructors' interests to minimise such differences, a number of techniques are used to improve female performance. Such disparate approaches as the presentation of problems verbally, the use of content more familiar or relevant to females, labelling categories by colour (a procedure which appears to help female candidates) and the use of certain types of scoring procedure are all used to enhance women's performance. Most reputable test publishers now examine each individual item in a test to identify whether males or females perform relatively less well compared to their score on the rest of the test, the assumption being that any differences relevant to the item but not to the test must simply be irrelevant by-products of gender. Therefore, the items on which females do relatively less well are excluded. Similarly, tests that produced greater than average differences between the sexes are less likely to be published than those which produce smaller differences.

All of these approaches are based on the assumption that observed differences between male and female scores are aspects of error and do not relate to ability to carry out numerical tasks. It is the standard perspective in the test design community but still has not done away with the sex differences in scores.

Any diminishing of the difference between male and female scores on numerical test scores over the last twenty to thirty years could be as much a product of the increasing skill of test constructors in creating tests as it is a result of genuine reductions in the difference.

Conversely, because numerical tests are designed to measure the content and style of numerical tasks as carried out currently, they are likely to reflect any biases inherent in the way numbers are currently used in organisations. Most tests are validated, i.e. assessed for their ability to measure relevant job dimensions, against current performance on the job. As we have seen, numerically oriented jobs are more likely to have been carried out by males than by females. Furthermore, they were seen as a predominantly male domain, and so it is likely that male approaches to numerical problems are accepted approaches.

Nevertheless, what is clear is that there can be no true measure of underlying ability if males and females respond differently to different assessment methods. Any test will fall somewhere between the extremes of maximising the relative performance of men on the one hand and women on the other, even if the possibility of such manipulation never occurred to the test constructor.

Recommendations

Many factors which affect the assessment, selection and promotion of women lie outside the control of the personnel practitioner; the standards and mores of society, the presentation of gender roles in schools, toys, the home and the media, and the existing and historical attitudes of the nation. However, there is also much that can be done to improve the current situation, thus making recruitment and selection both more just and more effective. Changes in the occupational world will in turn have their effect on other aspects of society, with the provision of more female role-models in a wider range of jobs, and a decay in the existing gender assumptions made about tasks, jobs, careers and employment sectors.

Practitioner awareness

In order for change to be effective we must begin with an understanding of the issues as they stand, and the better informed recruiters and selectors are about the effects of gender, then the more effective they will be in addressing erroneous practices and assumptions. Professionals throughout the field, be they personnel managers, occupational psychologists, advertising designers or assessors, should have a thorough grounding in how their work impacts differentially on males and females. This involves not only an awareness of what has been produced in the literature, but also an awareness of one's own assumptions, preferences and biases. This will be addressed in several of the following points.

Job definition

We have made the point that if the job definition is flawed, then everything that follows will be flawed. Job or competency analysis should be carried out by people with a good understanding of the subtleties of the task, and with an awareness of the dangers of simply defining the way the job is carried out currently, rather than taking a visionary approach.

1   One could begin by asking if there is a disproportionately large number of either males or females carrying out the job at present, and then ask, why? Does this indicate that the job is already gendered?

2   One should then identify whether males or females are rated higher in their performance in the job or in the tasks and personal characteristics identified, and again, if so, why? Is this based on assumptions about one gender being more suited regardless of the actual performance of staff? Is it based on a flaw in the current selection system resulting in only the very best applicants from one gender being appointed? For example, if the women carrying out a job tend to be better than the men doing the same job, perhaps this is because the selection process is biased in favour of men; an average male can pass the process but you need to be an exceptional female to get through.

3   Those providing information for the job/competency analysis might be invited to say whether they feel the job, and each individual task, is better carried out by males or females. This obviously has to be done with a great deal of sensitivity and be followed by an explanation of the reasons for it (to

guard against the suggestion that the enquiries are there to introduce [further] gender bias). However, it may provide useful information. If staff, supervisors or subordinates see one task as being better suited to one gender, you will want to know why. Is it because the way the job is currently done matches a popular perception of gender style? If so, you will want to investigate whether there are other approaches to completing the task which have not been attempted, be it due to a desire to maintain the *status quo*, staff having been selected to suit that style or maybe just a simple lack of imagination. Differences in the perceived ability of males and females to perform tasks and/or the job may also signal attitudes within the organisation that you will need to be aware of when working with it.

4   The person carrying out the analysis should then ask him- or herself whether the job and/or tasks seem better suited to males or females, at both a rational level and at an 'expectation' level, i.e. would you expect the incumbent to be a male or female. They should explore any inequality of suitability in their own minds to ensure that they themselves are not affected by biases, stereotypes or conditioned assumptions, as we all are to a greater or lesser degree.

5   In producing the written job description, the practitioner should be aware of how it will read to colleagues and applicants. It is worth presenting it to a panel who know nothing about the job and invite them to identify any content or wording that implies the job is more suitable for one or other gender, and then amend it accordingly.

6   More information is needed about the differences in male and female perceptions of, and approaches to, tasks. There is, therefore, a greater requirement for research such as that reported above by Sparrow and Rigg (1993), and for organisations to sponsor or support this work.

Advertising

The same processes described above need to be applied to the advertising. Does the person designing the advertising have a gender-specific view of the jobs? Is the wording, content or presentation of the advertisement more likely to attract the attention of one gender, and subsequently the interest of one gender? Will it send any messages to the potential applicant about the organisation's perception of the gender specificity of the job or the desirability of having applicants from one or other gender? All of these issues can be assessed by presenting the advertisements to mixed-gender panels, and they apply equally to all advertising media, whether it be a card in a job centre, a full-page spread in a national newspaper or magazine or a radio or television advertisement.

Application materials

Again, these need to be assessed for the message they send to applicants. Does the job seem more appropriate to males or females, and are any barriers that are created at selection stages (e.g. eligibility criteria) appropriate and non-discriminatory? Will differences in answering styles affect the way the application is completed or dealt with?

If self-selection questionnaires, job previews or other attempts to attract or put off potential applicants are included, they must be evaluated for the message they send to applicants and to different approaches to completing them. If male and female candidates differ in the way they answer questionnaires, assess their own abilities or present their interests and abilities, then they may well get different patterns of response which may act, unjustly, against one or other gender.

Selection

The differing performance of males and females on all selection systems must be considered, even if there is no apparent difference in profile or success rates. Assessments should be designed with reference to all of the factors discussed in the category of job definition above. The way that males and females differentially perceive selection instruments, be it their liking for or familiarity with them, or the perceived fairness or appropriateness of the tools, should be borne in mind. All aspects of the selection process should be scrutinised and presented to gender panels.

The risk component, most commonly seen in time limits to exercises (and cognitive tests in particular), should be minimised, to avoid tapping into gender-related areas you were not intending to measure. If you need to assess risk-taking then it should be assessed separately, not as a component of another assessment, otherwise how much of the score can you attribute to risk and how much to reasoning ability?

Severe sifts should be avoided if possible, as the lower range of female scores will tend to work against females as a group when the cut-off is over 50 per cent, and against men if it is lower. The more extreme the cut-off, high or low, the more extreme will be the penalty suffered by one gender.

Selection procedures and instruments must be chosen with reference to the requirements of the job. If there are found to be some areas of the job in which males tend to do better and some in which females are stronger, then the assessment should contain a balance of both types. The assessment should be as broad-based as possible to measure the whole job, not just those specifics which are easier to measure.

Assessors, and those making subjective judgements in particular (such as interviewers or raters of exercise performance) should be aware of their own preconceptions and of the scientific evidence relating to the interaction between gender, assessment performance and assessment and gender decisions.

Objective measures should be preferred to subjective ones where possible as any bias will be easier to identify. Cognitive tests should never be used in isolation for making selection decisions.

Feedback

Assessors should receive feedback on their performance in a non-critical environment to allow them to identify and evaluate any flaws in their technique.

Candidates can be invited to provide anonymous feedback on the process, assessors, tools, administration. etc., but should be asked to provide gender, age, ethnicity information. This is generally very helpful to those designing the selection process and has particular value in tracking patterns of bias, and gives the candidate the opportunity to express any feelings or concerns they may have.

Feedback to candidates on their performance has numerous benefits, but in the context of removing gender bias from selection there are two principal benefits. First, it allows the candidate to feed back to the organisation and identify any bias they may have felt. Second, by providing the candidates with realistic feedback on their performance, candidates may make better self-evaluations in the future and thus reduce some of the differences found between the genders in those applying for jobs.

Monitoring

Monitoring is essential to any recruitment or assessment process. Organisations should use the most sophisticated technology they can to evaluate whether, and where, bias is occurring in their process. This should be actively pursued, and the results made available to researchers where possible, to improve their knowledge of what factors are problematic. Companies may co-operate with each other to create larger data pools for analysis purposes.

It should not be assumed that an apparent lack of bias in the system confirms that there is no bias present. Simply identifying whether the same proportion of males as females is passing the selection process may tell us very little, for all of the reasons described above.

Monitoring needs to be intelligent and flexible. The statistical investigation of gender differences uses 'probability' values to state whether a difference can be confidently said to exist. By convention, if there is more than a 1 in 20 chance that the observed difference between male and female ratings could have arisen by chance when no real difference exists, then we say it is not proven. However, if the findings are anywhere near this level then one cannot be complacent, and investigation has to continue.

There should be a will to understand the process and identify problems, not simply to prove that the organisation and its tools and procedures are spotless. Monitoring organisations, be they head offices, Equal Opportunities divisions or the statutory bodies involved in, for example, ethnic and gender monitoring, need to be sympathetic and supportive of these efforts. Organisations that carry out thorough, detailed and systematic monitoring will find problems, and thus make themselves vulnerable to challenge. However, such organisations should be congratulated for expending the resources to identify problems and resolve them, and should not be penalised for producing accurate data. Otherwise, the safest route is to not look too hard for problems and to use procedures which are harder to audit because they are not standardised or systematic. A selector which records and evaluates every process it carries out, then makes the information public, is a much easier target for a monitor, but choosing these organisations for test cases or examples will do more harm than good in the long run.

Those taking creative approaches may also be more vulnerable to challenge. A defence which states that a procedure that impacts against women is valid because the job analysis shows the skill measured is relevant, may well be viewed as sufficient justification for its use. To go beyond that and say we felt the job analysis reflected the male *status quo* and we are using other tools to identify skills that may be equally valid, is to take a risk. Such visionary approaches must also be dealt with sympathetically if a sound theoretical model for following the procedures chosen has been developed. This would not provide a justification for trying any technique that caught the selector's attention, as it would have to be underpinned by sound a priori theoretical justifications.

Summary

There is no doubt that opportunities for women in employment have improved dramatically over the last half-century, but we must not be complacent and assume that the problems have all been resolved. Selection and recruitment which overcomes gender effects will not only be 'fairer' or more 'just', it will also be more effective. If we are passing people over for jobs or promotion on the basis of irrelevant information, be it their gender, age, race, disability or whatever, then we may not be getting the best person for the job.

References

Alban-Metcalfe, B. (1987) 'Attitudes to work: comparison by gender and sector of employment', *The Occupational Psychologist* (3). Special issue on gender issues in occupational psychology.

Baker, B. and Cooper, J. (1995) 'Psychometric assessment: selected findings from a survey of UK organizations' practices', *Selection and Development Review* 11(2): 4–7.

Benbow, C.P. and Stanley, J.C. (1980) 'Sex differences in mathematical ability: fact or artefact?', *Science* 210: 1262–4.

—— (1983) 'Differential course-taking hypothesis revisited', *American Educational Research Journal* 20: 469–73.

Burrell, G. and Hearn, J. (1989) 'The sexuality of organization' in J. Hearn, D.L. Sheppard, P. Tancred-Sherrif and G. Burrell (eds) *The Sexuality of Organization*, London: Sage Publications.

Cassel, C.M. and Walsh, S. (1993) 'Being seen but not heard: barriers to women's equality in the workplace', *The Psychologist* 6(3): 110–14.

Cattell, R.B., Eber H.W. and Tatsuoka M.M. (1970) *Handbook for the Sixteen*

Personality Factor Questionnaire (16PF), Institute for Personality and Ability Testing Inc, Illinois.

Civil Service Data Summary 1995 – Women Race Disability, Equal Opportunities Division of the Cabinet Office, London.

Cleary, T.A. (1968) 'Test bias: prediction of grades of negro and white students in integrated colleges', *Journal of Educational Measurement* 5: 115–24.

Curran, M. (1986) 'Stereotypes and selection: gender and family in the recruitment process', Equal Opportunities Commission, HMSO.

Deux, K. and Taynor, J. (1973) 'Evaluation of male and female ability: bias works two ways', *Psychological Reports* 32: 261–2.

Fennema, E. and Sherman, J. (1977) 'Sex-related differences in mathematics achievement, spatial visualization and affective factors', *American Educational Research Journal* 14(1): 51–71.

Fletcher, C. and Williams, R. (1992) *Performance Appraisal and Career Development* (2nd edition), Cheltenham: Stanley Thornes Ltd.

Franklin, U.M. (1985) 'Will women change technology or will technology change women?', Ottawa, Ontario: Canadian Research Institute for the Advancement of Women, Paper No. 9.

Heilman, M.E. and Stopeck, M.H. (1985a) 'Being attractive, advantage or disadvantage? Performance based evaluations and recommended personnel actions as a function of appearance, sex, and job type', *Organizational Behaviour and Human Decision Processes* 35: 202–15.

—— (1985b) 'Attractiveness and corporate success: different casual attributions for males and females', *Journal of Applied Psychology* 70(2): 379–88.

Herriot, P. (1987) 'The selection interview' in P. Warr (ed.) *Psychology at Work* (3rd edition), Harmondsworth: Penguin.

Kolata, G.B. (1980) 'Math and sex: are girls born with less ability?', *Science* 210: 1234–5.

Mabey, B. (1989) 'The majority of large companies use occupational tests', *Guidance and Assessment Review* 5(3): 1–4.

—— (1992) 'The growth of test use', *Selection and Development Review* 8(3): 6–8.

Marshall, S. (1984) 'Sex differences in children's mathematics achievement: solving computations and story problems', *Journal of Educational Psychology* 76: 194–204.

Morgan, G. (1986) *Images of Organization*, Beverly Hills: Sage Publications.

National Management Salary Survey (1996), Institute of Management/ Renumeration Economics.

Nieva, V.F. and Gutek, B.A. (1980) 'Sex effects on evaluation', *Academy of Management Review* 5: 267–76.

Parker, C. (1994) 'The OPQ: a closer look at its norms and scales', *Selection and Development Review* 10(4): 2–5.

Pattison, P. and Grieve, N. (1984) 'Do spatial skills contribute to sex differences in different types of mathematical problems?', *Journal of Educational Psychology* 76: 678–89.

Pema, M. and Scott, N.C. (1996) 'Gender impact on assessment centre decision making processes', *RAS report* 1(1), London: RAS.

Peterson, P. and Fenema, E. (1985) 'Effective teaching, student engagement in classroom activities, and sex-related differences in learning mathematics', *American Educational Research Journal* 22: 309–37.

Schmidt, F.L. and Hunter, J.E. (1977) 'Development of a general solution to the problem of validity generalization', *Journal of Applied Psychology* 62: 529–40.

Shackleton, V. and Newell, S. (1991) 'Management selection: a comparative survey of methods used in the top British and French companies', *Journal of Occupational Psychology* 64: 23–36.

Smith, M., Gregg, M. and Andrews D. (1989) *Selection and Assessment. A New Appraisal*, London: Pitman.

Sneath, F., Thakur, M. and Madjuck, B. (1976) 'Testing people at work', Institute of Personnel Management, Report No. 24.

Sparrow, J. and Rigg, C. (1993) 'Job analysis: selecting for the masculine approach to management?', *Selection and Development Review* 9(2): 5–8.

Swim, J., Borgida, E., Maruyama, G. and Myers, D.G. (1989) 'Joan McKay vs. John McKay: do gender stereotypes bias evaluations?', *Psychological Bulletin* 105: 409–29.

Top, T.J. (1991) 'Sex bias in the evaluation of performance in the scientific, artistic and literary professions: a review', *Sex Roles* 24: 73–106.

7

CHOICE: CAN WE CHOOSE IT?

Pauline Anderson

The choice of occupations can be approached in many ways, and various psychological theories have been formulated to account for how choices are made. Pauline Anderson reviews the major theories, none of which can be taken as supplying a complete and final answer. Choice cannot be considered simply as one event occurring at a particular point in time. The context that must also be taken into account includes the individual's history up to that point, and the structure and organisation of actual occupations, which are not necessarily static. In fact at the present time changes are taking place in the organisation of work which have important implications for the gender issue: for example, the increasing role of 'brain' as opposed to 'brawn' work, flexibility and other changes in working hours, short- and fixed-term contracts, and changes in the composition of the workforce itself. Educational and occupational choice must be redefined within a social and political context.

Introduction

The aim of this chapter is to present educational and occupational choice as a complex interaction of factors that affect women and men in different ways and at every point of 'choice' in the decision-making process. This complexity has important implications for the future of careers psychology, organisation development and, because of the nature of changes taking place in the job arena, society in general.

We only know how far we have travelled when we look back. The chapter therefore begins with a brief overview of the major theories that have influenced the field of occupational choice. No theory is without its drawbacks and limitations and, while we can learn from past approaches, there are methodological problems in researching this topic that must be discussed before considering contemporary approaches. It is from current research that the differing career processes for men and women will be explored, the complexity of choice expounded and traditional definitions challenged. However, the issue goes beyond individuals' cognitive and affective mechanisms to the external reality of organisational culture and how the manifestation of this affects choice and opportunity. The chapter concludes by considering the current and ongoing changes in the nature of work and organisations and their potential effect on the gender issue.

Major psychological theories of occupational choice

There are two broad categories of occupational choice theories; the differential and developmental approaches. The former have their roots in Parsons' (1909) 'matching men and jobs' approach to occupational decision-making and they seek to match aspects of the person with similar attributes in the job environment. Developmental theories, on the other hand, seek explanations through a process approach, usually involving several life-stages.

There are several differential theorists, for example Roe (1956), Ginzburg (1972) and Holland (1973), each of whom propose a different set of person–environment variables. Probably the most widely researched theory within this tradition is that of Holland (1973) who suggested that people seek out occupations that match, or are congruent with, their personality. According to Holland there are six categories of personality and occupation: *artistic*, describing self-expressive and creative people; *investigative*, describing scientifically oriented people who enjoy thinking through problems; *realistic*, describing practical, rugged people who enjoy working outdoors or with their hands; *conventional*, describing people who prefer highly ordered verbal or numerical activities; *social*, describing humanistic people concerned with the welfare of others; and *enterprising*, describing people who enjoy selling, dominating and leading.

A number of studies have given support to the psychometrics of Holland's model but most empirical investigations have been based on student samples that necessarily measure preferences rather than behaviour. Within the context of choice and gender, the main criticism is that the model is based on the assumption of a 'here and now, all things being equal' perspective, with no account being taken of external influences to occupational selection. A large proportion of women would neatly fit into the social category and seek out careers in social work, teaching or secretarial work and a large proportion of working-class men would be equally at home in the realistic category, seeking work as skilled or unskilled labourers. According to Holland's model this is a result of individuals' differing personality and environment relationship. This is a simplistic approach to the issue and does not at all explain why females and males, as social groups, tend to have different occupational patterns. However, the strength of the theory lies in identifying specific, measurable traits that allow occupational counsellors to acknowledge the here-and-now demonstration of interest which helps to improve the occupational choice process.

In contrast, developmental theorists seem to hold the view that by the time a person reaches late adolescence they usually have an identifiable pattern of occupational interests and preferences. Occupational choice is therefore seen as a process that begins long before any decision-making is required.

The most influential developmental theory of occupational choice belongs to Super (1953) in which he proposes that the central aspect is one of individuals seeking to implement their self-concept. This implementation is a function of progressing through six life stages: *exploration*, referring to childhood and adolescent development of the self-concept; *reality testing*, the transition from school to work and early work experiences; *trial and experimentation*, attempts to implement the self-concept by staking out a career; *establishment*, implementing and modifying the self-concept in the middle career years; *maintenance*, preserving and continuing to implement the self-concept; *decline*, new adjustments of the self-concept following termination of one's occupational role.

One criticism of this theory is that it implies a sequential and linear career path, which reflects the nature of work in the 1950s, as people clearly did experience work in this way. How relevant this is to the conceptualisation of work stages for both genders in the 1990s and beyond remains to be seen.

According to Super, each person has a different set of values, drives and motivations that are influenced by childhood experiences and serve as an initial set of goals that impinge on the process of choice. It appears his theory would predict that women and men have differing sets of values, drives and motivations and differing self-concept mechanisms to explain their respective careers. How and why this happens and identifying the important factors that influence difference is not so easily understood. By focusing on individual differences within an identifiable process, earlier developmental theories failed to home in on the importance of gender differences.

The last ten years or so have seen much research inclined towards the developmental perspective. In order to examine gender differences it has been necessary to redress the balance of research by focusing on the factors that relate specifically to the career psychology of women and attempting to explain its distinctive nature. In doing so, current theorists and researchers (e.g. Gottfredson 1981; Fassinger 1985; Osipow 1990) have embraced the crucial role of parental, societal and life-stage influences.

Methodological problems

As evidenced by the research which has been produced in the field of occupational choice, it is a topic fraught with methodological difficulties. Both the notion of occupation and that of choice are vague and ill-defined. The traditional approach was to consider that an occupation could be taken to be almost the same as a job, and that choice could be taken to be manifested by the fact of being in that job. Therefore the research design was primarily concerned with examining jobs, or groups of jobs, (the independent variable) to see if there were differences between them in terms of characteristics of the job holders, such as ability, interests, personality, gender, race and social class, etc. (the dependent variable). For example, see Harrell and Harrell (1945), Stewart (1947) and Strong and Campbell (1974).

From the point of view of rigour, such a research approach is, at best, a quasi-experimental design (Leedy 1989) and therefore considered to lack the hard edge of scientific exploration. This is, of course, hardly surprising. To examine any individual characteristic that might appear to distinguish those found in one occupational group from those found in another is to ignore the interaction between these characteristics. While it is possible to attempt to improve this traditional approach through the use of appropriate statistical methods to deal with the problem of interaction, little can be achieved. This is because the potential characteristics are not only almost infinite in number, but extremely complex in their psychological interaction. Statistical treatment is just not sensitive enough to explore the problem. Being black, male, and from a deprived inner-city area may all contribute in some measure to why an individual is more likely to be found in one occupational group than another. But so might interests, motivation, personality, family pressures and the chance meeting in a pub with someone having a job on offer. Some of these characteristics would be considered inherent in the individual, whereas others are imposed. Most of these characteristics are very difficult to quantify, none of them is independent of the others. To force them to fit into a format for statistical analysis would be to invite spurious interpretation of the results.

A further, but related, problem is the failure to differentiate between occupational choice and occupational incumbency. The traditional approach was that subjects just being in their jobs was good enough for the researchers. Both inherent and imposed characteristics were included, with no way of distinguishing between them. This means that it was impossible to investigate the psychological, as opposed to the political, determinants of occupational outcomes.

Much psychological research, when applied to naturalistic settings, has found that the complexity of the problem causes the traditional, rather positivistic, approach to the concept of scientific rigour to be seen as inappropriate. It often needs to be replaced by a more humanistic focus on the process of what is being investigated, rather than its content. Occupational choice is no exception. Later researchers have set out to try to understand the inherent and imposed influences on the decision-making process that results in someone's subsequent occupational choice (e.g. Taylor and Pryor 1985). This approach appears to overcome much of the criticism of earlier methods. Both inherent and imposed characteristics can be researched in a more focused way and the extent to which genuine occupational wishes are being obstructed by societal or economic influences might become more clear. The research design is, in part, the reverse of that used in the traditional approach. Here the researchers are using the different characteristics (the independent variable) to predict the type of occupation that people will go into (the dependent variable).

However, the way that the process-focused researchers have dealt with occupational choice issues is not beyond criticism. First, they have tended to use questionnaire-survey methods. These have been strictly pre-structured and statistically analysed. While this gives some insight to the different characteristics and the major interactions between them, it imposes restrictions on understanding the subtle, but important, connections that link them. Second, studies have focused overwhelmingly on students. There is, of course, a logic to this. They are a population that is experiencing both inherent and imposed pressures as part of the process of making occupational decisions. They are also accessible to academic researchers. But they are a population that may exhibit more inflated, fantasy-based, career aspirations than others of the same age group. They are also not a representative sample of the whole population. Their restricted age range, socioeconomic class, ethnicity and, until recently, gender dominance, means that it is unwise to offer a generalised theory of occupational choice from such a research approach.

The focus on process is clearly a promising route to understanding occupational choice, but maybe researchers have not gone far enough away from the traditional research paradigm. They have adhered too closely to conventional notions of internal and external validity. This has prevented them from getting near to what is really going on in the process of occupational choice. Those being researched may have great difficulty in reporting their true feelings about the internal and external pressures they are experiencing, especially when asked via a questionnaire. This will often need to be facilitated by the researcher. For this reason, the way forward may be to utilise a totally qualitative approach, for example, using hermeneutically based group discussions/interviews as the principal research method. This could be demonstrated to have both internal and external validity (Lincoln and Guba 1985) but would not be constrained by the need to use statistical analytical methods.

Challenging the concept of choice

In couching the issue of occupational behaviour within a choice framework, there is an inherent assumption that all people have to do is choose a particular job or career from a whole array of different options. To operate from this assumption simplifies the issue and implies some kind of deficiency on the part of those who appear to restrict their selection to specific fields.

The aim of this section is to demonstrate that educational and occupational choice is a complex process that is significantly influenced by environmental variables. Consequently, the current terminology and framework of choice, it will be argued, is inappropriate.

Environmental restriction and choice

The term 'career' was conceptualised by Super (1980) as a collection of roles that people perform throughout their working lives. This definition has been used by numerous authors as a shorthand way of describing people's achievement and progress through an organisation or occupation. However, sociologists are of the opinion that a career is a social role which is defined by society, linking individuals to the social structure (e.g. Barley 1989). The emphasis of social roles, rather than a sequence of jobs, suggests that the whole concept of a career means different things to different social groups. Meaning is derived from differential socialisation experiences related to membership of groups such as those of gender, socioeconomic status and ethnicity. This implies that when occupational self-concepts are developed, they are a function of the social relationships experienced throughout childhood and adolescence. Career choices can therefore only be seen meaningfully within the context of a person's entire social experiences.

It is the case that people have to make a series of decisions. Where they end up occupationally is largely a result of the educational routes into which they are channelled and the career opportunities to which this leads. Recent articles in the press have claimed that educational practices operate which ultimately disadvantage some pupils in the subsequent job market. It has been claimed, for example, that black pupils are channelled towards sporting activities rather than academic subjects, and working-class pupils are channelled towards the more practical end of the educational spectrum, to BTec and NVQ qualifications. It has been found that members of Asian ethnic groups are streamed educationally according to their language ability, which often does not reflect their intellectual capacity, and from then on their educational choices are limited (Anderson *et al*. 1993). Much has been written with regard to the differing pattern of educational guidance and opportunity available to girls and boys. However, although young children in the 1990s show less pronounced gender-stereotyping of school subjects than was the case a decade earlier (Archer and MacRae 1991), women still represent a low percentage of admissions to engineering, science and other primarily maths-based courses and careers. Thus, the early educational decisions which are made serve to narrow down people's occupational choices and these will inevitably match the social stereotypes of population subgroups.

However, it is likely that teachers and careers officers are attempting to facilitate the development of what they believe to be their pupils' educational and occupational *interests*. In my own professional practice, working with older individuals on career and personal development issues, I have found that people appear to limit their interests to a very narrow range of alternatives. Often, in retrospect, people are aware of this: 'Going to university was not something that people did in my family' is a phrase often used by people from working-class backgrounds. This, they explain, is why they did not choose university as an educational option and therefore restricted their choice of occupational field and, often, their level of achievement within their career.

For some time research evidence has indicated the significant influence of socioeconomic status on career orientation and success but this seems to have been recognised by only some authors. Gribbons and Lohnes (1968) found that social class is particularly influential when the individual is starting their working life, whereas a twenty-one-year longitudinal study (Super 1981) demonstrated its subsequent effect on career satisfaction and achievement of career goals. The children of working-class parents appear to opt for careers which are not too dissimilar from that of their father (Katz *et al.* 1968) and therefore, not surprisingly, are significantly less likely to aspire to a professional career than children of professional parents (Kelsall 1972). It is still the case that university entrants are predominantly drawn from a privileged sector of society and are likely to remain so as the disappearance of grants forces economic issues into the equation.

The children of working-class parents have no role-models for professional jobs and therefore may not identify with the notion of a career, with all its connotations of progression, achievement, development and satisfaction. This is also the case with black pupils, who may focus on sporting heroes such as Linford Christie, Tessa Sanderson and Ian Wright as role-models for success, since they may not be introduced to role-models of other occupational orientations. Consequently, people from certain subgroups may see little point in expending their time and energy on educational experiences. This was demonstrated in a classic study on 'why working-class kids get working-class jobs' (Willis 1977). It was found that working-class children operated a strong anti-school culture where the prevailing attitudes were anti-authority and anti-hierarchy. These attitudes were manifested by, among other things, lack of involvement in the formal aspects of school and an emphasis on out-of-school activities as their main interest. Similar attitudes and behaviours have been found to prevail among blue-collar workers, with studies demonstrating that work is not the central life interest of people from lower socioeconomic groups (e.g. Goldthorpe *et al.* 1968).

The middle-class child, by comparison, has numerous role-models both educationally and occupationally that extend beyond the actual roles that people occupy. Their role-models encompass a whole career-oriented way of life which emphasises the process of fulfilment through work activities. This seeming advantage does not necessarily have a positive effect since people's choices are often restricted in order to comply with family expectations, not least because gaining a university education is often automatically expected to be the individual's initial goal.

Thus, an individual's social background creates a value system about work and education that differs according to their specific set of experiences. It is likely that people of working-class backgrounds and those from certain ethnic groups do not have the sort of experiences which are conducive to thinking about themselves undertaking meaningful work, or valuing the type of intrinsic rewards that work can bring. They may not identify with the concept of education as a means of empowerment and are motivated to seek satisfaction and fulfilment through non-work activities.

Social class and ethnicity impact on both females and males but the nature of that impact is different according to gender. Consider, for example, the opportunities available to Asian males as opposed to Asian females. For many Asian women, education beyond school and career opportunities depend almost entirely on the views of their families, then their husbands and their husbands' families. Although many families in the UK are now fairly liberal in this respect, it is still the case that an Asian woman may have no occupational opportunities at all. Asian males, on the other hand, do not have the same restrictions (Anderson et al. 1993).

Many authors have written about the way in which differential socialisation experiences produce different sets of attributes and characteristics for females and males according to societal expectations (e.g. Chodorow 1979; Gilligan 1982; Miller 1986). For example, women are socialised to be peacemakers, facilitators, caregivers and sympathisers whereas males are aggressors, competitors and adventurers. There is a match between these stereotypical attributes and the occupations that people gravitate towards (Sachs et al. 1992). Men and women have different experiences in early life which prepare them for adulthood in different ways. Boys are socialised to have the skills that are valued by a patriarchal society which in turn allows them to participate within that society. Girls are primarily socialised to be of service to others and lack the experiences that allow them to participate equally with men. Thus, a woman of low socioeconomic status would be unlikely to be attracted to the job of a garage mechanic since it requires none of the attributes that she has to offer. The likelihood of her aspiring to a professional career is also very low. Consequently, people's early experiences serve to restrict the range of career alternatives which they perceive to be appropriate.

This notion was included in Gottfredson's (1981) model of career development which has two main components: circumscription and compromise. Circumscription refers to the progressive process of narrowing career alternatives according to society's expectations of what is appropriate on the basis of gender and socioeconomic status. This process produces a 'zone of acceptable alternatives' which demarcates the range of choices individuals would consider as available to them. Choices outside of this range are ruled out as incompatible with how a person has come to understand him- or herself. There are three main inclusionary elements: sex-type, which is the compatibility of the perceived sex-type of an occupation with an individual's developing sense of gender identity; prestige, which refers to the elimination of occupations that are either higher or lower than one's prestige boundary and is therefore related to social class; and interest, which refers to the elimination of occupations that are not compatible with one's interests and abilities. Gottfredson (1981) argued that these three criteria, when applied across fields of work, will outline a 'self-defined social space' within which an individual is more likely to consider vocational alternatives.

Compromise is the accommodation of personal job preferences to the realities of the world of work and deals with the implementation, rather than the development, of aspirations. The model proposes that in a vocational decision, an element (i.e. sex-type, prestige or interest) which has been internalised later on in an individual's development is fairly flexible and open to change. An element internalised at an earlier age will be more resistant to change. Consequently, interest is the first aspect to be compromised, because it is the most flexible, then prestige and finally sex-type or gender-appropriateness.

Studies have tended to test the circumscription and compromise aspects of Gottfredson's theory independently. Several studies have indirectly supported the compromise process (e.g. Anderson *et al.* 1983) and there are others, which have tested the process directly, that also lend some support. Taylor and Pryor (1985), for example, found that students tended to select future academic and career directions that were congruent with their dominant vocational interest only when their demand for prestige was met. Similarly Holt (1989) found that engineering and social-work students were more likely to select occupations of high prestige, regardless of their own area of academic interest.

There is some suggestion in the research findings that prestige is the most dominant of the three compromise elements as it is the one that people are most unwilling to give up. This is contrary to Gottfredson's model which predicts that sex-type is the most enduring factor because it is internalised at a much earlier age than the other elements. The main problem is the confounded nature of interest, prestige and sex-type. For example, interest in a scientific occupation leads to a high-status career, usually in a male-dominated environment. This makes it difficult to identify which factor is being compromised.

In focusing on the importance of sex-type and prestige, Leung and Plake (1990) showed that the degree of contrast between the two elements was important. They found that people allowed themselves greater scope in choosing occupations of higher prestige as long as the sex-type of the occupation was not in clear opposition to their gender. Despite such findings, the position with regard to prestige versus sex-type, and their relative positions in the compromise hierarchy, is ambiguous. However, what is clear, is that sex-type and prestige are important factors that influence career-choice behaviours.

The main methodological problem in empirically testing the circumscription part of Gottfredson's model is the difficulty of measuring and operationalising concepts such as 'self-defined social space' and 'zone of acceptable alternatives'. One attempt to address this used a retrospective method that involved asking participants to recall occupations that they had ever considered (Leung and Harmon 1990). This produced five indicators of their zone of acceptable alternatives. The results showed that zones of acceptable alternatives exist and that these zones are different for males than for females with respect to sex-type.

Gottfredson's model is a relatively recent addition to the career-choice literature and, as such, has not yet been subject to thorough empirical evaluation. However, results demonstrate the importance of gender-appropriateness and perceived prestige level of occupations to the career decision-making process. The interaction of these variables does appear to restrict the range of career alternatives that people are willing to consider in a way which is different for males than for females. Whether research findings support or challenge the model, researchers seem to endorse the view offered by Henderson *et al.* (1988) that it is useful, especially in helping people to challenge the premature elimination of educational and occupational alternatives.

Another current approach (Hackett and Betz 1981) proposes that career choice can be understood within the self-efficacy framework which emerged out of Bandura's (1977) social learning theory. Self-efficacy refers to the beliefs that an individual has about their performance capabilities. The degree to which someone believes themselves to be efficacious affects their attitudes and behaviour. Research demonstrates that self-efficacy is predictive of a range of occupationally related behaviour including academic persistence and achievement, career decision-making choices and willingness to engage in non-traditional career activities (e.g. Nevill and Schlecker 1988).

Lent *et al.* (1989) suggest there is a reciprocal relationship between self-efficacy and interests. In activities where individuals perceive themselves to be efficacious, interest will emerge from involvement in those activities. Interest, in turn, motivates the individual to seek out further activity exposure. This provides more opportunities for successful experiences and, hence, promotes feelings of competence and effectiveness.

It is reasonable to speculate that differential socialisation experiences will limit people's exposure to certain activities and enhance involvement in others considered to be more socially appropriate. If this is the case, we might expect to see significant differences in self-efficacy between females and males, people of different social classes and those of different ethnic groups. It is the case that significant sex differences have been found in a number of studies. These typically show that males have higher beliefs about their performance and achievement than females, especially in relation to mathematics and science (e.g. Lapan *et al.* 1989; Lent *et al.* 1991). Since it has been demonstrated that personal performance accomplishments constitute the most influential source of efficacy information (e.g. Bandura 1986), it is likely that males and females have differential efficacy-building experiences. The results of the study by Lent *et al.* (1989) are supportive of this view.

Thus, people's evaluation of their own performance may be limited to their experience of only those activities which are considered to be gender appropriate. Therefore, females and males may differ in terms of their perceived success in different occupations. This was demonstrated to be the case by Betz and Hackett (1981) who found that males had higher levels of self-efficacy for male-dominated occupations and females were significantly higher for female-dominated careers. Differential self-efficacy-building experiences may therefore promote choice behaviour which follows a stereotypical pattern.

Of course, no two females or males have the same set of experiences and will differ in the degree to which their behaviour is stereotypical. This difference, or degree of difference is often researched using measures of gender role orientation where people are typically sorted into groups according to their scores on the Bem Sex Role Inventory (BSRI) (Bem 1974). The BSRI was designed to measure psychological masculinity and femininity, although most researchers now prefer to use the terms instrumentality and expressiveness respectively to summarise these two BSRI components. So we might expect gender role orientation to be an important factor in career decision-making, with, for example, expressive women inclined to choose traditional female jobs, and instrumental women to be more likely to choose a non-traditional career.

A number of studies demonstrate the importance of gender role orientation in relation to career behaviour (e.g. Astin 1984; Fassinger 1990; O'Brien and Fassinger 1993). In general, results show that people who are highly stereo-typical in their attitudes are more likely to choose gender-specific occupations whereas the more liberal, or androgynous, their gender role attitudes the more they are prepared to consider non-traditional careers. Women with liberal gender role attitudes are more likely to be career oriented, to perceive themselves as being more confident in their abilities and to make choices with a high degree of congruence between aspiration and ability. Additionally, liberal gender role attitudes were found to be related to young women's self-efficacy for maths and careers. Thus, it is possible that women who are socialised into stereotypical behaviours and attitudes, may have fewer experiences on which to build self-efficacy beliefs and are more likely to be drawn to stereotypical occupations. However, researchers have not really begun to address the question of the development of self-efficacy beliefs, although preliminary results do indicate that, not surprisingly, background variables are very influential. For example, women whose mothers were employed outside the home exhibit higher levels of self-esteem and more liberal gender role attitudes than those with mothers who were homemakers (Betz and Fitzgerald 1987).

The aim of this section has been to demonstrate that educational and occupational choice is a complex process that involves interacting variables. These serve to restrict the interest and aspirations of people and channel them in directions considered appropriate. Educational and occupational choice can therefore only be seen meaningfully within the context of a person's entire social experiences. The concept of choice in this context is rather like saying to someone that they can choose any sweetie in the bag as long as it is the big red one in the left-hand corner. Thus, there is a case for redefining the concept of choice.

Redefining the concept of choice

Some people do have some choice and others overcome their social constraints through, for example, determination, courage, foresight or the encouragement of others. Yet, many others 'end up' in occupational areas for a variety of reasons rather than simply making a rational selection from a wide range of alternatives. What is needed is appropriate terminology and a framework that incorporates the constraints of the many instead of one that reflects the opportunities of the few. In this, we are constrained by language which does not supply a wholly acceptable alternative. The term 'occupational fate' is offered as an alternative label and a way to begin to reconceptualise the issue. Fate is usually viewed as predetermined, which is partly appropriate when used in the present context as we cannot control our sex, social class or ethnic origin, nor can we intervene in how we are socialised. Also, in line with most instances when fate is applied to the human condition, there is invariably an aspect of self-determination. The term may not incorporate the degree of self-determination that people bring to occupational behaviour and in this respect it is not wholly appropriate. However, if we conceptualise a continuum from choice to fate, the reality of occupational behaviour is considerably closer to the fate end of the scale. Occupational fate is therefore considered to be more accurate terminology.

The current choice debate seems to exist within a simplistic framework. This is reflected in the questions that are commonly posed, for example: 'why don't women choose scientific careers?', 'why don't more working-class people go to university?', 'why aren't there more black people in business?'. Explanations are offered for these restrictions which imply deficiencies on the part of those who appear to restrict their career alternatives, for example, women lack confidence or black people lack business acumen.

The incongruity of this approach begins to be demonstrated when we consider why secretarial work, hairdressing and beauty therapy are not overflowing with male incumbents. Roberts (1981) reflects this incongruity in his question 'Is the language of "choice" really appropriate in explaining why so few university graduates become bus conductors?' because he is reversing the direction from which choice is usually considered. The focus here is not on the deficiencies of individuals, but what they would have to *give up* in order to participate within these fields. If questions were asked such as: 'what is it about men that makes them want scientific careers?', 'why do middle-class people place such an emphasis on a university education?' and 'what is it about white people that makes them so focused on commerce?', the answer would be obvious to many people – the issue is one of economic and social power, not an abundance of motivation or confidence. The point here is that educational and occupational choice is ultimately a political issue and needs to be framed and conceptualised as such before any meaningful investigation can be undertaken.

Organisational culture and gender dominance

Up to this point, occupational fate has been discussed by exploring the environmental variables which influence people's inclination towards certain job or career categories. This has ignored the key issue of organisational culture which affects the perceptions that people have about different jobs and the environment in which they are carried out.

People differ in how they define and conceptualise organisation culture, although most include some notion that it refers to the prevailing pattern of values, beliefs, norms, activities, interactions and attitudes (e.g. French and Bell 1973) and perhaps can be thought of as the psychological nature of the organisation. Culture stems from top management as a result of their shared values, beliefs, etc. which translate into a philosophy of behaviours and general work operating style which they expect from others in the organisation. This philosophy is formalised within policies and procedures but is also ingrained in the day-to-day operation of the organisation.

Culture can change, for example, from being production-centred to one of service orientation, and the impetus is usually a strategy to address commercial issues such as increasing market share. This is often achieved by the appointment of someone new to the top of the hierarchy who imposes their own work philosophy on the organisation, thereby changing the pattern of beliefs, values and attitudes over time.

Since the key players in creating and maintaining organisation culture are predominantly white, middle-class males it is inevitable that the culture of the vast majority of organisations reflects their shared psychology. Nicolson (1996) describes this as a 'toxic context' and describes how it facilitates the development of the dominant group to the detriment of those outside it. Thus, people from other subgroups of the population may not be attracted to particular organisations, may not be selected for jobs within them or may not 'fit in' or thrive if they do commence employment. This is because they have not been socialised into white, middle-class masculinity.

One of the great barriers to women is the traditional culture of long working hours, required of those who are employed in professional, technical and managerial jobs, which increases with seniority. People are expected to give a level of throughput which they cannot contain within a standard working week and are often rewarded for the hours they work rather than their achievements. Such a culture is punitive to women because of their competing demands and commitments. It is still the case that women more than men take on other responsibilities such as the home, childcare, caring for family members and maintaining relationships with others. Men, on the other hand, typically see their careers as a central life-interest and organisation culture is structured in accordance with this perception.

Evidence shows that women report significantly more role conflict than men (e.g. Wiersma 1990), and that they anticipate this conflict prior to entering the employment field significantly more than their male counterparts (Karpicke 1980). This is likely to affect women and men differently in terms of their perceptions of work and the organisations to which they may be attracted. Not surprisingly, women and men value different personnel policies. In a study of married men and women with children, Wiersma (1990) found that women valued parental support policies such as flexible working patterns, days off for sick children, leave of absence for childrearing and company-run day care centres, significantly more than men did.

Preliminary research on the effect on organisations of implementing employee-centred policies indicates that they have a positive effect, for example Ralston et al. (1985) found that flexible working times increased productivity levels. Yet organisations disadvantage those whose career paths involve career breaks and commitments outside the organisation, and women often have to choose between the job and family concerns. Having been forced to choose, they are then criticised for leaving when so much has been invested in them in terms of training and career development. Organisations with cultures that do support flexible career paths tend to be the lower-paying public service industries, for example, education and health. It is possible that women gravitate towards these organisations because they have policies which are sensitive to their career needs.

Research does indicate that this may be the case. Using an expectancy theory framework, Hollenbeck *et al.* (1987) found that women placed a greater emphasis on work aspects such as control over work schedules and ease of movement in and out of the workforce than did men. They saw these aspects as being met by environments which were female dominated. Conversely, they were more negative in their perceptions of many aspects of male-dominated jobs than men were, for example, co-workers, security and promotional opportunities. The researchers concluded that females appeared to be both pulled towards female-dominated environments and pushed away from those which are predominantly male.

Some organisations are attempting to address these issues. Equal Opportunities policies have been implemented in a number of organisations and some have gone to great lengths to be more woman-friendly. From a survey of organisations, MccGwire (1992) was able to select fifty which she considered to represent the best UK companies to provide for women's needs in the workplace. The survey addressed policies and practices in areas such as maternity leave, sexual harassment, promotion, training and the proportion of women employed in management. It showed that some male-dominated corporate sectors, such as the oil industry, were taking positive action with regard to the employment and development of women. Those with the best policies on gender were found to be those more likely to be implementing positive policies with regard to ethnicity.

However, culture is not only about policies, it is concerned with the whole ethos of the organisation and as such permeates every aspect of job activity, including covert or unconscious processes. Relatively little work appears to be have been done in this area, not least because it is fraught with methodological difficulties that are best addressed outside the traditional positivistic paradigm.

Tannen (1995) begins to address this in her work on the differential communication patterns of women and men in the workplace. Drawing on available research and anecdotal evidence, Tannen explores the differential nature of women's and men's communication style within an organisational context and describes how these styles reflect the social processes involved in the construction and perpetuation of gender stereotypes. Men tend to engage in a style that is hierarchical, competitive, forceful and concerned with one-upmanship. In comparison, women are viewed as self-deprecating, conciliatory and indirect. The problem here is the value attached to, and the interpretation of, different styles and the power dynamics which they reflect. Because the culture of the organisation is essentially male and those who most often hold organisational power are male, the male communication pattern is the valued style and others are by defin-ition interpreted as deficient. Thus, women are disadvantaged because they have to operate within a context where success depends on how they are perceived by men, yet their experiences do not prepare them to communicate in the valued way. In meetings, for example, women's contributions are often ignored, credit for their ideas is given to men, or their participation is consciously reduced because of the desire to avoid having to compete with men for 'air time'. Such behaviours, which are more likely to be part of the culture in male- rather than female-dominated environments, have far-reaching consequences for women's careers including their visibility within the organisation and career development opportunities.

Covert organisational processes serve to maintain the *status quo* and diminish the power of different groups to influence change in culture. This hinders the selection and progress of subgroups and affects the perceptions that people have about particular organisations through the manifestation of these processes in observable phenomena such as lack of role-models, proportion of subgroup representatives at a range of hierarchical levels and public declarations of commitment to equal opportunities.

As Collinson and Hearn (1994) point out, men and masculinity are central to the analysis of work and organisations. Yet masculinity as an organisational issue is taken for granted and therefore remains largely unexamined. Researchers and authors are beginning to address the issue (e.g. Hearn and Parkin 1987; Firth-Cozens and West 1991; Nicolson 1996) but this does not seem to be having an impact in the management literature. As stated earlier, many organisations are beginning to address the more practical issues concerning the needs of different groups but it is far easier for them to institute policies such as flexible working time, career breaks or enhanced maternity leave than it is for them to deal with the real, covert issues of equal opportunity. However, the main reason they cannot deal with it is because they do not recognise that equal opportunity encompasses more than practical considerations. In a small survey of twenty organisations, Aitkenhead (1987) found that organisational barriers hardly featured as potential resistance to the development of equal opportunities. The most common response given as a resisting force was individual prejudice. Although this survey was conducted ten years ago, there is no published evidence to suggest that current views would be different.

There is a myth that organisations are androgynous, that they appeal equally to men and women and the only difference is the type of job they have on offer. This is clearly not the case and organisational choice as a concept compounds the complexity of the decision-making processes relating to occupations.

The changing pattern of work

The pattern of work and organisations is drastically changing and this could affect the occupational fate of men and women. Although it may seem to be 'crystal-ball gazing' to speculate about the future, it might be considered irresponsible to ignore the emerging pattern of change. This pattern could have significant implications for the issue of educational and occupational decision-making.

The 1990s has seen, 'creeping at a sprint' across the entire developed world, changes in the traditional patterns of work, perhaps mainly due to technological advances. These changes are apparent in four main areas: the nature of the market-place, the nature of work organisations, the nature of jobs and the nature of the workforce. Although largely ignored by politicians and educationalists, these changes have begun to make a noticeable impact on how, why and where people work.

In the marketplace, organisations strive to gain competitive advantage and the crucial factor in this is the quality of their human resources. It has recently been argued (Handy 1994) that, from now on, successful organisations need to acquire people who

> are well educated, well skilled and adaptable . . . who can juggle with several tasks and assignments at one time, who are more interested in making things happen than in what title or office they hold, more con-cerned with power and influence than status . . . who value instinct and intuition as well as rationality, who can be tough as well as tender, focused but friendly, people who can cope with these necessary contradictions.

Handy goes on to assert that it is women, who comprise half of the well-educated sector of society, who are more likely to possess these qualities. The implication is that women, at least those who are well-educated, are key to the future success of organisations. If this is the case, they will have an advantage over men in the employment market for the first time. Research shows that women are becoming more flexible about the range of occupations they are willing to consider (Betz *et al.* 1990). Over time, they have moved from a strong preference for female-dominated occupations to those which are spread across female-dominated, androgynous and male-dominated occupations. It is therefore a possibility that certain employment sectors will become more gender-balanced.

Men could be forced out of the traditional male-dominated occupations. However, contrary to the evidence on women, the shift in men moving along the employment spectrum towards traditionally female occupations is minimal (Betz *et al.* 1990). Gender boundaries appear to be more important to men than they are to women, which is likely to be the result of the greater emphasis placed on the masculisation of males than the feminisation of females during childhood (Nicholson 1993). There is, therefore, greater pressure on males to demonstrate gender-specific behaviour than there is on females. This inflexibility in males could well damage their employment prospects.

The most obvious change in the nature of organisations is reduction in size.

Expressions such as 'becoming leaner and fitter', and 'downsizing', used in relation to organisations, have become part of everyday language. Belief that this was
a temporary phenomenon, a product of economic recession, has been shown not
to be the case. The future, it seems, is that employment will be found in larger
numbers of smaller organisations. When this is considered together with other
organisational changes, such as the reduction of hierarchical levels and the dispersal from large, central head offices into 'distance-working' structures, a move
away from the conventional view of the onwards-and-upwards notion of careers
becomes necessary. The traditionally valued, onwards-and-upwards, approach to
careers has strongly advantaged men and disadvantaged women. This view
reflects the male, externally oriented, achievement pattern, i.e. competition with
others, status and hierarchical progression, for which men are psychologically
prepared and organisationally rewarded.

In the future, the more usual career path is likely to be one that offers people
lateral, rather than vertical, progression. Thus, the structure of organisations will
be flatter, with more dispersal of power and authority and a greater focus on
collaboration. There will, of necessity, be an emphasis on communication skills
and the ability to work well, and generally get on, with other people. This view of
a career path and organisational structure is one that women are more likely to
identify with.

Perhaps the biggest changes of all are to be seen in relation to the nature of
jobs. One such change is the rapidly growing practice of organisations offering
only short, fixed contracts of employment, with a gradual demise of the traditional cradle-to-grave employment. This can readily be seen when scanning the
advertisements on the appointments page of any newspaper.

A related issue is the emerging changes in the desired pattern of work.
Surveys have indicated that the workforce generally want to have a more flexible
working pattern and there is a strong wish to be able to work using different
sized 'chunks' of time, rather than following conventional patterns (Handy
1995). Indeed, for many this is already the case. Hewitt (1993) reports that
only 33 per cent of the actual workforce follow the traditional nine-to-five
pattern.

These job changes coincide with women's reported desire for greater flexibility
to move in and out of the workforce (Hollenbeck et al. 1987). The future view is
a situation that comfortably accommodates a more flexible career path, such as
career breaks. This will reduce the disadvantage to women and reduce the advantage to men who may have to learn to adjust to a career path which is very
different to the one they originally saw before them. Such changes may well alter
women's and men's perceptions of work and organisations.

According to Handy (1994) individuals will be required to build up their personal 'portfolio' of skills, achievements, clients and products which forms the
basis of what they use to market themselves from one employment contract to
the next. Women should hold the advantage over men as they are more likely
to have many of the qualities sought by organisations already within their

portfolios. This approach also favours women in that it reflects their, internally oriented, achievement motivation, i.e. feelings of personal accomplishment and development of skills.

In speculating on the consequences of emerging work patterns, a rosy picture can be painted for the future of women in the workplace. The picture for men appears to be less rosy but certainly is not bleak. There are dangers, however, in accepting this view. It ignores the factors previously discussed and assumes that organisational changes can eradicate the effects of interacting environmental variables. Simply considering what organisations will have to do shows up some crucial conditional factors. They will need, for example, to take appropriate action to ensure that organisational practices such as recruitment, selection and reward systems are genuinely driven in terms of equal opportunities. They will also need to take action with regard to covert practices, behaviour and attitudes that are gender-specific and potentially alienating. Can organisations become genuinely androgynous in how they operate, with all the awareness, sensitivity and courage that this implies?

Perhaps the greatest barrier that women will face is that these changes are taking place within a framework that is, essentially, male centred. The focus will be on self-promotion, aggressive networking and competition between individuals for contracts which may well be scarce. In addition, organisations take the view that people's productivity must be maximised. This no longer applies just to industry and commerce but to all private and public sectors, including health and education. In the United States, for example, people apparently work the equivalent of an extra month per year compared to twenty years ago. There is a similar pattern in the UK, where the strategy is to use half the number of people, making twice the effort, to produce three times the output of before (Handy 1994). This is far from a scenario that is likely to advantage women.

The discussion of the future has focused on those who are 'well-educated' and who therefore comprise a small, though increasing, percentage of the population. What does the future hold for the majority of society whose educational fate has not channelled them through the system? The commercial world has gradually seen what Handy describes as the 'up-valuing of brain' and the 'down-valuing of brawn'. The economic trend to replace heavy industry with service industry is at the root of this, considerably reinforced by the development of technology. Heavy manual jobs, traditionally performed by men, are those that have declined in number, whereas newly created jobs have been aimed at women. Over time, this may result in an underclass, of working-class males particularly, who are unemployable.

The main theme of this chapter has been to present educational and occupational choice as a psychological process. Understanding the complexity of this renders the language and framework of choice as inaccurate and inappropriate. Consequently, the issue has been redefined as one of occupational fate and framed within a social and political context. A speculative look at the future, given the nature of emerging work patterns, indicates that there may be

opportunities to discard the traditional notion of those occupations being designated as male and those designated as female.

References

Aitkenhead, M. (1987) 'Assumptions surround equal opportunities policies',
    Occupational Psychologist 3: 42–44.

Anderson, D.S., Stacey, B.G., Western, J.S. and Williams, T.H. (1983) 'Career
    development in four professions: an empirical study', *Psychological Reports* 53:
    1263–70.

Anderson, P., Lewis, C. and Avenell, J. (1993) 'Psychometrics and ethnic minorities: a
    feasibility study'. London Borough of Tower Hamlets and the Department of
    Employment.

Archer, J. and MacRae, M. (1991) 'Gender perceptions of school subjects among
    10–11 year olds', *British Journal of Psychology* 61: 99–103.

Astin, H.S. (1984) 'The meaning of work in women's lives: a sociopsychological
    model of career choice and work behaviour', *The Counseling Psychologist* 12:
    117–26.

Bandura, A. (1977) 'Self-efficacy: toward a unifying theory of behaviour change',
    Psychological Review 84: 191–215.

—— (1986) *Social Foundations of Thought and Action: A Social Cognitive Theory*,
    Englewood Cliffs, NJ: Prentice-Hall.

Barley, S.R. (1989) 'Careers, identities and institutions: the legacy of the Chicago
    School of Sociology' in M.B. Arthur, D.T. Hall and B.S. Lawrence (eds) *Hand-
    book of Career Theory*, Cambridge: Cambridge University Press.

Bem, S. (1974) 'The measurement of psychological androgyny', *Journal of Consult-
    ing and Clinical Psychology* 42: 155–62.

Betz, N. and Fitzgerald, L.F. (1987) *The Career Psychology of Women*, New York:
    Academic Press.

Betz, N. and Hackett, F. (1981) 'The relationship of career-related self-efficacy
    expectations to perceived career option in college women and men', *Journal of
    Counseling Psychology* 28: 399–410.

Betz, N., Heesacker, R.S. and Shuttleworth, C. (1990) 'Moderators of the congru-
    ence and realism of major and occupational plans in college students: a replication
    and extension', *Journal of Counseling Psychology* 37, 3: 269–76.

Chodorow, N. (1979) 'Feminism and difference: gender relation and difference in
    psychoanalytic perspective', *Socialist Review* 46: 42–6.

Collinson, D. and Hearn, J. (1994) 'Naming men as men: implications for work,
    organisation and management', *Gender, Work and Organisation* 1(1): 2–22.

Fassinger, R.E. (1985) 'A causal model of college women's career choice', *Journal of
    Vocational Behaviour* 27: 123–52.

—— (1990) 'Causal models of career choice in two samples of college women',
    Journal of Vocational Behaviour 36: 225–48.

Firth-Cozens, J. and West, M. (1991) (eds) *Women at Work: Psychological and
    Organizational Perspectives*. Milton Keynes: Open University Press.

French, W.I. and Bell, C.H. (1973) *Organization Development*, Englewood Cliffs,
    NJ: Prentice-Hall.

Gilligan, C. (1982) *In a Different Voice*, Cambridge, MA: Harvard University Press.

Ginzberg, E. (1972) 'Toward a theory of occupational choice: a restatement', *Vocational Guidance Quarterly* 20: 169–76.

Goldthorpe, J.H., Lockwood, D., Bechhofer, F. and Platt, J. (1968) *The Affluent Worker: Industrial Attitudes and Behaviour*, Cambridge: Cambridge University Press.

Gottfredson, L.S. (1981) 'Circumscription and compromise: a developmental theory of occupational aspirations', *Journal of Counseling Psychology* 28: 545–79.

Gribbons, W.D. and Lohnes, P.R. (1968) *Emerging Careers*, New York: Teachers College Press.

Hackett, G. and Betz, N.E. (1981) 'A self-efficacy approach to the career development of women', *Journal of Vocational Behaviour* 18: 326–39.

Handy, C. (1994) *The Empty Raincoat: Making Sense of the Future*, London: Arrow.

—— (1995) *Beyond Certainty: The Changing World of Organisations*, London: Hutchinson.

Harrell, T.W. and Harrell, M.S. (1945) 'Army general classification tests scores for civilian occupations', *Educational and Psychological Measurement* 5: 229–39.

Hearn, J. and Parkin, W. (1987) *Sex at Work: The Power and Paradox of Organisation Sexuality*, Brighton: Wheatsheaf Books.

Henderson, S., Hesketh, B. and Tuffin, K. (1988) 'A test of Gottfredson's theory of circumscription', *Journal of Vocational Behaviour* 32: 37–48.

Hewitt, P. (1993) *About Time*, London: Rivers Oram Press.

Holland, J.L. (1973) *Making Vocational Choices: A Theory of Careers*, Englewood Cliffs, NJ: Prentice Hall.

Hollenbeck, J.R., Ilgen, D.R., Ostroff, C. and Vancouver, J.B. (1987) 'Sex differences in occupational choice, pay, and worth: a supply-side approach to understanding the male–female wage gap', *Personnel Psychology* 40: 715–38.

Holt, P. (1989) 'Differential effect of status and interest in the process of compromise', *Journal of Counseling Psychology* 36: 42–7.

Karpicke, S. (1980) 'Perceived and real sex differences in college students' career planning', *Journal of Counseling Psychology* 27: 240–5.

Katz, J., Korn, H.A., Leland, C.A. and Levin, M.M. (1968) *Class, Character and Career: Determinants of Occupational Choice in College Students*, Stanford, CA: Stanford University, Institute for the Study of Human Problems.

Kelsall, R.K. (1972) *Graduates: the Sociology of an Elite*, London: Methuen.

Lapan, R.T., Boggs, K.R. and Morrill, W.H. (1989) 'Self-efficacy as a mediator of investigative and realistic general occupational themes on the Strong–Campbell Interest Inventory', *Journal of Counseling Psychology* 32: 176–82.

Leedy, P.D. (1989) *Practical Research, Planning and Design*, 4th edition, New York: Macmillan.

Lent, R.W., Larkin, K.C. and Brown, S.D. (1989) 'Relation of self-efficacy to inventoried vocational interests', *Journal of Vocational Behaviour* 34: 279–88.

Lent, R.W., Lopez, F.G. and Bieschke, K. (1991) 'Mathematics self-efficacy: sources and relation to science based career choice', *Journal of Counseling Psychology* 38: 424–30.

Leung, S.A. and Harmon, L.W. (1990) 'Individual and sex differences in the zone of acceptable alternatives', *Journal of Counseling Psychology* 37: 153–9.

Leung, S.A. and Plake, B.S. (1990) 'A choice dilemma approach for examining the relative importance of sex type and prestige preferences in the process of career choice compromise', *Journal of Counseling Psychology* 37: 399–406.

Lincoln, Y.S. and Guba, E.G. (1985) *Naturalistic Enquiry*, Beverly Hills: Sage.

MccGwire, S. (1992) *Best Companies for Women*, London: Pandora.

Miller, J.B. (1986) *Towards a New Psychology of Women*, 2nd edition, Harmondsworth: Penguin.

Nevill, D.D. and Schlecker, D.I. (1988) 'The relation of self-efficacy and assertiveness to willingness to engage in traditional/non-traditional career activities', *Psychology of Women Quarterly* 12: 91–8.

Nicholson, J. (1993) *Men and Women*, Oxford: Oxford University Press.

Nicolson, P. (1996) *Gender, Power and Organisation: A Psychological Perspective*, London: Routledge.

O'Brien, K.M. and Fassinger, R.E. (1993) 'A causal model of the career orientation and career choice of adolescent women', *Journal of Counseling Psychology* 40, 4: 456–69.

Osipow, S.H. (1990) 'Convergence in theories of career choice and development: review and prospect', *Journal of Vocational Behaviour* 36: 122–31.

Parsons, T. (1909) *Choosing a Vocation*, Boston, MA: Houghton Mifflin.

Ralston, D.A., Anthony, W.P. and Gustafson, D.J. (1985) 'Employees may love flexitime but, what does it do to the organizations' productivity?', *Journal of Applied Psychology* 70: 272–9.

Roberts, K. (1981) 'The sociology of work entry and occupational choice' in A.G. Watts, D.E. Super and J.M. Kidd (eds) *Career Development in Britain*, Cambridge: Hobsons Press.

Roe, A. (1956) *The Psychology of Occupations*, New York: Wiley.

Sachs, R., Chrisler, J.C. and Sloan-Devlin, A. (1992) 'Biographic and personal characteristics of women in management', *Journal of Vocational Behaviour* 41: 89–100.

Stewart, N. (1947) 'AGCT scores of army personnel grouped by occupation', *Occupations* 26: 5–41.

Strong, E.K. and Campbell, D.P. (1974) *Strong–Campbell Interest Inventory* (revised edition), Stanford: Stanford University Press.

Super, D.E. (1953) 'A theory of vocational development', *American Psychologist* 8: 185–90.

—— (1980) 'A life-span life-space approach to career development', *Journal of Vocational Behaviour* 16: 282–98.

—— (1981) 'Approaches to occupational choice and career development' in A.G. Watts, D.E. Super and J.M. Kidd (eds) *Career Development in Britain*, Cambridge: Hobsons Press.

Tannen, D. (1995) *Talking from 9 to 5. Women and Men at Work: Language, Sex and Power*, London: Virago.

Taylor, N.B. and Pryor, R.G.L. (1985) 'Exploring the process of compromise in career decision making', *Journal of Vocational Behaviour* 27: 171–90.

Wiersma, U.J. (1990) 'Gender differences in job attribute preferences: work–home role conflict and job level as mediating variables', *Journal of Occupational Psychology* 63: 231–43.

Willis, P. (1977) *Learning to Labour*, London: Saxon House.

8

AN EQUAL CHANCE TO SUCCEED?

Comparing women and men in management

Viki Holton

Men and women differ not only in choice of type of education and occupation, but notably in the level of achievement
that they reach. In nearly all fields there are relatively few
women at the top, and this certainly applies to management. In the UK, and generally in the world, there are very
few women who are senior managers. Viki Holton discusses
some of the reasons for this, as well as some of the attempts
that are being made to change it. Organisations wishing to
do so need to pay attention to numerous factors, including
a real commitment by existing management, changing attitudes towards women, modifying the role of both men and
women within the organisation and making considerable
investment in time or money or both. Progress so far is
encouraging but there is a long way to go to attain equal
opportunities.

Though women today in the UK have an equal right with men to choose a
management career, it is clear that they do not yet have an equal chance to
succeed. A number of major UK employers are recruiting as many female as male
graduates. However, there are still relatively few senior women managers in the
UK, and though the numbers are increasing, it is a very slow change (see Appen-
dix). An Ashridge survey revealed that among *The Times* Top 200 companies
women hold fewer than 4 per cent of director appointments.[1] Women are more
likely to be working in finance and banking or the service sector generally than in
industries such as pharmaceuticals and manufacturing and there is one trend that
is universal in any sector – the scarcity of women at middle and senior management levels. A summary of the European situation is highlighted in Table 8.1.

The scarcity of women at senior level is a UK trend and also an international
trend and Nancy Adler and Dafna Izraeli's introduction to *Competitive Frontiers:
Women Managers in a Global Economy* emphasises this point:

Table 8.1 The situation for women in Europe

Women make up 41% of the workforce	BUT earn less than men
AND hold fewer top jobs	Up to 40% less in manufacturing Up to 35% less in service sector 29% of all management jobs Less than 2% of senior management jobs Less than 1% of board seats (3% of board seats in the UK)

Source: Eurostat, Ashridge, ILO and *Business Week*, 15 April 1996

In each country a similar story is told of societies in which men control the centers of political and economic power and of management as a profession controlled primarily by men – a profession in which women remain relative newcomers, especially at the top.

(Adler and Izraeli 1994)

The current climate for women managers

Dame Sheila Masters, Partner at the major accountancy firm KPMG, is one of the most senior women in the company. Her career profile is typical of women who entered the professions back in the 1970s. When she joined KPMG in 1970 she was one of only four women among 100 recruits taken on that year. The attitude towards women she describes as one where 'women were looked on with suspicion', though this was a marked improvement to a few years earlier. She says, 'I think that coming in five years earlier would have been really tough. It was just at this time that women started saying they wanted to have professional careers and go on and do other things'.[2]

Now, in 1998 the situation for women has improved dramatically in one important respect, and that is the growing number of employers who see the need to take action in order to ensure women can compete equally. Many companies have joined the Opportunity 2000 campaign, a Business in the Community initiative aimed at improving the quantity and quality of women's participation in the workforce. Launched in 1991 with over sixty member organisations, there are now over 300 public and private sector employers involved in the campaign. The NHS, the Civil Service in England and in Northern Ireland, British Airways and major UK banks such as Midland Bank were among the early supporters of Opportunity 2000.

Opportunity 2000 has been instrumental in illustrating how equal opportunities can bring business benefits – something that was not widely recognised before. Research conducted by Ashridge for the launch of the campaign looked at this issue and also at why most equal opportunity programmes did not succeed. The Ashridge work concluded that changing policies was insufficient without changing the organisational culture.[3] A model of change was developed and tested, briefly, the following elements were required in order for equal opportunity to be successful:

- demonstrating commitment, that the issue was really important to senior managers;
- changing behaviour and attitudes towards women;
- building ownership among everyone in the company, not merely focusing action on women;
- making a considerable investment, either in time or money or both.

This model was used to help organisations joining the campaign to either review or implement equal opportunity programmes. In addition, there were also companies such as Rank Xerox UK and Midland Bank who were generous enough to share their considerable expertise and experience.

Contrasting the UK experience

The UK environment is better in some respects compared to other countries. Few other countries, for example, have similar campaigns to the Opportunity 2000 campaign. Recent data from Grant Thornton illustrates that the UK has the best record in Europe in employing women managers (see Figure 8.1). Nearly two thirds of small and medium-sized companies in the UK employ at least one woman manager,[4] a striking contrast to the Netherlands where only 30 per cent of companies employ women managers. The Scandinavian countries also have lower levels than the UK. Although there have been much higher gains in Scandinavian politics and in the public sector for women, women have made more limited progress in the private sector as highlighted by Anna Wahl's recent work in Sweden, *Men's Perceptions of Women and Management*. Her own view was that such progress could lead to complacency:

> In Sweden we take pride in having made considerable advances towards equal opportunities. This is partially true and it is something that we have every reason to feel proud about. This does not mean, however, that we can sit back. . .it is still the case that women and women's competence are not used to their full potential in working life. Women are not offered the same opportunities for development and promotion, and they do not receive equal pay . . .

> (Wahl 1995)

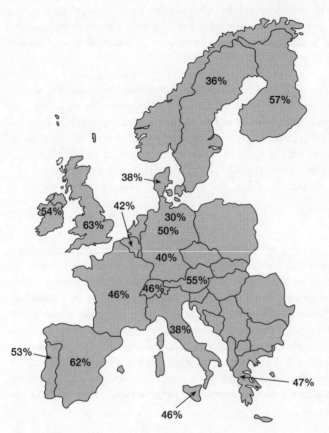

Figure 8.1 Small to medium-sized businesses with women in management

Hurdles to jump over

One of the hurdles that confronts women managers is isolation. The Grant Thornton survey mentioned earlier supports this, they found that very few companies, only 8 per cent of small to medium-sized companies, have more than two women managers. Even in a company with a comparatively high number of women employees, where women form the majority of staff overall, it is often the case that a woman at middle or a senior level may be the only woman at that level. Joanne Traves and Anne Brockbank's work (1996), looking at women managers in retail, makes this point. At one level being the 'first' woman to head a particular area or at a certain level creates a slide-rule against which all other women will be measured. Jean Sharpe, First Secretary and Consul in Bangkok, acknowledges this, ' I am aware, as are most women, that if we fail in a job it is more than just a personal failure – it reflects (unfairly) on the competence of all women'.[5]

Other problems of isolation are highlighted by Judi Marshall's research, looking at the experiences of women who have 'opted-out' of corporate life. She found isolation a key factor for the women she interviewed and found that,

> most of the managers had become more aware of organisations as male-dominated when they entered senior management. By this they meant descriptively that there were few women at these levels, but also that interactions tended to fit negative stereotypes of men's behaviour... many of the women reported being tested out in these cultures. They were in the spotlight, judged against gender stereotypes. People seemed to step back and see how (or if) they would manage without support.
>
> (Marshall 1995)

There is also still evidence of discrimination against women and figures from the conciliation service ACAS in 1996 showed a rise of nearly 10 per cent, compared with the 1995 figures, in the number of sex-discrimination cases. Research undertaken across a range of sectors – finance, retail, media, publishing and information technology (IT) – indicates that women face similar barriers in such critical areas as recruitment, assessment and career development. In 1994 the European Women's Management Development network (EWMD) looked at a number of these issues at a conference entitled 'Career Issues for Women in Management'.[6] Topics discussed included the dilemmas facing women working as international managers and the impact of organisational restructuring on women managers.

Information technology: a great place for women?

Back in the 1970s observers in the USA and the UK considered that the new information technology sector would be 'a great place for women'. With few established traditions and hierarchies it would be a place where women would be judged solely on ability. The extent to which this was true for women in the UK was the subject of research undertaken by Ashridge in a number of major information technology (IT) employers.[7] Sponsored by the Women into IT Foundation and companies such as IBM, ICL and BT, it was an ambitious project that lasted for eighteen months.

Part of the work surveyed individuals, one of the few studies to compare the experiences of women managers with a matched group of male colleagues. Some 400 individuals from over thirty major IT employers were asked about their career history and the current career environment within their organisation. Comparing men's and women's experiences revealed a number of crucial differences. Some of these are outlined as follows:

- Despite matched pairs being nominated, men were more likely than women to have gained greater responsibilities in the number of staff reporting to them; while women were more likely than men to want opportunities to lead a team.
- Training and development are not completely equal for men and women. Women were more likely to say it was not easy to find out what training was available in the organisation. Where training had been refused, the main reason reported by men was that it was regarded as inappropriate to their job. In contrast women were more likely to be refused due to budget constraints.
- The role of the immediate manager was found to be critical in the career development process. It was therefore worrying to find that men received more positive and supportive help from their manager compared to women. Men also appeared to be better at accessing information about training, job moves, promotions and career planning – key areas that ensure that individuals 'get on' in the organisation.

In addition to surveying individuals, we were also interested in what the companies thought about the situation. A number noted that there were few women applying as graduate entrants, or at senior levels – in one company only 5 per cent of senior managers were women. This was a concern for the organisations surveyed and the majority, 61 per cent, felt that they faced challenges in promoting women into senior appointments.

It was clear that organisations needed to consider ways to ensure the career development process was made more open and accessible to women, and that more positive support be provided for women at middle and senior management levels.

As mentioned earlier, it is evident that women face similar issues regardless of the sector. A publishing survey produced similar conclusions to the Ashridge work, finding that 'hidden barriers to career progression effectively form a glass ceiling, preventing women from achieving these jobs'.[8] One example of this is the assumption that working mothers will no longer want a career. Another respondent described how, 'equal opportunities is no different here from any other publisher: it's easy to get into management, impossible to get on the board'.

Company issues and action

Company action takes a number of different forms. Some have pooled energies in order to do this. The Ashridge IT research mentioned earlier was sponsored by a group of major employers such as BP, BT, British Airways, Digital, EDS, ICL, Shell and IT – The Post Office; a mix of IT users and IT suppliers who often compete to attract and retain the best graduates. However, the need to collaborate and exchange experience in order to help the situation for women was more important. It is a model of action that could be usefully developed in other sectors.

Finding out just what the issues are is important. As Post Office Chairman Sir Bryan Nicholson commented about the Ashridge IT research findings: 'we might believe that there are barriers, that "things are not quite right" but we don't know where to start putting things right unless we ask the individuals affected. We cannot claim that we know the answers yet but we now have a firm basis for targeting action.' The results of reviewing the current situation for women have in some cases surprised the organisations concerned. An example of this is work carried out by Ashridge with one employer surveying staff on many aspects of diversity. Men and women were asked about the environment for women within the company and though the majority felt that men and women worked well together as colleagues, fewer felt that men and women were judged equally. The fact that it was a minority, only one third of staff, who felt that men and women were evaluated equally in the organisation came as a considerable shock to the company.

The power of mentoring

BP Oil are one of a number of companies who have focused on issues for women at senior levels. The turning point at BP Oil came at a meeting of the European senior management in 1992, attended by 200 men and two women. Sabine Dietrich, from BP, explains that 'the manager responsible for this meeting thought that this ratio had to be changed and wanted some positive action in favour of women in the BP management'.

Sabine Dietrich was one of a group of senior women who undertook a review to make recommendations for change. Action has included family-friendly policies, a Europe-wide job-shadowing scheme and a mentoring programme. The mentoring programme provided a group of senior managers who agreed to act as mentors, to assist and coach women managers. It required a significant amount of time from the senior managers concerned and the fact that they were willing to help in this way undoubtedly created positive messages about the need to initiate support for women managers. The scheme has proved extremely successful in Germany where twenty-five women managers took part. It has since been offered in Belgium and is currently being adapted for the French operations.[9]

Mentoring is an approach that has been used in a number of companies to help women. The level of interest may be higher than might be expected. One organisation found that although less than 10 per cent of senior women managers were currently being mentored over half said that they would like such an option. Staffordshire University's mentoring programme is unusual in that it is offered to women at all levels – management and non-management. (Mentoring has traditionally been associated with managers or with graduate-entry staff.) After joining the Opportunity 2000 campaign, the University felt that work identified did not address individual women, who were left 'very much on their own'. In an effort to overcome this, Dr Christine King, Chancellor, considered that mentoring would be an ideal tool to provide help.

The programme has been successful and appears to address some of the particular issues women face within the University, as for instance a lack of confidence to aim high, or, alternatively, getting 'stuck' in jobs. Already one person has applied for, and been awarded, a promotion. Clearly though promotion is not the only outcome of the programme, as it will also enable women to broaden their skills within their current responsibilities.

Developing a family-friendly approach

A number of companies have become increasingly aware of the value of becoming more 'family-friendly', acknowledging the pressures of juxtaposing a career and family responsibilities.[10] Barry Morgan, Chief Executive of IBM UK, recently highlighted the link that he observed between work/family tensions and stress. As a result he has taken action within IBM to ensure that staff can discuss and acknowledge these issues, and that company action is taken to help. He advises other companies to ensure they similarly face up to such issues, as without such help the impact of stress will endanger the company's chances to be successful.

Shell recently undertook a major international survey to investigate the impact of dual careers and what the company might do to create improvements. Recent work by Ashridge for Lloyds Bank examined how well staff were able to balance home and work responsibilities.[11] We surveyed staff nationally, at all levels, and talked to both men and women, to those with childcare responsibilities and others with long-term care responsibilities such as for sick relatives or elderly parents. Regardless of whether Lloyds staff said they found it easy or difficult to achieve a balance between home and work, the vast majority supported the need for change and believed that the situation could be improved. As a result a number of action points and recommendations have already been implemented company-wide.

Compared with the majority of UK companies, Lloyds undoubtedly is a progressive employer. They were one of the first employers to introduce a career break in the UK and also were trend-setters as an early member of the Opportunity 2000 campaign. Their reason for undertaking the research was a concern to ensure that their provision of maternity, childcare and eldercare arrangements strikes the right balance between business priorities and the current and future needs of all staff.

We heard from staff at all levels in the Bank that the extent to which it was currently possible to balance home and work depends greatly on managers' discretion. When such an approach works well, all concerned can derive great benefit. We came across examples of caring, thoughtful managers who saw the benefits attached to helping staff manage their domestic commitments. These managers were invariably repaid by the increased commitment of their staff. In one instance a local school was completely shut down due to an outbreak of illness and the majority of staff in a small branch had to take time off. The effect on the branch was devastating and the skeleton staff who remained coped as best they could. When the school re-opened, the staff who had been away set up their own rota system to ensure that the extra time taken was paid back. There were no meetings concerning the incident as the rota was organised almost immediately. It was a voluntary gesture from the staff, in part to recognise how helpful the branch manager had been during the crisis.

The power of managers to either help or not help staff was most frequently mentioned with regard to paternity leave, emergency leave and compassionate leave. One of Ashridge's recommendations was to introduce some form of family leave to help people cope with unplanned emergency leave, another was to formally offer paternity leave, making it an automatic rather than a 'claimed' right.

Facing up to the future

There is a great deal to celebrate with regard to equal opportunities, and the fact that many leading employers in the UK are members of the Opportunity 2000 campaign creates a very positive environment. In spite of the positive changes underway there is a very long way to go before it can be said that men and women have an equal chance to succeed. Dame Sheila Masters, at KPMG, remains one of the few women in the company at senior level. The promotion of Petri Hofsté in KPMG earlier this year makes her the first woman partner in KPMG Holland.

Achieving progress with equal opportunities is not easy as most of those who have been involved in Opportunity 2000 would agree. There are a number of issues that can muddy the waters including the following points:

- Making progress will be tougher and take much longer than first envisaged. Even with a realistic time frame and action plans the advice from individuals who already have considerable expertise in the area is that organisations should not underestimate the issues.
- There is a danger of complacency when a company begins to collect a reputation for having achieved progress with equal opportunities.
- The rationale for equal opportunity action is misunderstood. It is possible that individuals believe action means women are given jobs simply because of their gender, while women resent what they mistakenly believe is remedial training. Emphasising the need to provide a 'level playing field' to ensure that men and women can compete equally, and that action for women is not action against men, is particularly important to overcome such issues.

However, it is good to see the level of research that has been undertaken about the work environment for women in the UK. To mention one recent publication, the work by Maureen Farish and colleagues looks in detail at the situation in three Higher Education establishments (Jayne 1996). Exchanging experience, particularly across national boundaries, will undoubtedly help to progress equal opportunities. Judi Marshall, mentioned earlier in this chapter, was a recent speaker at a New Zealand conference, 'Women and Leadership', which was organised by Massey University.

Finding out information about the topic can pose problems and often people searching for information about equal opportunities generally, or on a specialised subject, find it difficult to know where to turn. There is now much more written material available than previously was the case. Though Nancy Adler and Dafna Izraeli's book, mentioned earlier, remains one of the few to review the international scene for women managers, the number of books and articles grows continuously. A recent on-line search undertaken (on ABI/Inform) revealed some thirty articles using the search terms 'women' and 'leadership'. For those who do not have access to on-line facilities another source is a most valuable abstract service provided by *Women in Management Review*.[12] A special issue of the journal contains titles and summaries of articles published in the following key areas:

- Leadership styles and personality
- Recruitment and career management
- Dependent care and health/family issues
- Job evaluation, appraisal and equal pay
- Discrimination and equal opportunities

The Equal Opportunities Commission has published a number of important reports and surveys over recent years, not least of which is the 1993 'Women and Men in Great Britain'.

A recent meeting organised by EWMD (the European Women's Management Development International network) France on the topic of international careers illustrates the value of exchanging information:

> Depending on the country, the gender gap in salary for middle managers is small, but widens for senior level managers. In France, middle managers receive equal pay, but there is a national average gap of 30 per cent at the executive level (cadre dirigeant). However, multi-national companies use salary point grading systems which reduce the weighted average gap to 15 to 18 per cent. And the advice from workshop participants to women was that 'women need to be more demanding and assertive'.[13]

There has been a great deal of knowledge gained over the past few years through the Opportunity 2000 campaign, and this is now finding its way beyond the UK to help other countries. Recently, Lady Elspeth Howe, Chairman, and Liz Bargh, Campaign Director at that time, hosted a Dutch group who were keen to learn from the UK experiences.

It is important to ensure that action is taken at a macro level; an example is the

European Union's Equal Opportunities Programme launched in October 1996. The value of such efforts is evident. Sir Archibald Forster, Chairman of Esso UK, highlights the value of such work within Esso, and for other companies,

> ... that is not to suggest however that the business benefits of equal opportunities are just associated with a wider recruitment pool. The task of recruiting the best is dwarfed by the subsequent tasks of ensuring that the best are promoted and that all employees are able to develop to their full potential. It is those organisations that have quality employees that are the ones that meet their customers' requirements.[14]

Appendix 1: Stepping stones: key dates for women

Date	Achievement
1875	Women able to enter university on equal terms with men
1946	Women able to join the Diplomatic and Consular Services of the Civil Service
	The marriage bar was lifted and women were allowed to remain in Civil Service after marriage (previously women were required to resign)
1973	Women permitted to trade on the floor of the London Stock Exchange
1975	Sex Discrimination Act
	Equal Pay Act
1982	Sally Oppenheim-Barnes appointed, first woman Director at Boots the Chemist
1986	Lesley Knox appointed, first woman director at any City of London merchant bank
1989	Ashridge survey: 11 per cent of Times Top 200 companies have women directors
1991	Launch of Opportunity 2000 Campaign
	Kathleen O'Donovan appointed, BTR, first woman Finance Director of a major British company
1992	Rosemary Thorne appointed Finance Director and first woman Executive Director at retailers J Sainsbury
	Woman Director appointed to the court of the Bank of England, the first in 300 years
1993	June de Moller appointed, first woman CEO of a FTSE 100 company, the UK's top companies
	Ashridge survey: 25 per cent of The Times Top 200 companies have women directors
	For the first time women took the most senior jobs in HM Customs and Excise and the Crown Prosecution Service
1996	October, the official launch of the European Union's 4th Equal Opportunities Action Programme

Notes

1 Surveying the situation for women directors in the UK, by Viki Holton, *Corporate Governance Journal*, Vol. 3, No. 2, 1995.
2 'The Dame who is pitching for President', by Jon Ashworth, *The Times* 3 August 1996.
3 'A Balanced workforce? Achieving cultural change for women: A Comparative study', by Valerie Hammond and Viki Holton 1991. Published by Ashridge Management College.
4 Grant Thornton (1996) *International European Business Survey*.
5 Progress Report on Women in the Civil Service, 1984–1994, HMSO, 1994.
6 Special Edition of *Women in Management Review*, 'Career issues for Women in Management', Vol. 10, No. 3, 1995.
7 'Information technology environments: career development processes – policy versus practice', by Valerie J Hammond and Viki Holton 1992. Published by Ashridge Management Research Group.
8 *Still Grey Suits at the Top*, Book House Training Centre, 45 East Hill, London, SW18 2QZ.
9 'Spotlight on EWMD Corporate Member, interview by Angelika Poth-Mögele with Sabine Dietrich, BP Oil', *European Women's Management Development Network Newsletter*, Summer 1996.
10 *The Family Friendly Employer*, by Christine Hogg and Lisa Harker 1992. Published by Daycare Trust, UK.
11 'How to become a family-friendly company: balancing home and work responsibilities at Lloyds Bank', by Viki Holton 1996. Ashridge Management Research Group.
12 'Special Abstracts Issue', *Women in Management Review*, Vol. 11, No. 7, 1996.
13 'International careers: what's hot, what's not' by Rissa Seigneur, *European Women's Management Development Network Newsletter*, Issue 48, Autumn 1996.
14 *From Equality to Diversity: A Business Case for Equal Opportunities*, by Rachael Ross and Robin Schneider 1992. Pitman.

References

Adler, Nancy and Izraeli, Dafna (eds) (1994) *Competitive Frontiers*, Blackwells.
Equal Opportunities Commission (1993) *Women and Men in Great Britain 1993*, London: HMSO.
Jayne, Edith (1996) 'Book review of equal opportunities in colleges and universities towards better practices', *Women in Management Review*, Vol. 11, No. 6.
Marshall, Judi (1995) 'Working at senior management and board levels: some of the issues for women', *Women in Management Review*, Vol. 10, No. 3.
Traves, Joanne and Brockbank, Anne (1996) 'Women retail managers', *European Women's Management Development Newsletter*, Issue 48, Autumn.
Wahl, Anna (ed.) (1995) 'Men's perceptions of women and management', Sweden: Fritzes.

9

WHY CAN'T A WOMAN BE MORE LIKE A MAN, OR VICE VERSA?

John Radford

Professor Higgins's lament has become almost a caricature of outdated male attitudes, yet reviewing the papers in this volume as well as other research, it is clear that men and women are widely considered to be different in respect of education and occupation; they tend to be treated differently; in many ways they regard themselves differently; they make different choices; and they end up in different jobs. These are all differences on average; they do not apply to every individual. I argue that individuals differ along a bundle of traits which can be approximately characterised as 'male' and 'female', and that much the same applies to subjects for study and to occupations. Individuals generally make approximate matches between themselves and their preferred activity. Men tend to gravitate towards the 'male' end of the spectrum, and women to the 'female' end. But there are no sound reasons in terms of ability, or of any other sort, to exclude either group from any opportunity.

Meanings of 'gender'

In May 1995 there was a brief correspondence in *The Times* over the appointment of a Professor of Gender Relations at the University of Dundee, or rather, over the title, one reader regretting that 'a great university' was not aware that only words have gender – living beings are of different sexes. In the social sciences, this was in fact true until about twenty-five years ago. Udry (1994) refers to a bibliography of 12,000 titles for marriage and family literature from 1900 to 1964, in which the form 'gender' does not appear once. The current usage seems to stem from Money and Ehrhardt (1972). Udry suggests that most commonly 'gender' is now used as a synonym for biological sex. But not all writers agree. Diamond (1977) for example distinguishes 'sexual identity', defined as 'the individual's personal and private assessment of his or her gender' from 'gender role' which is 'stipulated by society'. Deaux (1985) uses 'sex' to refer to 'the biologically based categories of male and female', and 'gender' for 'the psychological features frequently associated with these biological states, assigned either by an observer or by the individual subject'. This is more or less the same usage as Leonard Holdstock adopts in this volume, closely following that of Halpern (1992). Hoyenga and Hoyenga (1993) on the other hand object to the use of two separate terms at all, on the grounds that this establishes 'an arbitrary and undesirable dichotomy' – we are products of both biology and environment. Another *Times* reader suggested that 'gender' was only used at Dundee because the University felt unable to appoint a Professor of Sex Relations. In bookshops, 'gender' is almost a synonym for 'feminist'.

In a book whose title (perhaps rashly) starts with the word 'gender', it would seem desirable to be clear about what this means. Perhaps, contrary to Udry, it most often refers (in psychological publications including this one) to the two obvious groups of men and women, to one of which most of us feel we clearly belong. This is not facetious; the existence of some individuals who do not experience this clear identity is important. It may be said that we are now referring simply to biological sex differences. These are what constitute 'men' and 'women'. But this is not so. Rather, I suggest that we have, as so often with behaviour, to consider, at least in principle, three levels of analysis, with the approximate labels of physiological, individual and social, related in rather complex ways. Nor do I mean that gender or sex roles or identity are 'constructed' and have no other reality, in the way that Hoyenga and Hoyenga for example argue that gender-related traits are situation specific, and that 'there can be no "transcendent" sex differences'. As Leonard Holdstock points out, what actually happens (in our society) is that we are initially, that is at birth or very shortly after, assigned membership of one of the two groups, normally on the judgement of medical personnel. The basis is physiological – anatomical (normally external), to be precise – but the membership is social. In the United Kingdom, once this membership has been formally recorded on a birth certificate, it is legally impossible to change it. In 1997 an appeal against this to the European Court of Human Rights, by two transsexuals who had undergone sex-change surgery, was unsuccessful. Modern techniques mean that such changes are by no means uncommon. There is a (small) proportion of individuals who identify so strongly with membership of the group to which their anatomy did not initially entitle them that they are prepared to undertake this long and difficult route. There are others whose anatomy is initially ambiguous. It is often modified to be more clearly one or the other, but there are cases in which such physically assigned identity does not correspond to the individual's experience, and at least sometimes it is later changed around. In any case, every individual shares characteristics of both sexes, and only approximates, more or less, to the modal type of one or the other.

The importance of this is that even at the most basic level we have to deal not with an absolute dichotomy but with a bimodal distribution, or two overlapping distributions. As has been said, this distribution is the initial basis for the classification, but it is not the normal basis in social interaction. (One recalls Gore Vidal's reply to the question as to whether his first sexual encounter was with a man or a woman, 'I was much too polite to ask'.) We very seldom classify individuals whom we meet as male or female on the basis of primary sexual characteristics. Secondary characteristics – beard, breasts – are indicative, and so are cultural ones such as hair length, clothes, or make-up. According to Serbin *et al.* (1993), children as young as five months can discriminate male and female pictured faces, apparently relying on hair-length cues. Even so, it is not unusual to come across individuals who are at least momentarily puzzling. Misidentification is frequently the subject of comedy, from Shakespeare to *Charley's Aunt* and *Some Like It Hot*, as, in a different way, is caricature of one side by the other – the Betsy of morris dancing, pantomime dames, Les Dawson, Edna Everage. Societies vary greatly in their insistence on a sharp dichotomy. On the one hand, they may more or less systematically define two sets of behaviour; on the other, they may or may not tolerate the existence of ambiguity.

Social dimensions

Many societies have more or less formal arrangements to accommodate individuals of indeterminate gender assignation, or those who are physically in one group but behaviourally and/or experientially in the other. The term 'berdache' has become familiar for the latter case, from anthropological studies in North America. Goulet (1996) shows that this term has in fact been used in several different ways to refer to various permutations of male : female and morphology : psychology. In some of these, at least, occupation in a broad sense is involved. For example, cases are reported of parents who, having failed to produce a son, brought up a daughter to fill this role, specifically to hunt for them in later years. In other groups the berdache may fill some unusual role, for example of a shamanistic type. In our own society, folklore and song are replete with examples of (usually) women taking male roles – the 'female drummer', the 'handsome cabin boy', and so on, often based on real life stories (for some of these see Fraser 1994), as was Henry Fielding's *The Female Husband* of 1746. Many of these cases date from the seventeenth and eighteenth centuries, when, it has been suggested, the role of women as wives and mothers was beginning to be more sharply delineated (Friedli 1987). Such behaviour was severely punished when discovered, indicating the force both of social opinion and of the needs of individuals prepared to risk it. Quite recently the category of 'homosexual' has emerged as a way of encompassing ambivalent patterns (see e.g. Bleys 1996; Boswell 1995; Spencer 1995). Those so classified (or classifying themselves) are not officially assigned any particular occupation, but are certainly excluded from some, such as some armed forces and priesthoods.

Here we move into the other aspect of the dichotomy, the fact that classification can function in a way analogous to caste: specific functions and behaviour are thought to be appropriate to one group or the other, and the 'wrong' ones may be forbidden. An extreme case is seen at the present time in Afghanistan, where under the Islamic Taleban regime women are barred from all education and employment. Less outrageous systems, however, have operated in probably all societies, often marked by rites of passage in which the individual is accepted into the appropriate adult group. For example, in the Jewish faith there are different naming ceremonies for boys and girls shortly after birth, and at thirteen and twelve respectively they celebrate *bar mitzvah* or *bat mitzvah*. The latter receives less attention because the religious role of women is less public than that of men, for example, a boy after the ceremony can be counted as one of the ten men who make up a *minyan* for prayer (Unterman 1994). Being a man or a woman is often associated with legal or customary obligations and restrictions of many kinds. On the whole, there is little doubt that this has historically most often operated to the detriment of women, even when their role has not in itself been a particularly oppressed one. In Classical Greece, for example, women had many recognised and valuable functions in the household and family, and their religious rites were no less important than male ones; but they did not have access to political life and the role of citizen (Blundell 1995). At the same time it should be remembered that there have been many variations. Women in medieval Europe, for example, were in some ways better off than more recently. Chaucer's Wife of Bath – independent and widely travelled, to say nothing of her five husbands 'at church door' – hardly needed 'liberating', while at least some real life women achieved successful and influential careers in what we would now call administration or management, as heads of great estates or religious houses, or in trade or business. An interesting case is that of brewing, one of the most important of medieval trades, and largely a female one. By 1600, however, it had been taken over by men. Bennett (1996) shows that this coincided with the trade becoming more prestigious and profitable. She argues that women lacked access to capital, but also that cultural notions of the proper role of women changed.

Contrariwise, even partial equality has been achieved in our society only recently. In 1869 John Stuart Mill proclaimed 'that the principle which regulates the existing social relations between the two sexes – the legal subordination of one sex to the other – is wrong in itself, and now one of the chief hindrances to human improvement; and that it ought to be replaced by a principle of perfect equality, admitting no power or privilege on the one side, nor disability on the other'. In the United Kingdom it is still within living memory (1929) that women gained equal voting rights with men. In 1993, female entrants to university for the first time exceeded male in the UK (as they do in most advanced countries). The Church of England has only just (1994) admitted women to the priesthood – with numbers of adherents consequently defecting to the Roman church which does not. Actual discrimination in employment against either sex has been illegal in the UK since the early 1970s (see Chapter 6 by Neil Scott and Paul Creighton), but complaints of it continue. In 1995 for the first time the Equal Opportunities Commission received more of these from male job applicants than female (*The Sunday Times*, 5 May 1996).

We must distinguish opportunity from achievement, and from ability. It is well documented that in many fields – though not all – women currently do less well, in status and salary, than men, as discussed by Viki Holton in Chapter 8. At the top financial level, *The Sunday Times* list of the richest persons in Britain (6 April 1997) shows that only sixteen, 3.2 per cent, of the top 500 are women, and this includes some who merely inherited their wealth from a successful husband. In the Civil Service, whose official commitment to equality actually goes back several decades, only 8.6 per cent of posts in the top three grades (known as the senior open structure) were in 1994 held by women (*The Times*, 3 February 1994). Even in the USA the corresponding figure was only 10.1 per cent. The General Election of May 1997 produced almost twice as many women Members of Parliament as before, but thanks partly to the Labour Party instituting all-female shortlists in selection. In academic life, where again there is a general commitment to equality, only 8 per cent of professorships are held by women (*The Times Higher Education Supplement*, 6 June 1997) – up from 5 per cent in 1995. But they are very unevenly distributed between disciplines, ranging from 29.4 per cent in librarianship and information studies to 1.4 per cent in engineering and technology. This of course reflects differential recruitment as well as lack of promotion. Female graduates in 1996 gained 9 per cent more 'good' degrees (upper second or first) than men; yet almost twice as many men as women gained places on graduate training schemes, and male graduate starting salaries were 16 per cent higher than those of females (*The Times*, 29 March 1997). We cannot, however, infer lack of either opportunity or ability simply from lower achievement. In the case of the graduates for example, it appears that men tended to put more effort into job-hunting, women into their studies.

There is a complex relationship between achievement and mode or direction of activity. There has been a tendency for male-dominated occupations to be better paid than female. One aspect of this, of course, is that the latter have often been subservient to the former: secretaries as against managers, nurses as against physicians. Men have been unwilling to take on the lower-paid and 'female' jobs; women have been willing, partly on the basis that the job is only ancillary to a role as wife and mother. Most employees still spend most of their work time in predominantly single-sex jobs; and jobs at the upper levels, both manual and non-manual, are predominantly male (Scott 1995). To put it another way, women as a class still tend to be disadvantaged both because they cluster in lower-status occupations, and because in many occupations they tend to fill the lower ranks.

It is important to remember that while both discrimination, positive or negative, and social or legal rules may be in terms of a dichotomy, actual educational and social differences are matters of central tendency, and generally of overlapping distributions. This is of course generally, perhaps universally, true of human behaviour and human characteristics, as has been realised for 150 years, though not, apparently, by everyone. The simple model is that of height. No one questions that while men are *on average* taller than women (and the tallest and shortest recorded individuals are respectively male and female), large numbers of females are taller than large numbers of males. Nevertheless, popular, and even academic, pronouncements frequently appear to the effect that 'men' are like this and 'women' are like that. So appealing are such statements that large fortunes are to be made from them, for example John Gray's *Men Are From Mars, Women Are From Venus* (1992) has sold 10 million. Conversely, when some finding is reported in the press that men or women *tend* to be one thing or another, it is invariably accompanied by a quote from a (usually well-known) individual, to the effect that, 'This is all complete nonsense. I'm not like that at all!'

In so far as the causes of differential achievement exist at the 'social' level, they are to an extent amenable to change, if this is thought desirable, as by legislation for equal opportunities, or private initiatives such as those of the Labour Party (although in some cases such attempts may backfire, as apparently in post-Communist Eastern Europe [Occhipinti 1996]). Complex issues are then raised about the rights and wrongs of positive discrimination. Some of these are related to the question of differences between men and women: for example, whether they are actually equally well equipped for, or suited or inclined to, various occupations. Most societies, probably, have believed them not to be, or at any rate acted as though they were not, although the actual allocation of roles has not always been the same. Levine (1991) asserts that sexual dimorphism in certain adaptive characteristics is universal in human populations, for example in reproduction and nurturing, strength, and probably aggression; though none of these is uniformly translated into adaptive outcomes, in other words, behaviour. (Murder rates vary in different societies from under one per million to over 900 per million; but the typical pattern is of young men killing young men – *The Sunday Times*, 5 May 1996.) The idea that roles were more or less flexible became popular partly through a perhaps oversimplified reading of the enormously influential anthropological works of Margaret Mead (e.g. *Coming of Age in Samoa*, 1928, *Growing Up in New Guinea*, 1930), which seemed to show that patterns of male and female behaviour were culturally determined. While her fieldwork has largely been discredited, what she actually argued for on the basis of it was the need for education for choice, and equality of opportunity, in our own very different society. A huge literature has subsequently developed carrying a more or less explicit assumption that there are few if any 'real' differences between men and women. And as our own society has, perhaps, become less insistent on rigid distinctions, reports have abounded of 'opposite sex' behaviour, from male nannies to female bullfighters (*The Sunday Times*, 3 July 1994, 18 May 1997). The distributions overlap a little more. A more subtle argument is that there are, for whatever reasons, differences of various kinds such as intellectual or emotional, and that these would result in women changing the nature of fields in which men excel, if only they were allowed to enter them (e.g. Haste 1988; Wertheim 1997; Helena Kennedy, 'Prisoners of Gender', *The Times Higher Education Supplement*, 3 November 1995). It is perhaps not very easy to see how to test this hypothesis (a criterion of male science).

Biological factors

This inevitably leads to the physiological level of analysis. Cochrane (1994) for example refers to 'the subsidiary nature of biological influences compared to the overwhelming impact of social expectations and social traditions'. Golombek and Fivush (1994), impressed by the differential treatment that boys and girls receive from birth onwards, conclude that gender differences are not inevitable; biological differences are slight and can be exaggerated or diminished by cultural beliefs, and gender-related behaviour has changed in many ways, especially in the last two decades. These points have force. However, in the same year that Mill made the case for legal equality of the sexes, Francis Galton set out 'to show . . . that a man's natural abilities are derived by inheritance, under exactly the same limitations as are the form and physical features of the whole organic world'(Galton 1869). One of the most dramatic developments of the last decade or two has been the rapid accumulation of evidence that Galton was, broadly, on the right track. There can be no doubt that a substantial part of the variance in human behaviour is due to genetic factors. Evidence is summarised in, for example, Plomin *et al.* (1988); Wilson (1989); Short and Balaban (1994). From the point of view of choice in education and occupation, the aspects that are of particular importance concern possible differences in abilities and interests between men and women, and possible physiological bases, or potential, for any such differences. As Rutter (1997) and others point out, a genetic contribution does not necessarily determine the outcome. Rutter quotes an increase in height of boys in London of some twelve centimetres this century, almost certainly due to improvements in nutrition. At the same time, human height has historically only varied within fairly narrow limits. Behaviour is more flexible, but how much so is at present unknown.

Males and females are genetically different and this is the basis of the primary physiological difference, although as we have noted this is not a precise dichotomy. It does, however, result directly in important influences on occupation, specifically due to childbearing and nurturing. The first, wholly, and the second, largely, (that is, in breast-feeding) remain female activities, and short of genetic engineering will continue to be so. (Actually, male breast-feeding is theoretically possible, *The Sunday Times,* 27 April 1997.) A legal ruling by the House of Lords (*The Times,* 5 July 1996) held that 'mothers are generally better fitted than fathers to provide for the needs of very young children'. Having children does not fit well with the current structure of many occupations – some more than others. Of course these structures *are* amenable to change, but the radical shift that would be necessary seems unlikely in the foreseeable future. More important, there are clear genetic influences in the two groups of characteristics that affect education and occupation, namely abilities and interests.

However, not all of these by any means show clear differences between males and females, or what might seem obvious. Galton thought that men must be better at taste and smell, because tea-tasters were always male; in fact women are greatly superior. Perhaps the greatest controversy has been aroused, as so often, over the question of intelligence. Even defining this has always proved problematic. The simplest line seems to be to consider it as a core set of cognitive abilities, involved to a greater or lesser extent in all intellectual tasks; approximately, what has been known since the work of Spearman (1904) as 'g', for 'general intelligence'. A substantial genetic contribution to this is very well-established (e.g. Neisser *et al.* 1996; Vernon 1993). Without going into the complexities of measuring 'g', including the perhaps insoluble problem of establishing 'fair' measures when what we are interested in is differences, there would seem to be some evidence, summarised by Eysenck (1995), for a small male superiority. He also quotes evidence for larger brain size, which correlates with intelligence. More important, perhaps, is the fact that the distribution of intelligence – and indeed other characteristics – in females tends to have a smaller range; there are fewer very high or very low scores. Extremely high intelligence is sometimes referred to as 'genius' level. Genius as generally recognised certainly cannot be only a matter of intelligence, but the fact is that there are almost no recorded females to whom the title has been widely accorded. The view of Eysenck (and others) is that the exceptional achievements of genius must result from the interaction of many factors each having a high value. He points out that if this interaction is multiplicative, even a small difference in one factor would have a substantial effect on the outcome. Genius is, however, by definition, far removed from the educational and occupational choices most of us make, and even if such differences do exist, they would have no bearing on the ability of individual men or women to succeed in any normal occupation.

What may be more important are differences in type of intellectual ability. There is a long history of studies showing different patterns of scores for men and women. Lynn (1992) for example reports results of the eight sub-tests of the Differential Aptitude Test for 10,000 British 13–18-year-olds, compared with similar American samples. In both countries males scored more highly than females on verbal, abstract, numerical and mechanical reasoning and spatial relations; females were better at clerical speed and accuracy, spelling and language. Feingold (1992), reviewing a large number of such studies, concluded that on average:

1   males score more highly than females on tests of general knowledge, mechanical reasoning and mental rotations (indicative of spatial ability);
2   females score more highly than males on tests of language usage (spelling and grammar) and perceptual speed;
3   there are no notable differences in general verbal ability, arithmetic, abstract reasoning (perhaps most akin to 'g'), spatial visualisation and memory span.

He concludes also that differences between the two groups have decreased markedly over the past generation (in the USA). A further point stressed by Feingold is one we have already noted: we have to deal with distributions, not merely with means. Not only do the distributions overlap, they tend not to be of the same form for males and females. Males, for example, as usual are consistently more variable than females, in quantitative reasoning, spatial visualisation, spelling and general knowledge – in other words there are more very high and more very low scorers. This is very consistent with extensive studies of the mathematically gifted in particular. Benbow and Lubinski (1993) for example show that over the previous twenty years there have consistently been many more highly able males than females at least from age thirteen, as identified in the extensive Study of Mathematically Precocious Youth (SMPY) centred at Johns Hopkins University (low scorers don't come into this).

Of course, there is ample evidence that boys and girls are reared differentially from the start – as a student once wrote, they are dressed in blue and pink respectively – but it is unclear to what extent this is a matter of adults responding to differences that are naturally there. Serbin *et al.* (1993) state that gender schemas, that is, networks of characteristics associated with males and females, begin to form in infancy, and a notion of sex roles, as shown by knowledge of occupation-related, sex-typed objects such as a hammer or a broom, exceeds chance levels as early as two or two-and-a-half years. Again, it is well-established that boys and girls tend to receive different treatment at school, for example, teachers pay more attention to boys (Hamilton *et al.* 1991; Kelly 1988; Colley, this volume). Lynn (1992), however, argues that it is implausible to suppose that differential treatment alone would produce the quite subtle differences in cognitive development that are found. This seems particularly true if we consider the distributions. We would have to suppose not only that families encourage specific abilities more in boys, but that they do so much more in some boys while discouraging them in others. Differences in potential seem likely. It has been suggested, for example, that spatial ability has been of evolutionary advantage to males in exploring a wider territory and thus gaining access to more females, which is of more value than the converse because of the different length of the reproductive cycle (Gaulin 1993).

It is not just a matter of genetics. There is now convincing evidence that other biological factors in development, especially the hormone balance, affect the pattern of abilities. This is discussed in detail by Ernest Govier in Chapter 1. Udry (1994) summarises other research showing how differential exposure to hormonal influences can affect the development of more feminised or masculinised behaviour. From this and his own studies he concludes 'with increasing confidence we can now say that individual women' (and men, by implication) 'differ in their average biological propensity to sex-typed behaviour. We can also infer that males and females differ from one another in their average biological propensity to the same behaviours.'

Halpern ([1986], 1992) reviewing the whole question of sex differences in cognitive abilities, concludes cautiously that there are data that cannot be explained by psychosocial hypotheses, other data that cannot be explained by biological hypotheses, and still other data presenting difficulties for both. Few people, probably, would suggest that one type of explanation is likely to be sufficient by itself. What is clear is that there appears to be a biological *basis* for cognitive differences, which are thus unlikely to disappear altogether although modified by familial, social or educational influences. Such differences alone are far from sufficient, of course, to account for educational or occupational choice. Not only do the distributions largely overlap, there are many other factors in play. However, some of these also appear to have partly genetic foundations, as Ernest Govier shows. Lykken *et al.* (1993) report a substantial twin study (over 1,000 pairs) of vocational and recreational interests, which showed that about 50 per cent of the variance could be attributed to genetic factors. This does not mean, of course, that an interest in, say, history or physics is inherited. The authors point out: 'Because specific interests are undoubtedly learned, these findings must be interpreted to mean that the experiences people seek, and the effect of those experiences on their developing interests, are influenced by traits of physique, aptitude and temperament – and perhaps by certain not-yet-identified primitive or primary interests – that are themselves substantially genetically influenced'. One might say more generally that individuals come into the world with different patterns of potential, which may be modified by various environmental elements. Some of the complexities of what happens are set out by Rutter (1997). As Plomin and others (e.g. Plomin and Neiderhiser 1992) have shown, these elements are themselves to an extent selected and modified by the individual. This is very consistent with biographical accounts of exceptional individuals which describe them actively seeking out experiences appropriate to their developing talents (e.g. Radford 1990). Bouchard *et al.* (1992) quote evidence that work attitudes and job satisfaction are partially genetically influenced, although environment is the larger factor. As they point out, the acceptance of genetic influence in individual development does not imply a kind of fixed determinism. On the contrary (one might say), we are all born unique, and diverge further as we select from and modify our environment. The philosopher Mary Midgley (1978) has made much the same point: it is only because we inherit individuality that we can avoid being socialised into uniformity.

Choice and the individual

Choice, in education, occupation or anything else, is obviously an individual matter, although it may be constrained to a greater or lesser extent by factors over which the individual does not have control. Leonard Holdstock mentions the continuing usefulness of the 'Seven-Point Plan' of the National Institute of Industrial Psychology (Rawling 1985) as an *aide-mémoire* for the major factors in such choices. The points are: physical make-up; attainments; general intelligence; special aptitudes; interests; disposition; and circumstances. They refer primarily to vocational guidance, that is, usually to a decision to be made at a particular point in time. However, the educational/occupational career of an individual is a series of such decisions, whether conscious or not and whether made by that person or by others for them, as discussed by Pauline Anderson in Chapter 7 and well illustrated by Estelle King in Chapter 5. The general pattern of career choice seems to be one of considerable stability, both in the individual and between groups – specifically, men and women. Each of the seven points is liable to change: even physical make-up may radically alter for better or worse; general intelligence may effectively increase or decrease with changes in motivation (disposition) or circumstances or indeed health. But generally there will tend to be consistency, partly of course in a self-fulfilling way. Each decision in a particular direction tends to make that direction more likely, and may close-off others (hence the dictum of Alec Rodger, who originally devised the Seven Points sixty years ago, 'planned procrastination and occupational versatility'). A very apposite case at the present time is the choice of secondary school subjects. Until 1988 British governments had refrained from controlling this, but the Education Reform Act of that year introduced a National Curriculum allegedly to provide a 'broad, balanced education' for all children. As no criteria were mentioned for either breadth or balance the phrase was strictly meaningless, and the actual curriculum was effectively that of the Board of Education of 1904. It was subsequently modified, but boys and girls must now follow the same route up to age thirteen. However, it has long been established that preferences for school subjects vary substantially between boys and girls, and that these preferences begin quite early on, certainly before secondary school (e.g. Archer and Macrae 1991), and tend to persist. An extensive literature explores the stereotyping of school subjects, e.g. Archer (1992); Colley, this volume; Durndell *et al.* (1995); Martin and Murchie-Beyma (1992); Weinreich-Haste (1981). Sex stereotypes in education and occupation are widespread and persistent across many nations (Williams and Best 1982, 1990). The question that arises is whether the pattern will be altered by compulsion. In the UK it is still too early for a clear answer. Hendley *et al.* (1995) found some persisting differences in attitudes, with boys still more positive towards science, technology and mathematics, girls to reading and writing in both English and science, but less positive to all other aspects of the latter. Watson *et al.* (1994), concluded from a study of over 1,000 sixth-formers that subjects are chosen on the basis of students' interest in them and the perceived academic freedom offered by them. These are not affected by a uniform curriculum. Girls continue to choose science less often than boys, once they are free to do so, and the pattern seems to be quite robust. This key stage of educational choice, with obvious consequences for occupation, is discussed further by Pauline Lightbody and Alan Durndell in Chapter 3, and by Ann Colley in Chapter 2.

The notion of changing the pattern has been prevalent for at least the last forty years. At a conference on 'Careers for Girls in Engineering' in 1957 the then Minister of Labour and National Service, Iain Macleod, argued that girls were needed to meet demands for more trained engineers. A succession of initiatives has followed aimed at altering the balance, with, as Leonard Holdstock makes clear, little or no effect. In 1994 one more was launched, a development unit under the auspices of the Office of Science and Technology, with a remit to 'tap a vastly underused resource to the benefit of the nation's science, engineering and technology' (*The Times*, 14 November 1994). The results have yet to be seen as of June 1997. Apart from lack of positive results, a couple of other points seem to be overlooked in such initiatives. One is that women and men might simply prefer to do different things, and a democratic society might be expected to accept such preferences whatever their basis. In a series of publications Hakim (e.g. 1994, 1995, *The Times Higher Education Supplement*, 26 April 1996) has shown, *inter alia*, that a real decrease in obstacles to female employment has not produced a major shift away from choice of a role as homemaker. The other point is that if more of one group are attracted into a particular area and thus away from other areas, someone else, presumably from the other, will need to take up the slack. More female engineers means more male nurses, who are equally hard to come by.

Academic segregation (male and female choice of different subjects or disciplines), as has been suggested, appears to be quite persistent. Ransom (1990) presents data from Higher Education in the USA for 1960, 1977 and 1984. There is little decline in segregation, possibly some increase, over the period. Data in the UK are very similar (e.g. Holdstock and Radford 1993, unpublished; Radford and Holdstock 1996). As has been indicated, this is unlikely to be mainly due to differences in ability. Interests are more important. Students who are asked an open-ended question as to reasons for their choice of subject invariably state 'interest' as the major item (e.g. Radford 1991; Tebbutt 1993), consistent with the finding of Watson *et al.* (1994). This 'interest' needs to be unpacked, and while more needs to be done, two points do seem to emerge. One is that there seems to be a widely held and consistent view that subjects, and related occupations, vary in their suitability for men and women, as reported by Leonard Holdstock in Chapter 4 (and consistent with the literature on stereotypes already mentioned). A recent replication (Radford *et al.*, in preparation) with university and pre-university students in Suzhou, China, yielded almost identical results, except that almost no respondents took the option of declaring that the subjects were all equally suitable for men and women. Of course, this does not explain why the views of suitability are held, and there is reason to think that, despite official policy, social attitudes on segregation are more rigid in China than in the UK. Hooper (1991) reports that only one-third of university students are female, with no change since 1973, and that they tend to cluster in lower-status areas, especially teacher training. As here, numbers of women are low in science and technology and high in humanities and languages.

The other point however is that broad subject areas do not reveal the actual facts of segregation. Thus many different activities tend to be lumped together as 'technology', sometimes also combined with science or with engineering. Overall, female recruitment to these broad areas is low; for example only 12 per cent in 'engineering and technology' in 1995. But female recruitment is high in some areas of technology such as polymers and textiles (81 per cent), nutrition (88), food science (69) and radiography (79) (Holdstock and Radford 1997). It is tempting to suggest that the common factor is something like 'homemaking/caring'. In engineering, the most popular area for girls was civil engineering with 14 per cent, while electrical, electronic, mechanical and aeronautical each had less than 9 per cent. Perhaps civil engineering is seen as more to do with people. More than half the admissions to medical schools are women, but the female proportion of surgeons is very small – only two per cent of consultants (*The Times*, 27 May 1993). It may be that surgery involves work conditions that are particularly difficult for women, and it may be that they are actually discouraged by men. But it also seems obvious that surgery involves rather different activities compared to, say, paediatrics or general practice. The guess would be that the latter are, or are seen as, more personal and more caring as compared to surgery. All this requires further investigation; although twenty years ago Bottomley and Ormerod (1977) for example concluded, from a middle-school study, that 'girls like science best when it is nurturative – caring for plants and animals – rather than analytical'. Ebbutt (1981) found that girls liked science with aesthetic values and an end product (such as extracting plant scents), while boys preferred developing rules from observational work on elements, electrical circuits or air pressure (and see Ann Colley's chapter). A study of 10–15-year-olds found that their image of 'a scientist' tended to be a bald man in a white coat who hated children and animals; whereas 'a cancer researcher' was a caring woman with glasses, who loved children (*The Times Higher Education Supplement*, 22 October 1993).

The range of subjects that are taken for university honours degrees does seem to resolve rather neatly into a continuum from those that are in some sense 'more male', to those that are 'more female'. This is both in numbers recruited, and in a prima facie consideration of what they are for or 'about' (rather than what they consist of, so to speak). Nursing (around 90 per cent female) is generally about caring for sick people (of course in practice it is by no means always so); engineering is broadly about producing machines. Law (approximately equal numbers of males and females) is partly about formal procedures, documents, legal theory, but also partly about face-to-face interaction with (often worried) clients. Medicine combines scientific/technological knowledge with caring for individuals.

One of the earliest studies of personal values, by Allport and Vernon (1931), presented almost a mirror image for men and women. Men were high on theoretical, economic and political values, women on aesthetic, social and religious values. This does not tell us about the distribution of values within groups. And we must continue to remember, as Golombek and Fivush (1994) point out, that gender-related characteristics are multidimensional in nature. As far as education is concerned, Radford and Holdstock, in the studies of psychology and computing students described in Leonard Holdstock's chapter, found that the latter tended to be more 'masculine' than the former, and that in psychology it was the more 'feminine' elements that were more popular among both boys and girls. This corresponds to the fact that the two subjects recruit approximately three-quarters female and male students respectively. What we have, once again, is a set of distributions which, as Udry (1994) shows, is the conclusion that follows from the assumption that individuals are biologically predisposed towards at least some gendered aspects of behaviour. Conversely, if gendered behaviour were entirely learned, we would hardly get more 'feminine' men and more 'masculine' women.

Conclusions

Education and occupation are gendered, to a greater or lesser extent, in probably all societies. This is partly due to economic, legal, social, religious or other factors over which the individual has relatively little control. It is also due to the series of choices – decisions – that the individual makes, or that are made by others for him or her. There is more freedom of choice in our society than in some others. These choices are also gendered to a greater or lesser extent, and this in turn is due to individual make-up, which begins with inherited potential and is developed by physiological, familial, educational, social and other influences. These result in individuals being each somewhere along a 'masculine–feminine' continuum as regards physical make-up, abilities, interests and values: a whole bundle of loosely but positively correlated traits. Men tend to be more masculine and women more feminine. Education and occupation are also gendered in a similar way; they are made up of various components each of which is somewhere along a dimension. Other things being equal – opportunity, for example – individuals will tend to make approximate matches between themselves and their educational and occupation choices. The more 'feminine' individuals – preponderantly women – will gravitate towards the more 'feminine' activities, and vice versa. All the dimensions, probably, overlap to a large degree. A man can be 'more like a woman', or vice versa, and many are but on average there are fairly stable differences which are likely to persist.

As Udry (1994) points out, most societies have always accepted the idea that there are biological predispositions towards some behaviour. But they have not therefore regarded the behaviour as unalterable; childrearing, education, social norms, laws are largely established with this in view – with, of course, very varying degrees of success. To what extent efforts should be made actively to reduce differences in gender-related characteristics is debatable. Research suggests that success will be limited. This is quite a different question from that of equality of opportunity and reward. This too is a matter of policy; what research shows here, however, is that there is no sensible basis for differential treatment of individuals on a principle of group membership. At its simplest, this is merely because of the statistical overlap of such membership. It is also because of the complexity both of individual development and of educational and occupational patterns. There is no justification for holding that men or women ought, or ought not, to be nurses or engineers, although there are reasons why they may continue to choose differentially. There is every justification for making education and occupation equally available to all, as J.S. Mill urged back in 1869. In this regard, our society still has some way to go.

References

Allport, G.W. and Vernon, P.E. (1931) 'A test for personal values', *Journal of Abnormal Psychology* 26: 231–48.

Archer, J. (1992) 'Gender stereotyping of school subjects', *The Psychologist* 5: 66–9.

Archer, J. and Macrae, M. (1991) 'Gender-perception of school subjects among 10–11-year-olds', *British Journal of Educational Psychology* 61: 99–103.

Benbow, C.P. and Lubinski, D. (1993) 'Consequences of gender differences in mathematical reasoning ability and some biological linkages' in M. Hang, R.E. Whalen, C. Aron and K.L. Olsen (eds) *The Development of Sex Differences and Similarities in Behavior*, Dordrecht: Kluver Academic Publications.

Bennett, J. (1996) *Ale, Beer and Brewsters in England*, Oxford: Oxford University Press.

Bleys, R.C. (1996) *The Geography of Perversion: Male to Male Sexual Behaviour outside the West and the Ethnographic Imagination 1750–1918*, London: Cassell.

Blundell, S. (1995) *Women in Ancient Greece*, London: British Museum Press.

Boswell, J. (1995) *The Marriage of Likeness: Same-Sex Unions in Pre-Modern Europe*, London: HarperCollins.

Bottomley, J.M. and Ormerod, M.B. (1977) 'Middle school science activities in their association with liking for science', *Education in Science* 74: 23.

Bouchard, T.J., Arvey, R.T., Keller, L.M. and Segal, N.L. (1992) 'Genetic influences on job satisfaction: a reply to Cropenzano and Jones', *Journal of Applied Psychology* 77: 89–93.

Cochrane, R. (1994) 'Introduction' in G. Siann *Gender, Sex and Sex and Sexuality: Contemporary Psychological Perspectives*, London: Taylor and Francis.

Deaux, K. (1985) 'Sex and gender', *Annual Review of Psychology* 36: 49–81.

Diamond, M. (1977) 'Biological foundations for social development' in F.A. Beach (ed.) *Human Sexuality in Four Perspectives*, Baltimore and London: Johns Hopkins University Press.

Durndell, A., Glissov, P. and Siann, G. (1995) 'Gender and computing: persisting differences', *Educational Research* 37: 219–27.

Ebbutt, D. (1981) 'Girls' science: boys' science revisited' in A. Kelly (ed.) *The Missing Half: Girls and Science Education*, Manchester: Manchester University Press.

Eysenck, H.J. (1995) *Genius: The Natural History of Creativity*, Cambridge: Cambridge University Press.

Feingold, A. (1992) 'Sex differences in variability in intellectual activities: a new look at an old controversy', *Review of Educational Research* 62: 61–84.

Fraser, A. (1994) *The Warrior Queens*, London: Weidenfeld and Nicolson.

Friedli, L. (1987) '"Passing women": A study of gender boundaries in the eighteenth century' in G.S. Rousseau and R. Porter (eds) *Sexual Underworlds of the Enlightenment*, Manchester: Manchester University Press.

Galton, F. (1869) *Hereditary Genius*, London: Macmillan (reprinted: Fontana 1962).

Gaulin, S.J.C. (1993) 'How and why sex differences develop, with spatial ability as a paradigm exemplar' in M. Hang, R.E. Whalen, C. Aron and K.L. Olsen (eds) *The*

Development of Sex Differences and Similarities in Behavior, Dordrecht: Kluver Academic Publishers.

Golombek, S. and Fivush, R. (1994) *Gender Development*, Cambridge: Cambridge University Press.

Goulet, J.-G.A. (1996) 'The "berdache"/"Two-Spirit": a comparison of anthropological and native constructions of gendered identities among the Northern Athapaskeans', *Journal of the Royal Anthropological Institute* 2: 683–701.

Gray, J. (1992) *Men Are From Mars, Women Are From Venus*, New York: HarperCollins.

Hakim, C. (1994) 'A century of change in occupational segregation 1891–1991', *Journal of Historical Sociology* 7: 435–54.

—— (1995) 'Five feminist myths about women's employment', *British Journal of Sociology* 46: 429–55.

Halpern, D.F. (1992) *Sex Differences in Cognitive Abilities*, Hillsdale, NJ: Lawrence Erlbaum (second edition; first edition 1986).

Hamilton, V.L., Blumenfeld, P.C., Akoh, H. and Miura, K. (1991) 'Group and gender in Japanese and American elementary classrooms', *Journal of Cross-Cultural Psychology*, 22: 317–46.

Haste, H. (1988) 'Legitimation, logic and lust: historical perspectives on gender, science and ways of knowing, review of *Reflections on Science and Gender* by Evelyn Fox Keller, New Haven: Yale University Press, 1985, and *Rhetoric as Philosophy: The Humanist Tradition*, by Ernesto Grossi, University Park, PA: The Pennsylvania State University Press, 1980', *New Ideas in Psychology* 6: 137–45.

Hendley, D., Parkinson, J., Stables, A. and Tanner, H. (1995) 'Gender differences in pupil attitudes to the National Curriculum subjects of English, mathematics, science and technology in Key Stage 3 in South Wales', *Educational Studies* 21: 85–97.

Holdstock, L. and Radford, J. (1993, unpublished) 'Gender segregation by field in United Kingdom Higher Education'.

—— (1997) 'An unsuitable job for a woman?', *New Scientist* 8 February: 48.

Hooper, B. (1991) 'Gender and education' in I. Epstein (ed.) *Chinese Education: Problems, Policies and Prospects*, New York and London: Garland Publishing Co.

Hoyenga, K.B. and Hoyenga, K.T. (1993) *Gender-Related Differences: Origins and Outcomes*, Boston: Allyn and Bacon.

Kelly, A. (1988) 'Gender differences in teacher–pupil interactions: a meta-analytic review', *Educational Research* 39: 1–23.

Levine, R.A. (1991) 'Gender differences: interpreting anthropological data' in M.T. Notman and C.C. Nadelson (eds) *Women and Men: New Perspectives on Gender Differences*, Washington, DC: American Psychiatric Press Inc.

Lykken, D.T., Bouchard, T.J., McGue, M. and Tellegen, A. (1993) 'Heritability of interests: a twin study', *Journal of Applied Psychology* 78: 649–61.

Lynn, R. (1992) 'Sex differences on the Differential Aptitude Test in British and American adolescents', *Educational Psychology* 12: 101–6.

Martin, C.D. and Murchie-Beyma, E. (1992) *In Search of Gender-Free Paradigms for Computer Science Education*, Eugene, Oregon: International Society for Technology in Education.

Mead, M. (1928) *Coming of Age in Samoa*, Harmondsworth: Penguin (1943).

—— (1930) *Growing Up in New Guinea*, Harmondsworth: Penguin (1942).

Midgley, M. (1980) *Beast and Man: The Roots of Human Nature*, London: Scientific Book Club.

Mill, J.S. (1869) *The Subjection of Women* reprinted: Wordsworth Editions 1996.

Money, J. and Ehrhardt, A.A. (1972) *Man and Woman, Boy and Girl: The Differentiation and Dimorphism of Gender Identity from Conception to Maturity*, Baltimore: Johns Hopkins University Press.

Neisser, U. (Chair), Boodoo, G., Bouchard, T.J., Boykin, A.W., Brody, N., Ceci, S.J., Halpern, D.F., Loehlin, J.C., Perloff, R., Sternberg, R.J. and Urbina, S. (1996) 'Intelligence: knowns and unknowns', *American Psychologist* 51: 77–101.

Occhipinti, L. (1996) 'Two steps back? Anti-feminism in Eastern Europe', *Anthropology Today* 12: 13–18.

Plomin, R. and Neiderhiser, J.M. (1992) 'Genetics and experience', *Current Directions in Psychological Science* 1: 160–3.

Plomin, R., DeFries, J.C. and Fulker, D.W. (1988) *Nature and Nurture During Infancy and Early Childhood*, Cambridge: Cambridge University Press.

Radford, J. (1990) *Child Prodigies and Exceptional Early Achievers*, Hemel Hempstead: Harvester.

—— (ed.) (1991) *The Choice of Psychology*. Occasional Papers of the Group of Teachers of Psychology of the British Psychological Society, Vol. 12.

Radford, J. and Holdstock, L. (1996) 'Does psychology need more boy appeal?', *The Psychologist*, 8: 21–4.

Radford, J., Holdstock, L. and Wu, R. (in preparation) 'Attitudes of Chinese university and pre-university students towards Higher Education'.

Ransom, M.R. (1990) 'Gender segregation by field in Higher Education', *Research in Higher Education* 31: 477–91.

Rawling, K. (1985) *The Seven-Point Plan by Alec Rodger. New perspectives fifty years on*, Windsor: NFER/Nelson.

Rutter, M. (1997) 'Nature–nurture integration: the example of anti-social behavior', *American Psychologist* 52: 390–8.

Scott, A.M. (1995) *Gender Segregation and Social Change: Men and Women in Changing Labour Markets*, Oxford: Oxford University Press.

Serbin, L.A., Powlishta, K.K. and Gulko, J. (1993) *The Development of Sex Typing in Middle Childhood*. Monographs of the Society for Research in Child Development, 58: No. 2.

Short, R.V. and Balaban, E. (eds) (1994) *The Differences Between the Sexes*, Cambridge: Cambridge University Press.

Spearman, C. (1904) '"General intelligence", objectively observed and measured', *American Journal of Psychology* 15: 201–93.

Spencer, C. (1995) *Homosexuality: A History*, London: Fourth Estate.

Tebbutt, M.J. (1993) 'Sixth formers' perceptions of A level and degree courses in physics and mathematics', *Research in Science and Technological Education* 11: 27–37.

Udry, J.R. (1994) 'The nature of gender', *Demography* 31: 561–73.

Unterman, A. (1994) 'Judaism' in J. Holm with J. Bowker (eds) *Rites of Passage*, London: Pinter Publishers.

Vernon, P.A. (ed.) (1993) *Biological Approaches to the Study of Human Intelligence*, Norwood, NJ: Ablex Publishing Co.

Watson, J., McEwen, A. and Dawson, S. (1994) 'Sixth-Form A Level students' perceptions of the difficulty, intellectual freedom, social benefit and interest of science and arts subjects', *Research in Science and Technological Education* 12: 43–51.

Weinreich-Haste, H. (1981) 'The image of science' in A. Kelly (ed.) *The Missing Half: Girls and Science Education*, Manchester: Manchester University Press.

Wertheim, M. (1997) *Pythagoras' Trousers*, London: Fourth Estate.

Williams, J.E. and Best, D.L. (1982) *Measuring Sex Stereotypes: A Thirty Nation Study*, Beverly Hills, CA: Sage.

—— (1990) *Measuring Sex Stereotypes: A Multinational Survey*, London: Sage.

Wilson, G. (1989) *The Great Sex Divide: A Study of Male–Female Differences*, London: Peter Owen.

INDEX

ability: defined 64; mean sex differences 65; verbal 3, 5; visuo-spacial 3–4, 64
ability distributions: cut-off 65–6; male/ female differences 64–5; variances 66–8; *see also* frequency distribution
Access courses 85, 96, 97, 101
achievement 178
advertising 135
alienation 91
Anderson, P. 141–59, 184
assessment techniques: adverse impact 114, 119–20, 125, 128; objective 107, 113–14, 136; *see also* cognitive tests; employment selection process

behaviour, socially determined 176–7
Bem Sex Role Inventory (BSRI) 9, 150–1
berdache 176; *see also* transsexuals
brain organisation 1–2
brainsex 10–13

career: aspirations 23–4; defined 145–6; development 148–9; and domestic responsibility 47, 153–4; lateral path 157; *see also* job; occupation; professions; work
Chaucer, Geoffrey 177
childhood 88–93, 129–31, 143, 182
choice: conceptual problems 143–4; environmental restrictions 145–51; factors affecting 183; *see also* occupational choice; subject choice
Civil Service 105
Cognitive Developmental Theory 20–1
cognitive differences 128–9, 181–3
cognitive psychology 2–5
cognitive tests: cut-off 119–20, 136;

four-fifths rule 120, 124; gender effects 114, 115–19, 126–7, 128–33; intercept bias 123–4; manipulate sex differences 132–3; monitoring 125; performance levels 117–18; performance ranges 118–29; pressured context 131–2; research problems 126; sampling effects 131; validity of 121–7, 133; *see also* assessment techniques
collective self vs. personal self 46
Colley, A. 18–33, 38, 84, 182, 184, 186
communications 154–5
company action 167–8; downsizing 156–7; family-friendly approach 168, 169–70; *see also* organisational culture
compromise and circumscription 148–9
computer studies 70, 71–3; female participation 24; gender stereotyping 40; nature of 71; sex-segregation ratio 72
Congenital Adrenal Hypoplasia (CAH) 11
Creighton, P. 104–38

de Moller, June 172
developmental theories 142–3
dichotic listening tests 1–2, 7–10
Dietrich, Sabine 168
differential theories 142, 143
discrimination 166, 178; difficulty of proving 107; direct and indirect 112–13; positive 179
Durndell, A. 37–55, 70, 184

earnings 105–6
education: delivery and curriculum 26, 32; learning environment 26–31; *see*